THE COMPLETE BOOK OF BASEBALL INSTRUCTION

THE COMPLETE BOOK OF BASEBALL INSTRUCTION

By

Dell Bethel

Contemporary Books, Inc.
Chicago

Library of Congress Cataloging in Publication Data

Bethel, Dell.
    The complete book of baseball instruction.

    Includes index.
    1. Baseball.   I. Title.
GV867.B457   1978   796.357   77-91148
ISBN 0-8092-7741-7 (cloth)
ISBN 0-8092-7740-9 (paper)

Photos by Marvin L. Axelrod

Copyright © 1978 by Dell Bethel
All rights reserved
Published by Contemporary Books, Inc.
180 North Michigan Avenue, Chicago, Illinois 60601
Manufactured in the United States of America
Library of Congress Catalog Card Number: 77-91148
International Standard Book Number: 0-8092-7741-7 (cloth)
                                       0-8092-7740-9 (paper)

Published simultaneously in Canada by
Beaverbooks
953 Dillingham Road
Pickering, Ontario L1W 1Z7
Canada

This book is dedicated to the Bethels, Cowgills, and Halters, wherever they are. Their love, understanding, and sacrifices over the years made this book possible and a joy to write.

Contents

Acknowledgments

I wish to acknowledge the great baseball players, coaches, and managers I have had the pleasure to play under or work with side by side. I have learned much of what I have written in the pages to follow from these men, who through their love and dedication have made baseball the great game it is today.

These men are William Leslie Bethel, Fred Warburton, Ray Ross, Ed Burke, Dick Siebert, Ray Gestaut, Angelo Giuliani, Andy Gilbert, Carl Hubbell, Bubber Jonnard, Paul Deese, Ron Oestrike, George Medich, Chick Genovese, Tom Heath, Jack Fisher, Leo Durocher, Don Kirsch, Cliff Dorow, John Kasper, Dave Kosher, Larry Starr, Al Campanis, Grady Hatton, Jim Fitzharris, Rosy Ryan, Don Pries, Charlie Fox, Chuck Tanner, Rollie Hemond, Bill Veeck, Hal Middlesworth, Ed Katalinas, Rich Rollins, Ralph Kiner, Charlie Lau, John Sain, Wally Moses, Whitey Herzog, Dick Howser, George Brophy, Eddie Yost, Ray Berres, Brooks Robinson, Clete Boyer, Bud Harrelson, Mickey McConnell, Cliff Kachline, Harry Walker, Ted Williams, and Andy Cohen.

I also wish to express my sincere appreciation to Herman Masin, editor of *Scholastic Coach*, for his encouragement and assistance in my writing endeavors from the beginning, and to Prudy Heritage for her hard work and help with this manuscript.

Introduction

Coach Bethel made me feel I could make it in the major leagues. His teaching approach to the mental aspects of this game helped me become a winning pitcher.

Dell knows the mechanics of pitching and is a real student of the game. He helped change my grip and style of pitching, so all my pitches now have movement. He is one of the best pitching coaches in the country.

Nothing can replace the desire to play the game. Desire is the key to discipline. Dell instilled the desire and discipline I needed to make the major leagues. With his enthusiasm and love for the game, he taught me the value of *fun* in baseball.

Vern Ruhle, Pitcher
Detroit Tigers

Dell was a tremendous influence on me when I was a young pitcher starting out in baseball. Through his encouragement and interest, I made it to the major leagues.

I am now a pitching coach myself, and in working with the Seattle Mariners, I always keep in mind the value of a good coach, the good coach that Dell was to me.

His ideas for teaching baseball are major league! If anyone has the talent and knowledge to put forth the ideas that will help you learn baseball, it is Dell.

I'm sure you will find this book of real value in helping you accomplish your goal.

Mel Stottlemyre
Coach, Seattle Mariners

1 | What Does It Take to Become a Baseball Star?

"The sheer joy of being involved, surrounded, and enveloped by baseball is its greatest reward."

These words of my former manager in Japan, Ray Gestaut, say it all for me. He further stated, "Those days when I played and managed were the happiest days of my life because I was close to the sport I loved, and to the good people who shared that feeling."

Baseball skill requires two traits: a real love for the game and the ability to have fun playing or being involved in any aspect of baseball, whether it be as a player, coach, scout, or manager. This feeling for the game of baseball has been common in fellow players or students of the game I've had the privilege of coaching.

Roy Campanella of another era said it very well when he remarked, "There has to be a lot of a little boy in a major league player." Reggie Jackson put it beautifully today when he autographed a baseball for my son, "Happiness is a way of living."

In mastering baseball, love of the game and the fun of playing it are the basis for the other important ingredients needed to reach your full potential. Total dedication to practice and the desire to condition your body to its fullest are almost equally important. When I played for the Giants, they did a study which found it took ten thousand hours of practice to make a professional prospect. Think about that a minute. Ten thousand hours of practice; this doesn't even include game time. If this amount of time is taken from one's life and devoted to another area, you could become an expert builder, a talented architect, or whatever you choose.

There are many, many stars of baseball. They each have achieved their goal in their own style. I'd like to share with you some of the

Willie Mays signing autographs for the kids at the Hall of Fame Baseball Camp in the sweltering heat. Willie loves the kids—he had fun making another kid happy.

thoughts, feelings, and actions of outstanding baseball players I've been fortunate enough to meet through pitching, teaching, coaching, playing, and just being a fan of the greatest game.

Andy Cohen used to take the young Ted Williams (Williams was 19 years old at the time) down to a city park near our home. Ted would hit baseballs by the hour, until his hands were literally bleeding, then he and Andy would go to Nicollet Park (home of the old Minneapolis Millers) and play a double header. This is why he became one of the greatest hitters of all time. What used to anger him more than anything in later years was to have someone come up to him and say, "You sure are a natural hitter." In addition to this regular season practice, during the winter he spent long hours swinging a leaded bat hundreds of times a day. He would follow this with fingertip pushups to develop more strength in his wrists and arms.

Willie Mays showed his love for the game and kids a few years ago when he was finishing his career with the New York Mets. We asked him to speak to the kids at our baseball school in the mountains of New York State. He got up at 4 A.M. and drove to the camp. Willie was dressed in sharp clothes, but he didn't hesitate to take off his shoes and demonstrate hitting in his stocking feet. For several hours he went over all the aspects of the game, kidding around and demonstrating all facets, as well as answering the questions of the eager students. After lunch he sat in the sweltering sun and signed autographs for every kid who had come to this mountain retreat from miles around in the name of baseball. They numbered in the hundreds.

Later that afternoon, he drove to Shea Stadium and hit a home run and almost put another one in the cheap seats for one of his best nights as a Met. Willie had already hit a home run for baseball and all those kids earlier that day.

Mel Stottlemyre and Vern Ruhle, two young men I had the pleasure of coaching, both made the major leagues. They both had a burning desire to become major league pitchers—to master the art of pitching. Each man kept himself in tremendous physical condition in season as well as off season. They always gave unstintingly of themselves to other pitchers and to youngsters. Both Mel's and Vern's cap sizes remained the same as when they were kids.

Rich Rollins, after retiring from his major league career, was managing a rookie league team. Rich believes "you win with class people.

The author and Vern Ruhle, pitcher, Detroit Tigers.

The author and Mel Stottlemyre, coach, Seattle Mariners.

Dennis Leonard, pitcher, Kansas City Royals.

A class person will do a little more than he has to do."

Rich had 35 ball players on his team. To find out how many of them really wanted to play the game, Rich would call an extra practice early in the morning. This practice was not mandatory. Out of the 35, 8 to 11 players would show up for the practice. Those were the players who advanced in baseball.

"Confidence increases in direct proportion to the preparation you put into an endeavor," said Vince Lombardi. A young hitter who went four for four during a particular game said to Stan Musial, "Did you ever have the feeling you were going to get a hit every time?" "Yes, every day," Musial replied.

Dennis Leonard of the Kansas City Royals told me, "I had a coach in high school who made me run, sprint, and really get in shape. As I moved through baseball, this training became tremendously important to me because it helped me get in the best condition possible, to help get the most from my ability. Also, after you make it, if you don't keep in top condition, you may slip back into the minors. If you can't run fifteen foul line-to-foul line sprints in the majors, you don't belong there."

Baseball also takes courage—courage to work hard to attain your goal. As Winston Churchill said, "Courage is the greatest virtue because it makes all others possible." Every major leaguer has had tremendous courage to pursue and attain that goal.

George Toporcer, a former major league player who went blind after his retirement, has stayed near the game he loved. Although blind, he still gives lectures and writes on baseball. He couldn't see the two hundred bug-eyed kids whose baseballs he autographed at our baseball school.

Buck Leonard, who is in the Baseball Hall of Fame, still gives freely of his time to talk with kids. And Johnny Bench signs autographs for major league players. Jim Bouton said it correctly in his book *Ball Four:* "I found all my life I was gripping the baseball, but when it came to the end of my career, I found that it was the other way around." A little noted statement that will someday be a classic.

Bang the Drum Slowly, a beautiful baseball story by Mark Harris, was made into a movie in 1973. As technical director, I helped four actors "make the majors" in two months. Two of them, Robert DeNiro and Michael Moriarty, came out to Central Park in New York every morning at 6 A.M. Bob, playing a catcher, had to learn to do just that—catch the ball and throw it back to the pitcher, Mike Moriarty. Bob and Mike did all the baseball scenes themselves. They had to learn all the mechanics of baseball: catching, pitching, sliding, hitting, signals, and infield and outfield play. Bob learned slides—hook, right, left, straight in, and head-first—and all this while learning to chew tobacco. He'd get sick as a dog, but kept it up until he could finally chew and play baseball.

A real classic: major league players asking Johnny Bench for his autograph.

Actor Robert DeNiro and Technical Director Dell Bethel at Yankee Stadium during the shooting of *Bang the Drum Slowly*. Bob's total dedication and professionalism was the key to his success as an outstanding catcher for this baseball movie.

Mike worked on his pitching form until it was down perfect. His arm was so sore he couldn't even comb his hair. He had to see a doctor.

They all went through the same conditioning and workouts as any major league player. Often my phone would ring, and it would be one of them wanting to "pick my brains" on multiple signs, take-offs, or little mannerisms that would make them more like a major league player.

They each knew they had "made the majors" when Bob boomed a triple in the alley to the wall at Shea Stadium, and Mike threw a ball with such velocity that he broke the plexiglass in front of the color filter in the camera behind home plate, while grinning from ear to ear.

This dedication and professionalism is what helped them rise to the top of their field as actors—and authentic baseball players in the movie. Total dedication and love of what they were doing equaled Oscar.

A radio sports authority and personality in Cleveland, Pete Franklin, has a special "Real People Philosophy" to which I subscribe. Pete says simply: "What I respect more than anything else is excellence, professionalism. The greatest thing I've ever seen in my life was when I was a kid, going to college, and on a lunch hour in New York City, I saw this old Italian guy with an enormous handlebar mustache, swinging a pick and singing. When he took his lunch break, he had a hero sandwich and a bottle of wine. Now, that man loved what he was doing and was a happy man. That was a one-shot thing, haven't seen anything like it before or since, but it had a tremendous influence on me. If you're happy in a job and doing it well . . . that's probably the closest any of us ever come to the meaning of life."

Excelling in baseball means reaching a goal to each player who has made it. It also means there is a real love for the game, the ability to

Willie Mays working with the young kids at our baseball school. Willie enjoys the love and esteem of the young, and it shows in these pictures.

have fun playing the game, with total dedication to practice and the desire to condition your body to the fullest extent. The professional has class and you win with class. He has confidence because he is prepared. He knows in his own mind that he has given it his best shot in hours of batting practice, extra conditioning, running, weight lifting, and special practices. He has courage—the greatest virtue—to pursue and attain his goal. And most of all, there is the greatest desire to share with one and all this tremendous love and knowledge of a game that has been the life and breath of the man. A master of baseball . . . a love of a lifetime.

Young players who really want to learn and improve themselves listening with total dedication and concentration.

2|John Sain—Genius Pitching Coach in Residence

A great coach is a tremendous confidence builder and knows how to inspire his players. He builds with patience, compassion, respect for the players' individuality, technically sound knowledge usually based on experience and put into a language a player can understand, empathy, rapport with players, and his own love of the game.

He will also think long and hard on ways to improve the game himself and discuss it with his protégés. He never stops learning. He inspires his people to shoot for the stars and then gives them the tools and methods to utilize every ounce of their ability to reach that goal. Once you ask him for help, he will talk to you forever on pitching, hitting, or whatever facet of the game concerns you. He stands up when his ideas are challenged.

John Sain moves into the clubhouse several hours before game time to visit with the players and plant some more "seeds" into their minds. Sometimes the harvest of these seeds may be a year or two later, but the coach enjoys seeing his protégés succeed, no matter when the time.

One of the truly great satisfactions in playing and coaching is living the development and success of your own career and that of each player you coach. In contrast to your own success as a player, whether it be for five, ten or even fifteen years, your career is only once in a lifetime. Sain shows us a perfect example of a successful career of his own and the development of successful careers in his many players. John has a rare talent born in all great coaches, and his talent has been developed to the fullest extent.

John's philosophy of coaching is as individual as he is. He makes it a practice to offer two or three suggestions to a player, based on the man's ability. Sain would say, "I put myself into their place and ask how I would pitch with this man's ability. I'll offer two or three suggestions. He'll pick out the thing that fits him, and it becomes his idea. If he says, 'I can do it this way,' then he'll have a good chance of doing it. If you offer him only one method and tell him to do it, he builds up a wall against it. You've hurt him. The man who succeeds is the man who follows his own plan."

John develops a friendship with a player through long conversations about topics of mutual interest, as well as on pitching. When the pitching questions stop and the conversation turns to other topics, Sain knows he has the player's confidence.

In working with many types of ball players, knowing the mechanics of pitching is not enough. Sometimes you must let a player have a little success and let him start to go backwards before you can help him go forward again.

The mental aspects of pitching also play an important role. Casey Stengal once asked Sain why the Yankee pitchers enjoyed throwing to Elston Howard. Sain thought about it for a month. Then it dawned on him that before a game or when Howard came to the mound, he would say to the pitcher, "What's your plan? What do you want to throw? What are you trying to do?" Elston gave them credit for using their head for something besides a cap rack.

Give the player some credit for sense. One of the essential thoughts a successful coach or manager must keep in mind is that *for a manager to get the maximum from his twenty-five men, he must make them feel important.*

Former Minnesota Twins third-baseman Rich Rollins thought Sain revolutionized the game in the 1960s with his hard slider. "When you batted against a pitcher Sain had worked with, you knew it because they all had that 'hard slider.' When Sain was with us, he had that great intangible ability to build tremendous confidence in you even if you were not a pitcher. Sain would talk to me about his Walnut Ridge car agency. I might have been in a slump, but he had a great way of putting the game of baseball in a long-range perspective. 'Have fun in the game, and give it your best shot,' Sain

John Sain, pitching coach.

would say. After listening to this man philosophizing, and knowing exactly how you felt, your eyes would light up and you'd be out of your slump. If the media were writing or saying critical things about you, and the coaches were treating you like you had the plague, and all these pressures [this is where the problem lies at the major league level—these tremendous pressures and how you react] built up in you, John would sit down and say, 'Criticism is everywhere in baseball. Any time you let criticism or a derogatory remark get you down, the only person who will be dragged down is yourself, if you let it bother you.'"

The key words in John's teaching philosophy were success, idea, plan, and simplification. Make the player feel you're with him and he's got sense. You can learn an idea anywhere. A stopped watch is right twice a day. His philosophy about players was the players are kings. There wouldn't be a game if you didn't have them.

Some star players have had great praise for

Coach Sain
at work.

their coaches. Denny McLain felt that "Sain taught me that the only way to accomplish great ideas is thinking about them persistently and never stop learning. When I saw a 50 year-old man like him still carrying around school books, I knew I could still learn something."

"Sain knows more about winning a baseball game than any man I know" remarked Mickey Lolich. "He gave me confidence without letting me jump over the line where cockiness starts." Jim Bouton felt that John Sain was the most outstanding person he'd ever met. "That man Sain," said Jim "Mudcat" Grant, "sure puts biscuits in your pan."

What are John's feeling about his players? Here are some quotes: "Pitchers have to have an arm. "You can't make chicken salad out of chicken manure." "The world wants winners and results. People don't want to hear about labor pains, they want to see the baby." "Pitchers get lonesome on the mound. When they're in trouble they start walking around out there wondering what to do, wondering what the guy on the bench wants them to do. There's the trouble. They've got to do it themselves. My job is helping them plan ahead so when they're on the mound, they know what to do."

The testimony of the relationship between coach and pitcher can be seen in Sain's twenty-game winners:

New York
Yankees
1961   Whitey Ford
1962   Ralph Terry
1963   Whitey Ford, Jim Bouton

Minnesota
Twins
1965   Mudcat Grant
1966   Jim Kaat

Detroit
Tigers
1967   Earl Wilson
1968   Denny McLain (31 wins)
1969   Denny McLain

Chicago
White Sox
1971   Wilbur Wood
1972   Wilbur Wood, Stan Bahnsen
1973   Wilbur Wood
1974   Wilbur Wood, Jim Kaat

Sain's own record boasted four seasons of winning twenty games or more. Why is John Sain one of the greatest pitching coaches of all time? The reason is very basic. He will show a pitcher how he can get maximum performance from himself and still make the game fun.

John's students encompassed all types, but they usually fell into three categories: 1) players who could learn and figure things out for themselves, 2) those who could watch a demonstration of an idea and carry it through them-

selves, and 3) ballplayers who needed to have an idea repeated over and over again and maybe once more. He could handle them all.

Sain's unique approach to coaching may be the reason he is one of the best in his field. A typical example is the turnaround in the career of Dick Radatz, a 31 year-old pitcher who had lost his control and was sold by the Cleveland Indians to the Chicago Cubs. The Cubs released him eventually, and six other teams couldn't find a spot for him. Radatz was invited to the training camp of the Tigers by the club's general manager, and the pitching coach went to work. Radatz came up with a new pitch with a drop that caused hitters to swing off balance. His control was unequaled in his career, as he retired the first twenty-one batters he faced during that spring training.

Throughout spring training Radatz' coach, John Sain, would stand behind him, spitting tobacco juice and pointing out every flaw in the pitcher's movement. In addition, Sain sold his "power of positive pitching" philosophy to Radatz. "The woods are full of pitchers going back to the minor leagues and bullpens who throw just as good a fast ball and curve as the guys who're winning in the big leagues. Why? They've all got a thousand reasons why the sun's liable not to come up tomorrow. Well, the world wants winners and results. People don't want to hear about labor pains, they want to see the baby." He would continue, like a sales manager at his Monday morning salesmen's meeting: "Look, you can go stomping through weeds and popping birds out of the sky if you're a good shot and shoot subconsciously. But, if you stand there all nerved up like you are in a ball game and say, 'Step number one, put finger on trigger, step number two, do this—well, you couldn't hit a sleeping elephant.' It's the same in pitching. And the only reason a good arm can't pitch in the big leagues is not thinking you can do it. But praying isn't going to get that ball across the plate. You've got to know it's going to go there and have a program to get it there."

An appreciative player with the Tigers once said, "Look, I've had nine other pitching coaches, and except for one of them, all they wanted to do was run you to death or holler, 'Pound that ball up and in, baby,' or 'Pound low and away, baby, no problem.' Sain lays it on the line. He says you're in the business to fool people and explains how you can do it." Sain had his work cut out for him when he joined the sixth-place Twins in 1965. Working with an underachieving staff, the coach took control and turned out Jim "Mudcat" Grant, winning twenty-one games, and Jim Kaat, winning twenty-five games that season. The remaining pitching staff, including Jim Perry and his new spinning pitch, Dave Boswell, Bill Pleis, Jerry Fosnow, Jim Merritt, Camelo Pascual, and Al Worthington, pulled the team through despite mononucleosis, torn muscles, and tendonitis incapacitating the four starting pitchers. The Twins won their first pennant in 1965 and followed that success with a second-place finish in 1966. The credit went to the pitching coach.

In 1967, Sain moved to the pitching-poor Tigers. Working with Denny McLain, Mickey Lolich, and Earl Wilson, he improved the Detroit pitching staff to the point of finishing a close second in that first season, in which Wilson won twenty-two games, and McLain, seventeen games. The latter, claimed from the White Sox earlier for $8,000, developed a tricky sidearm pitch (see story in pitching chapter about how this pitch was developed). In 1968, the Tigers won the World Series. McLain claimed thirty-one victories, becoming the first thirty-game winner in thirty-four years. (Lefty Grove won 31 in 1931, and Dizzy Dean, 30 games in 1934.)

That winning hard slider pitch which changed the game was a tremendous asset to Sain and his pitchers. "I consider the spinning pitch a bonus," said Sain. "Look, you decrease the speed of your pitch when you throw a curve, and if it doesn't curve just right, somebody will knock it into a parking lot. But, if you throw a fast ball that spins without reducing the speed, and it slides only two inches in either direction, then you've got people swinging at four inches of air. You're not just in business, you're

running the business. Anything you can conceive or believe, you can achieve."

He practices what he preaches with his pitchers. As a pitcher warms up, Sain watches the ball approach the plate from behind the batter's box. By standing behind the plate, he quickly observes any mistakes, such as pitchers favoring the outside of the plate. "Don't be afraid of hitting the batter," he would call out. "If you low bridge me, it's my fault."

Sain also has his own philosophy on running for pitchers. "Look, there's been a lot of money made running pitchers," Sain says, "and nobody can prove these guys wrong. When I played they had me believing that you had to run until you grabbed your sides, and I'm sure I nearly ran to Arkansas and back. Sure, you've got to run enough to get in shape, but when you've abused your body pitching eight or nine innings, you need three days to recover. If you're looking for ways to kill time, doesn't it make more sense to practice the mechanics of pitching than it does to run? If it didn't, pitching coaches could go to track meets and get all kinds of star pitchers."

Once the season begins and Sain has given his pitchers the knowledge and confidence to get the ball right where it needs to go, he discourages outside advice or instruction, either directly or through team meetings. "A pitcher must usually adjust during a game to pitches that work most effectively for him on that day. If it turns out that he must throw something other than what was planned, players tend to ask, 'How come you're not following the game plan?'"

Sain never hesitates to defend his pitchers when a pitch does not go as expected. "Don't let anybody tell you that was a bad pitch. That guy might have hit something else farther." A pitcher must have confidence in his judgment and ability.

Sain believes that visiting the mound during a game breaks the pitcher's concentration, and that its only justification is to stall while a relief man warms up. "You shouldn't interfere with a pitcher's judgment if you've coached him right. Nobody knows the hitter better than the pitcher, and he has the pulse of the game a lot better than the guy coming out to the mound. Now a few of these guys think they are great advisors. One major league pitcher said he had a coach who liked to get on TV and would come out to the mound and say, 'This guy's a good long-ball hitter, so don't give him anything good to swing at. But don't walk him either.' Finally, he had enough and hollered at the coach as he strutted off the mound, 'Hey, what'd you want me to do, pitch to him or walk him?' "

His pitchers talk freely with him after a game. This is one reason Sain dresses with his players, not with the manager or other coaches, so he is readily available for their questions or conversations. In a baseball tradition, Sain doesn't congratulate a winning pitcher in the dugout, but reserves it for private moments. As he observes from the dugout, he evaluates the pitcher's performance and watches the spin and velocity of pitches so he can answer the player's questions about the success or failure of certain pitches. It is easy to talk with a friend sitting next to you. Mickey Lolich recalled, "I've pitched such lousy games that nobody could find anything positive to talk about. But Sain would say, 'Remember that curve ball that turned so and so around? Well, though you might have lost, you realized some gain from it. Your curve ball might be improving.' He gave me self-confidence."

Sain challenged an old idea and axiom: the value of scouting reports on batters. "It sounds good to say we're throwing to a batter's weak spot, but it makes more sense for a pitcher to use his strength against the hitter than it does to match his weaknesses against what somebody guessed is a batter's weakness."

Sain will defend his pitchers to the end. In a tense moment in Minnesota, a curve ball was hit so hard that the Twins left fielder had to leap against the fence to catch it. "Anybody who grooves a pitch like that," interjected Billy Martin (then the Twins coach), "ought to be fined."

"Any pitch that gets the batter out," Sain said, "is a good pitch." "Anything less, when people jump on my pitchers," he said later, "would have been a double cross."

In a pitching career that spanned twenty years in the majors and minors, Sain accumulated a vast store of knowledge and know-how. Because "I never had the power to throw it past the hitters," he had to learn to confuse the batters to win. He developed seven different kinds of curves.

Early in his career, Sain was released by four different teams. He then spent several years pitching for $50 a month in organizations like the Cotton States League and Northeast Arkansas League. He got beat in one game by a score of 17-2. He knew then he had to figure out a way to improve himself. He then joined the navy, and there began his concept of the power of positive pitching. He became known as Silent John, a straight-faced, mean-looking man who would stare menacingly at the batter and, after a few confusing motions, throw a ball that would cross the plate in a split second. The next time he would pitch in a similar manner, but have the ball reach the plate a little sooner. His greatest season came in 1948 when he and Warren Spahn won thirty-nine games between them and pitched the then-Boston Braves to a pennant. Using his confusing ways and curve balls, he had the batters swinging at air. If the batter expected a change-up, Sain would throw a pitch that resembled a fast ball, but slid or dropped just before it reached the plate. His record spoke for itself.

John is presently doing his thing with the Atlanta Braves, in his best style of a great coach.

All the great coaches I've known have also displayed these same outstanding traits, including people like Ted Williams, Charlie Lau, Wally Moses, Ralph Kiner, Ray Berres, Dick Siebert, Andy Cohen, Buck Leonard, Branch Rickey, Mickey McConnell, Rich Rollins, Whitey Herzog, Dick Howser, Eddie Yost, Rosy Ryan, and Ed Katalinas. They all have mastered coaching.

3 | John Sain on Pitching

After a brilliant career with the Braves and the Yankees, tall, quiet, gentlemanly John Sain moved his gear into another part of the locker room and launched another dazzling career, this time as a pitching coach. First with the Yankees, then with the Twins, Tigers, White Sox, and now with the Atlanta Braves, the Arkansas traveler has established himself as the nonpareil of pitching coaches. Jim Brosnan, an outstanding pitcher before he turned writer, has said that Sain's approach may have done as much for pitching in the 1960s as the lively ball did for batting in the late 1920s and the 1930s.

Nobody has ever known more about pitching than John Sain. Nobody has ever been able to articulate or teach it as well. And probably nobody in baseball has ever been more candid about his knowledge and more willing to reveal everything he knows. The result has been a

bonanza for everyone who has ever talked pitching with him.

The writer presented himself to Sain and received the typical Sain hospitality—several hours of fabulous pitching talk! Some of the highlights of this conversation, in question-and-answer form, follow.

How would you go about developing a young pitcher?

I'd first determine the boy's natural way of throwing. One way of doing this is by hitting fungoes to him in the outfield and watching him throw the ball back. That generally will be his natural way of throwing and the way he should pitch.

I'd then try to develop his pitching motion—a simple, smooth, free, and rhythmical delivery. Coaches who disregard these basic mechanics

Notice how both Dave McNally and Nolan Ryan have their arms into a perfect position to throw and now everything becomes a quick downward motion. Have someone in your family or your coach take a picture of you; if you are not in this position at your release point, your pitching mechanics are basically wrong.

and principles of pitching form and let the boy abuse his arm will wind up with ineffective and sore-armed pitchers.

What do you stress in a smooth motion?

I want the pitcher to put his hip pocket into the hitter's face. This is especially important for the sidearm pitcher. Although the overhand and the three-quarter pitchers also must emphasize this point, it is not as imperative.

This sort of pivot or turn allows the arm to keep up with and work with the body. If this isn't stressed, the pitcher's body can be too quick for his arm, thus destroying his rhythm and power, as his arm will have to hurry to catch up with his body.

What are the pitcher's chief tools?

Velocity, rotation, change of speed, and deception with control. At the same time,

pitching must be simplified. The pitcher should always be thinking of how to make everything simpler.

Rotation can be practiced anywhere off the field with the John Sain Spinner [See Chapter 4]. This device enables a coach to show any young pitcher the proper spin from any pitching angle.

How important is spin?

It's the spin that makes a curve ball curve; a slider slide; a sinker and a screwball sink; and a fast ball rise. And remember—good breaking stuff always must go down.

The reason is simple. If a curve stays on a horizontal plane, the batter's line of vision won't be too badly disconcerted. Even if he's fooled by a pitch, he can continue to bring his bat around on a horizontal plane—pulling it in or reaching out—to meet the ball.

Mel Stottlemyre puts it all together.

In this sequence Vern Ruhle illustrates the smooth, balanced delivery which is a key to good control. Notice in photo 7 how the body and arm are together perfectly at the release point. In photo 8, you can see how the pitching shoulder is "buried" in the ground. Study this excellent sequence and see how the rhythm and timing are merged for maximum use.

Wayne Garland pitching from the stretch—a fine sinker-ball pitcher with excellent form. He finishes up in splendid fielding position. Notice in photos 1, 2, and 3 how he stretches and gets himself set in a relaxed position. In photos 6, 7, and 8, you can see how Garland bends his back knee and really launches his body from the rubber. In the last photos, you can see the excellent pitching form. In picture 13, Wayne is in perfect fielding position.

Paul Splittorf shows his outstanding pitching fundamentals from the left side. (Port-siders always seem to have classic pitching form.) Paul is loose in his preliminary windup with his arms free, the ball well hidden. Notice in picture 8 a real key teaching point, if you are a tall pitcher, in keeping the ball low. You must bend your back leg at the knee, which allows you to lower your body and drive off the pitching rubber (much as a plane shooting off a catapult on an aircraft carrier). In photos 10 and 11, he has the toe of his front foot pointing down to help keep his shoulders level. Also note that he's kept his front shoulder closed. In the last two pictures, Splittorf is really burying that pitching shoulder in the ground.

Al Hrabosky demonstrates his all-out pitching delivery which has made him one of the top relievers in recent years. In the last three photos, his total use of his body is apparent, which helps him get that little extra on the pitch. This will help it to move. In the first picture, note how relaxed the wrist and fingers are so that he will get maximum whip and snap from them. (Al is not trying to squeeze the juice out of the ball.) Picture 2 is a classic for young pitchers, an excellent illustration of hiding the ball. You can't even see the top of his wrist with a telephoto lens. In photo 5, we see demonstrated all the pitching fundamentals we have been talking about. Notice Hrabosky's total concentration; his *head* and *eyes* are glued on his target in each step of his delivery.

Bert Blyleven, one of the best curve-ball pitchers in the game today, shows his splendid form. In photo 4, notice how his fingers are hooked around the ball for maximum spin. His thumb is tucked to be able to flip the ball out and give it extra spin at the last second. Also see how the narrow part of his arm is going to be facing the hitter as he releases this curve ball.

When the ball sinks, however, his visual line must suddenly change from the horizontal to the vertical. And if he has been bringing his bat around on a horizontal plane, he'll now have to quickly dip it to meet the ball. This takes some doing, particularly if he has already committed himself to a flat swing.

What kind of grip do you advocate for the curve ball?

The grip should be light but firm, not tight, with the two top fingers fairly close together and the thumb directly underneath them. An overly firm grip tightens the muscles on the underside of the forearm, partly locking the wrist. And if there's anything that a good curve-ball pitcher needs, it's a good flexible wrist to get the necessary spin on the ball.

Your fast curve or slider has revolutionized pitching. How do you teach it?

The fingers are moved slightly to the right of the fast-ball grip, and the fingers are pulled over and straight down on the ball. The elbow is slightly bent and closer to the body and head. The smooth delivery and good follow-through place hardly any strain on the elbow.

The thumb doesn't grip too tightly, as this can spoil the wrist action. In fact, the thumb can sometimes be flipped from underneath the ball to provide even more spin.

The faster the rotation, the sharper the drop. The motion is so easy and the strain so little that Whitey Ford started throwing this pitch from almost the first moment he tried it.

The fast curve is really a fast ball with a break at the end. The break may take a little off its speed, but it's a highly effective pitch to go along with the regular fast ball, curve, and changeup.

What is your theory on the release of the ball?

You must have a quick forearm and wrist action. The White Sox pitchers did this real well. I like to have the pitcher think curve ball on every pitch until just before the release. If it's a curve ball he's throwing, he just thinks curve ball all the way through. If it's going to be a fast curve, he thinks curve ball until just before the release and then thinks fast ball the rest of the way. Quite obviously he must have command of all his pitches.

What do you do with the pitcher who seems to have lost his stuff for no apparent reason?

A pitcher will lose a pitch when he begins neglecting it. If he has three or four pitches, it would be wise for him to spend 50 percent of his time on his best pitch.

How do you go about teaching pitchers to work on the hitters?

I don't feel that you can teach each pitcher a different way to pitch to the hitters. Basically, the pitcher should work to his power, which usually is from the waist down. And he should put his best stuff on the ball. If he then makes a mistake high, he may get away with it. If he's just pitching to spots, however, he'll be in real trouble if he misses.

What are your thoughts on working from the stretch position?

In holding a man on first, it's important to have the knees bent. If you keep them straight and then bend them in the delivery, you'll be giving the runner a good tip-off.

It is also essential, of course, to develop quickness to the plate, and you'll have to experiment until you arrive at the best way to do this. As a pitcher, I closed my stance by moving my front leg way over toward third.

With a man on third and the steal or the squeeze a distinct possibility, the pitcher should work from a stretch. Being able to see the runner, (if he's right-handed) he can take his time and put something on the ball. When pitching from his regular stance, he'll be inclined to hurry his pitch for fear of the runner taking off on him.

What are the important mental aspects of pitching?

I like a pitcher who, after losing, doesn't

blame it on the breaks, but goes on trying to find ways to improve himself. The pitcher must always stay loose, particularly in a jam.

How many times have you seen a pitcher in a tight spot make up his mind to blow the ball by the hitter? Just before the release, he'll really muscle up and then let go. The result is an unnatural delivery with a poor wrist action that puts less, rather than more, on the ball.

A smart catcher can be a big psychological help to the pitcher. The catcher who really knows how to handle pitchers will come out to the mound and ask "What's your plan? What do you want to throw?" or possibly "What are you trying to do?"

This kind of catcher is giving the pitcher credit for having some sense and thus builds his confidence. It takes a special temperament to pitch. The two people who really look bad whenever they show emotion on the field are the pitcher and the manager.

Concentration is another big item—it must be total. This is where pressure and second guessing visit the mound. Also the worry about how tough the particular hitter is or about the last good hit he got off you.

The pitcher must think positively. Instead of thinking about the hits, he should think of the success that he's had against the hitter or against other hitters in similar situations. And anytime he gets the hitter out on a line drive, he shouldn't think of it as luck. He should think of it as a good pitch. He must feel that he's the master of the situation.

About how often should a pitcher throw?

Contrary to some theories, I want him to throw some every day—enough to get loose but not enough to abuse his arm. You must develop your pitcher's arm and one of the best ways of doing this is by having him throw. I feel that the typical pitcher is ready, mentally, to pitch every third day, though I realize that, physically, this schedule would be difficult to maintain over a season.

We often hear the term that so and so is a five- or six-inning pitcher. What are your thoughts on this?

It's possible that the pitcher simply lacks stamina, that he fatigues easily. The more likely cause, however, is that the pitcher hasn't enough equipment; the batters begin catching up with him after five or six innings. What he needs, as a rule, is another pitch.

What use do you make of pitching charts?

We can discern several things from a good chart. Generally, a batter will hit his ground balls and pop outs in one direction and his line drives in another. And it's a big help to know which pitches he hits where. Also, if the pitcher feels he's getting killed with one of his pitches, we can go to the charts and see what's really happening with that pitch.

The pitching chart in Chapter 23 shows the type of chart we use. We use red for base hits and blue or green for fly outs and ground balls.

What do you try to do in coaching and working with pitchers?

First, I like to put myself in the pitcher's shoes. I say to myself: "How would I pitch with this man's style and stuff?" Then I suggest two or three ideas which might help him. Most of the time he'll try them out and find the one which helps him most. Once he's satisfied that it can help him, he'll adopt it and work on it.

If I tried to force him to throw one way, he'd probably resist me. This is the one flaw of many otherwise fine pitching coaches—they try to make all pitchers throw the way they did, even though their physiques and tools are completely different.

How should a pitcher get ready for spring training, especially in a winter climate?

The two drills I particularly like for this purpose are bench jumping and cement-block drill. In the first drill, the pitcher jumps up and down on a bench or chair (whose surface is about three feet off the floor) fifty times. Later, he can increase the repetitions and do it with both legs. This not only builds up the legs but simulates the pitcher's leg kick.

The cement-block drill can be used in a basement, gym, or any other area. After obtaining or making up a solid three-foot square cement block, you should smooth one side so that it won't scuff your baseballs and paint the strike zone on it. You should then run two pipes from the top down to the floor.

You can then either pitch to the painted target, working on your different pitches (particularly the low strike), or you can set up the block as first, second, or third base and work on your pick-off moves. These two aids really helped me in preparing for the season.

4 | John Sain on Spinning Pitches

It isn't exactly a secret that the first checkpoint on a pitching prospect is the velocity of his fast ball. With rare exceptions, a youngster must have a strong arm to rate a chance for the majors. Speed is the one quality nobody can teach him. He either has it or he doesn't, though he might slightly improve it with better mechanics.

As important as it is, however, speed isn't the entire answer to pitching success. It's merely the beginning. Few pitchers can get by in fast company with just a fast ball. The prospect must also develop control, a curve ball, and a change of pace. And, in time, as the arm starts losing its elasticity or the batters start catching up with the basic pitches, the smart hurler will develop an "extra" pitch—a slider, sinker, screwball, or some other offbeat pitch.

The moral is fairly obvious: any young pitcher who wants to get anywhere in baseball shouldn't rely on one good pitch, unless he can throw the ball as hard as a Walter Johnson or pitch "butterflies" like Hoyt Wilhelm. The more rounded a pitcher's repertoire, the better his chances for advancement.

I believe the learning process should begin as early as possible; the earlier, in fact, the better. The high school coach might immediately protest: "Do you mean you want me to teach my kids how to throw sliders, sinkers, and knucklers?"

My answer is yes—with reservations. I realize most coaches and physiologists have always discouraged youngsters from fooling around with "freak" deliveries. They believe that the youthful arm isn't strong enough to be "strained" in this fashion, and that it might be permanently injured. They also believe that the boy, at this age, should be concentrating wholly on control of his basic pitches.

I have no quarrel with this reasoning. It is sound, as far as it goes. But I believe this: the earlier a boy starts learning anything, the faster he's going to master it. Why wait until a boy is eighteen or nineteen before teaching him the mechanics of the various types of breaking pitches? You'll be retarding his progress. He's going to need one or more of these pitches in the not-so-distant future, and instead of having them at his command at that time, he's going to have to start learning them.

I don't mean to imply that a 12-, 13-, or 14-year-old boy should be sent out on the mound and taught the curve ball. I do mean that he should be given an understanding of the proper mechanics of all pitches—why rotation is important, how it is applied, what it does to the ball.

How can this be done? For a long time, I used to demonstrate rotation by holding a ball in my left hand and showing the various types of spin with the other. This left something to be desired. The different mechanical actions and rotations were not only difficult to demonstrate, but could hardly be remembered and much less practiced without abusing the arm.

One afternoon I noticed Ralph Terry on the bench practicing spin by flipping the ball easily in various ways. I said, "Ralph, I'm going to fix up a ball so that you can spin it a whole lot easier and better than that."

Thinking about it on the way home, an idea occurred to me. When I got home, I went into the living room, picked an apple out of the fruit bowl, then plucked the end out of one of the "rabbit ears" (indoor antenna) of my television set. I stuck the thin bar through the apple, and I now had a "baseball" I could spin to my heart's content. The next step was the development of the patented Baseball Spinner.

With this Spinner and our illustrations, I feel every boy can practice the correct way of spinning a baseball for all types of pitches. I realize that this sort of practice won't guarantee instant success; you won't be able to go out the next day and start snapping off sharp-breaking curves, rising fast balls, and deceptive sinkers. It will, however, provide an understanding of the spin you must apply to make the ball do these things.

It's the spin that makes a curve ball curve; a slider slide; a sinker and a screwball, sink; and a fast ball, rise. And always remember: good breaking stuff must go down.

In the old days, a distinction was made between curves and "drops." The curve was usually a flat, breaking pitch, while the drop did just that. The distinction has long vanished. Since a flat curve isn't usually effective, the good curve ball breaks down. In short, a curve ball, in modern parlance, is a breaking pitch that goes down. The "hanging curve," which is so often stroked out of the park, is merely a curve that hasn't been spun sharply enough to make it drop.

The reason is simple enough. If a curve stays on a horizontal plane, the batter's visual line won't be too badly disconcerted. Even if he's fooled by the pitch, he can continue to bring his bat around on a horizontal plane, pulling it in or reaching out to meet the ball.

When the ball sinks, however, his visual line must suddenly change from the horizontal to the vertical. And if he has been bringing his bat around on a horizontal plane, he'll have to quickly dip it to meet the ball. That takes some doing, particularly if he has already committed himself to a flat swing.

Now let's see how the various spins can be taught with the Baseball Spinner. The handle is held in the non-pitching hand, while the proper spin on the ball is sharply imparted with the pitching hand. The direction in which the handle is pointed is of vital importance, since it puts the baseball in the correct axis for the specific type of delivery and spin.

The grip should be light but firm, not tight, with the two top fingers fairly close together and the thumb directly underneath them. An overly firm grip tightens the muscles on the underside of the forearm, partly locking the wrist. And if there's anything that a good curve-ball pitcher needs, it's a good flexible wrist to get the necessary spin on the ball.

Now, let's proceed to the photos. They show how the Baseball Spinner can be used by both left and right-handed pitchers in the overhand, three-quarter, and sidearm motions. They dem-

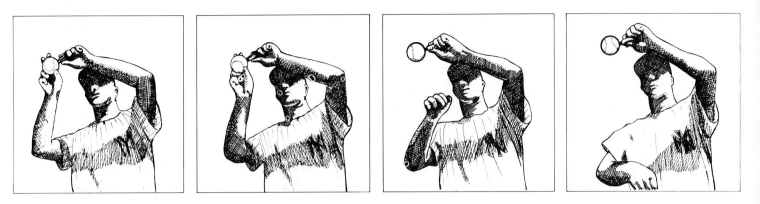

Johnny demonstrates the correct spin for a three-quarter arm fast ball on his unique Baseball Spinner.

After changing the axis of the Baseball Spinner, Sain applies the correct spin for a three-quarter arm curve ball.

onstrate the correct axis for each type of spin, as well as the direction in which the spin should be applied.

FAST BALL

Holding the Spinner in the position shown, apply the spin in the direction indicated by the arrow. This will make the ball rotate back toward you.

It's the speed and spin that makes a fast ball move or hop. The real good overhand fast ball will level off or rise. Both the three-quarter and the sidearm delivery, when thrown with enough speed and spin, will move in on the hitter (right-handed pitcher to right-handed hitter or left-handed pitcher to left-handed batter).

While a fast ball can sometimes be improved through practice and the development of coordination, the best fast balls seem to be rare gifts of nature.

CURVE

Check the direction of the Spinner handle for the proper axis. Place your finger on the ball and then sharply apply spin in the direction of the arrow.

Most pitchers apply this spin by simultaneously pulling down with the fingers and flipping up with the thumb, spinning the ball in the direction of the arrow. The youngster can try spinning the ball with only the top fingers, using a light pull downward in the direction of the arrow. Next, he can try flipping the ball upward, using only the thumb.

The lesson is clear: if he can apply a small amount of spin with each of these methods, the coordination of the two should give him a faster rotation.

After learning to get good rotation on the Spinner, don't immediately start on sharp-breaking curves. After a preliminary warm-up, try throwing about half-speed, applying the spin you've learned on the Spinner. Since you no longer have the ball on a handle, you must now watch the spin while the ball is in flight. In your early attempts, be satisfied if the ball merely spins in the right direction, even if it doesn't curve.

Before trying to throw faster and sharper breaking curves, make sure you have a smooth delivery and that there's little strain on your arm. As mentioned before, the mechanics should be learned at about half-speed. Most arms are hurt when a pitcher starts losing his temper, showing off, or throwing hard without a proper warm-up.

SLIDER (FAST CURVE)

The slider is really a fast ball with a break at the end. The break may take a little off its speed, but it's a highly effective pitch to go along with the regular fast ball, curve, and change-up.

The axis, or handle, of the Spinner is now pointed downward and to the left side of the plate for a right-handed pitcher, and downward and to the right side of the plate for a left-handed pitcher. Apply the spin by pulling down in the direction of the arrow. This provides an off-center fast-ball spin whose axis is downward in the direction of the break.

If this doesn't work, you can experiment with your own ideas. Just remember that most mechanical pitches should be practiced at about half-speed, and that you should wait until you're better coordinated and understand the mechanics before trying to make a pitch break sharply.

SINKER

Compare the three-quarter sinker and the three-quarter fast-ball pictures. You'll notice that the axis in the sinker is downward and slightly forward as the fast-ball spin is imparted. Turning the wrist produces a loss of some forward speed, which is why a sinker is slightly slower than a fast ball.

Now compare the sidearm sinker and sidearm fast-ball photos. Again note the axis change and how the fast-ball spin is applied in both instances.

SCREWBALL

This is a very difficult pitch to learn and maintain with consistency. It is produced by a combination of spin, change of speed, and motion. The ball acts like a reverse curve, moving out and down when delivered by a left-handed pitcher to a right-handed batter, or by a right-handed pitcher to a left-handed batter. To be effective with this pitch, you must properly coordinate the three aforementioned factors.

Compare the three-quarter screwball and the three-quarter fast-ball photos. Notice that the axis changes slightly in each, creating a change in the wrist position. Since the wrist and forearm are sharply turned in—an unnatural action—most people believe the screwball puts a lot of strain on the arm. This strain can be reduced by proper mechanics and a proper delivery.

This applies to all mechanical pitches, plus the fast ball. If the pitcher is unable to realize when he's abusing his arm, a coach or some other knowledgeable baseball man must help supervise his throwing.

When should a boy actually start throwing breaking pitches? I've often been asked this question and I admit it's hard to answer. It's such an individual matter—depending upon the boy's age, build, strength, intelligence, experience, and coordination—that the coach, an experienced baseball man, or perhaps even the boy himself will ultimately make the decision.

I can tell you this, however: every good curve-ball pitcher I know has told me they started throwing curves at an early age. Most of us started by spinning the ball with extreme cau-

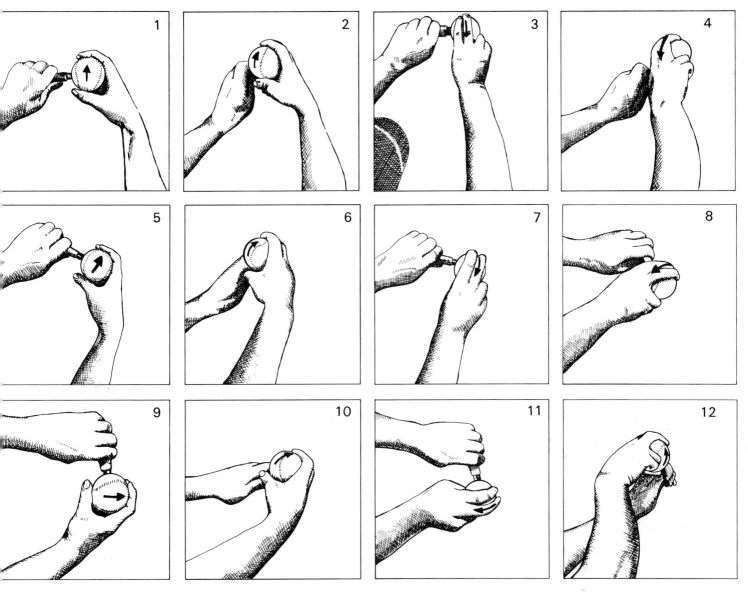

The positions for hands for right-handed pitchers: curve ball, slider, fast ball, and sinker.

1. Overhand curve ball
2. Overhand slider
3. Overhand fast ball
4. Three-quarter sinker
5. Three-quarter curve ball
6. Three-quarter slider
7. Three-quarter fast ball
8. Side-arm sinker
9. Side-arm curve ball
10. Side-arm slider
11. Side-arm fast ball
12. Screwball

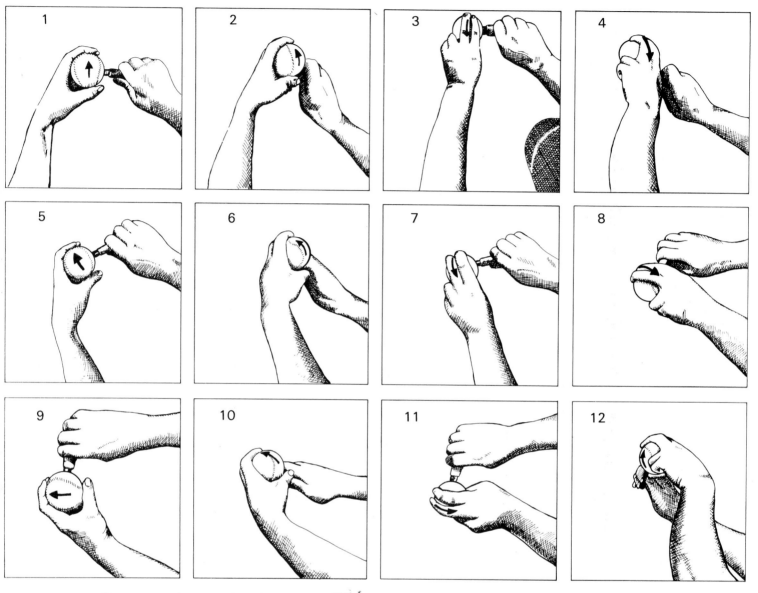

The positions for hands for left-handed pitchers: curve ball, slider, fast ball, and sinker.

1. Overhand curve ball
2. Overhand slider
3. Overhand fast ball
4. Three-quarter sinker
5. Three-quarter curve ball
6. Three-quarter slider
7. Three-quarter fast ball
8. Side-arm sinker
9. Side-arm curve ball
10. Side-arm slider
11. Side-arm fast ball
12. Screwball

tion, putting as little strain on the arm as possible until the muscles were coordinated and strong enough for the actual execution.

The "secret" lies in careful planning: (1) give the boy a thorough understanding of the mechanics, (2) start him slowly, having him merely spin the ball at half-speed, (3) see that he warms up properly before attempting any hard throws, (4) make sure he has the coordination and strength to attempt these pitches, (5) supervise him carefully to see that he doesn't abuse his arm. And always remember this about the final point: a boy can hurt his arm throwing fast balls just as easily as he can throwing curve balls.

FIRST THINGS FIRST: DEVELOP A SMOOTH DELIVERY

With nobody on base, take a stance squarely facing the batter. Place the front spike over the edge of the rubber, slightly angled to the right to facilitate the pivot. Set the other foot a few inches back of the rubber. Keep the body fairly erect, with the weight forward and the shoulders level. When taking the sign, hide the ball from the batter. You may place it behind the thigh of the pitching foot. A short windup—one or at most two pumps—loosens the arm and helps bring the weight behind the pitch. Swing the arms up past the hips and join them overhead,

making sure to keep the back of the glove turned toward the hitter, thus concealing the ball.

Now the pivot begins. Slide the pitching (front) foot diagonally forward into the hole and turn your body to the right. Then, as the arm goes back, swing the left leg up and around so that you face the batter over the left shoulder. Don't kick the left leg too high; it may throw you off-balance. As you can see, you're now in a perfectly balanced position; in fact, at this point you should be able to come to a stop without falling either forward or backward. Just before bringing the pitching arm forward, start the forward stride with the left leg. Hit the ground with it flat, not on the heel, and point the toes directly at the plate. The arm is brought through in a free, easy, but powerful motion with the weight flowing from the rear to the front foot, the unwinding of the hips providing both momentum and power.

Don't stop jerkily after the ball leaves the hand. Bend the back and let the arm relax as soon as the ball is released, thus relieving the tension on the entire arm. As the arm follows through to the opposite side, the right leg comes forward into a squared-off position and the glove is brought around to the front of the body. You're now in perfect fielding position, ready to move right, left, or forward with equal facility. Now check the head. Note how it remains fixed from the start to the finish of the delivery.

Coach Sain demonstrates
the development of a
smooth delivery.

Don Gullett illustrates the perfect sequence of pitching from the stretch. Photo 5 shows his perfect balance.

5 | Mastering Control: The Key to Pitching

What is the key to pitching? *Control.* How do you teach control? How can a pitcher be improved in this area? When can a pitcher hope to develop some consistency in his control? What is real control in pitching?

In recent years I have come to believe that the mental aspect of pitching has a great deal to do with control. Even on the major league level, you may have noticed that a pitcher may be struggling along and be wild and perhaps walk one or two hitters, but as soon as there are some base runners his control becomes much sharper and he doesn't have any trouble finding the strike zone. I believe the big reason for this change is the pitcher's mental attitude. Now, instead of trying to overpower the hitter and blow it by him, he wants to fool the hitter, getting him off-balance so he will hit out in front of the pitch or behind it. The result is often a groundball for a double play or a pop

up. His main idea now is to fool the man with the lumber at the plate, either by taking a little off the pitch or putting a little more on it.

There are several ways of improving a pitcher's control. I like to use the examples of the golfer and bird hunter. A golfer who aims right at the pin on a green has a much better chance of hitting the larger green area, even if he misses the very small actual target, the pin. The same concept applies to pitching—by aiming at a small target you may miss the actual target but still get a strike. I use the bird hunter analogy to point out that a hunter reacts instinctively in aiming his rifle and firing as the birds are flushed. He doesn't slowly aim to ensure hitting the target. Many pitchers do develop this pattern of trying to carefully aim the ball over the plate.

Control is more than the ability to throw in the strike zone; it also entails mastery of the

John Hiller, premier Detroit relief pitcher. In
pictures 12, 13, and 14, John is really burying that
shoulder. In the last picture he has really let his
body go to get that little extra on the pitch.

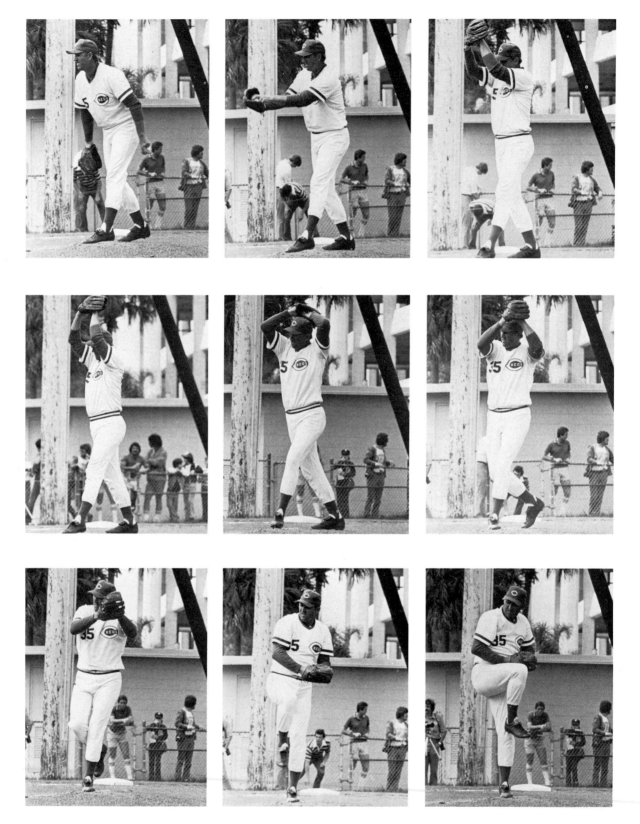

Woodie Fryman reviews all the points we've talked about in pitching with this sequence. Notice especially the perfect "L" angle of the arm in pictures 14 and 15.

Tug McGraw of the Philadelphia Phillies demonstrates perfectly the pitching fundamentals of burying the pitching shoulder in the ground, to ensure getting your maximum body power into the pitch. The last four photos really show the perfect balance before launching to the plate. Note the toe of the raised foot pointing toward the ground in photo 2. This will help you keep your shoulders level throughout the delivery. In photo 4, Tug demonstrates the classic position of every great pitcher at this key point in his delivery.

corners and the low strike. The strike low and away comes closest to being the unhittable pitch.

Relaxation at all times is a must. For example, most young pitchers grip the baseball much too tightly, especially with the thumb, which destroys good wrist action and creates arm tension. Try this yourself by gripping a ball hard with the thumb—notice the difference in the range of movement of your wrist and hand. We like to tell our pitchers to think of a ball as an egg when gripping it. To assist in relaxation, take a deep breath before pitching. A pitcher should know what pitch has been signaled for and where it should be delivered. Concentration toward delivery of the pitch should be keen. If you can do this about one hundred times a game, you should be a consistent winner.

SOME OTHER AIDS IN GAINING CONTROL

Try to split the heart of the plate with a low first pitch (possibly aiming at your catcher's crotch). If you have your good stuff that day, the ball should take off and catch one of the corners. Many professional pitchers try to be too fine in aiming the ball for a corner of the plate. If they just miss, they are in the hole. Falling behind in the count leads to real control problems; then you have to either come in with a real fat pitch or walk the hitter.

Always throw at a target. This requires concentrated effort. Satchel Paige developed control by practicing with a matchbox for a plate. If he could cut the corners of the small matchbox, home plate would appear to be a very large and easy target to hit after pitching at one so small.

Try to visualize the anticipated path or groove of the pitch before delivering.

Start with the pivot foot on the middle of the rubber. If your pitch is wild inside or outside, simply move over on the rubber and keep using the same motion.

When you are wild high, you are releasing the ball too soon. When you are wild low, you are holding the ball too long.

Develop a groove so that your lead foot lands in the same spot every time—don't become a scatter foot. Sandy Koufax could warm up twenty minutes and yet only leave one mark with his striding foot.

Throw each pitch from the same angle. Use your natural throwing motion on all pitches.

Work with one pitch at a time (first the fast ball, then the curve, etc.) until you can place it anywhere in the strike zone.

Learn first to throw at the catcher's mitt, then his shoulders, knees, and finally the lettering on his uniform.

Use the plate in practice, throwing at the corners.

Know where every pitch is going and why it is going there.

Keep your head up and still.

When pitching with men on base, be certain you have picked your target before starting your motion to the plate.

Spend half of your time in practice throwing from the stretch.

Draw a seven-foot line from your pivot foot toward home plate. On the delivery (if you are a right-handed pitcher), your left leg should always end up on the left of this line. This will prevent you from throwing across your body.

Discipline yourself mentally. Anger destroys your concentration.

Throw the ball hard, don't aim it.

Run, run, and run some more. Lack of control late in the game is usually attributable to poor physical condition.

Chart every pitch you throw in practice and games (after you are warmed up). This will give you the true facts in regard to your control.

Check the wind conditions as soon as you arrive at the park. Wind at your back helps your fast ball; wind directly in your face helps your curve.

Don't be "cute" or try to pitch in and out until you are ahead of the batter. Put something on the ball and get it over (you have eight men behind you and even a .300 hitter fails seven out of ten times).

Vida Blue bringing it from the left side. Working from the stretch in this sequence, Vida shows a real smooth head fake to first in photos 6 and 7 before picking up his target in photos 8 and 9, and delivering to the plate. Notice the classic pitching position in picture 12 that we've talked about so often in relationship to the perfect form. The pitching shoulder is buried toward the ground so well in photos 14 and 15.

Talk to yourself on the mound; for example, say "low and outside" over and over. This helps shut out all distractions.

When your pitches are coming in higher than you want, aim at the hitter's shoe tops.

Dip the knee of your pivot leg; this gives you a chance to push off as you start your forward motion.

If you are tall, you must dip the knee of your pivot leg to consistently keep the ball low. The dip lowers your projected trajectory and improves the follow-through of your arm and back.

A lazy back leg produces high pitches.

Challenge the hitter with your best pitch, even if it is to the hitter's strength. If a pitcher spot-pitches without his best stuff and makes a mistake, he is in real trouble, but by going with his best stuff he may make a mistake and still get away with it.

Concentration must be total on the mound. Carl Hubbell once told me that if I came to the mound and asked for your home phone number and you could not tell me, your concentration was then total and had reached the desired point. This is where pressure and second guessing visit the mound to disrupt total concentration. One great pitching coach would rather not visit his pitchers on the mound in most instances, his thinking being that he will partially upset the pitcher's concentration which must be total.

Do not worry about how tough the hitter is or the last good hit he got off you. Instead, the pitcher should think of the successes he has had against the hitter in similar situations. You have to feel you are the master of the situation.

The result of this thinking will be splendid control, the key to pitching.

6 | Developing as a Pitcher

What causes sore arms? How can a coach avoid or minimize them? What is the best way to condition pitchers? How long and how often should a young pitcher throw at the start?

Coaches are always pondering such questions, particularly when organizing preseason practice. The early-spring routine is critical for pitchers. In fact, most baseball men feel that they can minimize or even eliminate arm trouble by breaking in their pitchers' arms properly in the spring.

The writer threw these questions at baseball's premier pitching coach, John Sain, and the wizard of arms came through (as usual) with several splendid ideas on the art of pitching and working with pitchers.

First, Sain feels that every youngster must pitch from his natural throwing angle or he'll eventually end up with arm trouble. There are two ways of determining a boy's natural style.

One is to have him catch some fly balls in the outfield and throw hard to a relay man. As long as the boy doesn't know he's being observed, he'll throw with his natural motion.

The second method is to have the boy work at a pick-up drill (to be explained in Chapter 19) until he becomes tired and then observe how he returns the ball to the thrower, especially with respect to his arm angle and release point. Once the young pitcher's natural motion is determined, that's the way he should pitch to minimize arm trouble.

Knowledgeable coaches are now giving much thought to the arm angle and release point that will produce the most power for the individual pitcher. You can experiment with your pitchers by standing in front of them and clasping their pitching hands at the different release points and angles and see from which point (straight overhand, three-quarters, sidearm, or under-

Mel Stottlemyre, the former Yankee ace who was coached by the author, demonstrates a smooth, relaxed, and highly functional delivery. Notice how he steps directly toward the batter, delivers with a fluid but powerful full arm motion, and finishes in perfect fielding position.

Mel Stottlemyre's loose, relaxed grip helps avoid forearm, wrist, and finger tension.

Mark "The Bird" Fidrych doing his thing. In photo 3, he has lifted his front knee to help get his throwing arm in position. Even though Mark supposedly has an unorthodox pitching style, notice the perfect balance in photo 4. His pitching fundamentals are perfect. In photo 5, Fidrych demonstrates perfectly the pitching mechanic of bringing your pitching hand back with the palm facing the ground. This allows the hand and the wrist to act like a whip. Photos 6 and 7 demonstrate free arm action and burying the shoulder in the ground to get that extra velocity.

hand) they can deliver the most force against your hand.

Sain makes another point which is often overlooked in young pitchers—arm tension, especially in the reach back. Some boys have a tendency to grip the ball too tightly at the start of the delivery.

A related problem is gripping the ball too hard with the thumb. This destroys the wrist action and helps increase arm tension. Sain suggests that you have the pitcher think he's gripping an egg rather than a baseball. He then won't be so prone to squeeze tightly, especially when taking the ball out of his glove at the beginning of his delivery. He'll thus come to his release point with a relaxed forearm and wrist, which will help him develop a fast arm.

Sain has some highly convincing ideas on how to bring pitchers along in the spring, particularly with respect to the amount and frequency of work. He offers a program which any coach can use, even those who must condition their pitchers in the gym before moving outside.

His method is one of cautious preparation. He uses a stopwatch to make sure of his work schedule; he won't allow a pitcher to throw a minute over the allotted time. That extra pitch or two could be just the ones to strain the arm.

Once a pitcher has gradually worked his arm into condition, he can pitch so hard and long (from two to three hours) that it may become frighteningly stiff. The pain and stiffness will reach such a peak on the second day that the nervous pitcher will begin to think he's had it.

On all balls hit to the left, the pitcher is responsible for covering first base. Although first-baseman Jason Thompson fielded the ball, Vern Ruhle sprinted to the bag as quickly as possible. From this sequence of pictures, can you tell why there are no other base runners?

The discomfort will subside somewhat on the third day, but not enough for some pitchers to believe that they'll be able to throw the next day. The fourth day brings the "miracle." The arm suddenly feels so loose and strong that the pitcher loses all doubt about going nine innings.

Some words of caution: too much rest can be just as risky as too little rest. Some pitchers, after taking more than their normal rest, become so strong that their pitches tend to straighten out or become so alive as to cause control problems.

Pitchers who develop pains very early in spring training, usually through throwing too hard too early, will tend toward recurrent soreness all season. They may not be able to pitch effectively for months or, sometimes, ever again.

Sain makes sure to prevent his pitcher from throwing too long too early. He has them begin training by warming up slowly for five minutes and then lobbing the ball in batting practice for another five minutes. (He puts a stopwatch on them.) Then the pitchers run sprints, do exercises, and discuss with Sain the mechanics of pitching.

After four days of the five-five program, the pitchers are excused from throwing for a day. Then, every other day, they warm up for ten minutes and throw batting practice for another ten. After being on the ten-ten program for two or three days, the hurlers warm up for fifteen minutes, then throw fifteen minutes in a controlled situation, either in the batting cage, gym, or on the mound (if outside). The pitcher, after a day's rest, is now ready to go three or four innings in an exhibition game.

This type of conditioning program will have all the pitchers ready for a complete effort with a strong arm at the opening of the season.

Another major league team offers the following ideas on the conditioning of pitchers:

1. Pick ups are beneficial to the arm and the back muscles, especially during spring training.

2. Keep your legs in shape by running.

3. A pitcher must be the best athlete in the club and, therefore, should be in better shape than anyone else.

4. The first ten days are the danger period. In two week's time, a pitcher should be able to throw as hard as he likes for two or three innings without any aftereffects. He should throw every day until he's ready to pitch batting practice and start spinning the ball the first day. (Different muscles come into play in throwing breaking pitches and must be strengthened too.)

5. After a player pitches batting practice (in spring training), send him to the bunting cage (if available) or use him in pick-off plays. This should be done while the pitcher's arm is warm. Never use a pitcher in a throwing drill when his arm is cold. (Don Drysdale spent much time fielding balls placed everywhere in front of the plate and throwing to every base. He felt that this type of practice helped him win one or two games a season.)

6. Keep your pitchers as busy as possible. Let them participate in pepper games if they choose, but don't let them stand around and stiffen up.

To make our pitchers aware of their control, we have our stats man mark every pitch on the pitching chart in Chapter 23 (actually used by major league clubs). We start out with 30 pitches, 15 from the stretch and 15 from the wind-up. We then increase it to 40, 60, 80, and so on until we reach 120 pitches, half from the stretch and half from the windup.

After using these charts for awhile, you'll find that your pitchers will fall into a definite groove with respect to strikes and balls, and you'll be able to quickly spot potential problems—they show up in the form of sudden changes in the ball-strike ratios. Charting every pitch from the first day of practice can be a real aid in improving a pitcher's concentration and control.

When should a boy actually start throwing breaking pitches? Sain admits this is hard to answer: "It's an individual matter—depending upon the boy's age, build, strength, intelligence, experience, and coordination—and the coach or an experienced baseball man probably will have to make the decision.

"I can tell you this, however: every good curveball pitcher I know has told me that he started throwing curves at an early age. Most of us started by spinning the ball with extreme caution and with as little strain on the arm as

Jim Lonborg shows perfectly some of the pitching fundamentals we've been discussing. In photo 6, he breaks his hands (glove and ball separate). In the next picture, he lowers the ball as far as possible, allowing his arm to make the longest arc possible for the maximum whip and use of the arm. Notice the cocking of the wrist in photo 8, and in photo 9 you can see perfectly the palm of the pitching hand facing the ground. This provides the maximum whip and use from your wrist, hand, and fingers at the release point in your delivery. In the last picture, Lonborg has gotten everything into the pitch.

possible, until the muscles were coordinated and strong enough for the actual execution."

Isn't it strange that years ago, before Little League, thousands of kids threw heavily taped baseballs or pitched heavy, waterlogged baseballs for hours without ever injuring their arms!

Most of our preseason conditioning drills for pitchers are done at the end of practice or on days when they aren't working. We run our pitchers about two miles a day for stamina and have them do wind sprints (thirty, from foul line to foul line) for speed. We also have a bench drill wherein the pitcher stands sideways in front of a locker bench and jumps up and down, alternating feet. We begin with a two-minute stint and increase both the time and intensity of the drill as the season progresses. We feel that this helps strengthen the leg muscles used in pitching.

"Pickups" provide another good drill for the early season. Pitcher A, with two baseballs, faces pitcher B. He rolls one ball after the other about ten feet to B's right and left. B fields the balls and returns them to A, and the drill is repeated. We start with 50 tosses and go up to 150 as the conditioning season progresses.

Weighted baseballs have become quite popular with pitchers today. You may fill a baseball with buckshot or buy a commercial lead baseball weighing between four and five pounds. One of the best exercises is to have the pitcher stand on his toes and reach as high as he can with his weighted ball, as if screwing in a light bulb. A simulated pitch makes another good exercise with the weighted ball. The pitcher goes through his regular motion while holding the ball in his pitching hand and supporting the arm at the elbow with the other hand. This exercise benefits strength, stretching and flexibility.

Upon moving outdoors, we convert all of our pitchers to infield and outfield fungo hitters. We feel that this hitting action over the course of a season has a positive effect on the shoulders and arms.

Each pitcher keeps a bottle of rubbing compound in his locker. This contains a fifty-fifty mixture of wintergreen and alcohol, which we expect the pitcher to vigorously rub on his entire shoulder and arm area a half hour before pitching, as well as after his post-game shower. With a little food coloring, this is Satchel Paige's "Snake Oil" compound.

The young pitcher with a real herky-jerky motion must be carefully watched. No matter how good he is, he has to abuse his arm and it will be just a matter of time before serious arm trouble crops up. The wise coach will smooth out his motion before this occurs.

7 | Charlie Lau on Hitting

We'd like to take you behind the scenes for a seminar on hitting with one of the most outstanding hitting coaches in the world, Charlie Lau of the Kansas City Royals. We move from the Royals' clubhouse to their dugout three hours before game time on a good summer baseball night. The weather is hot and muggy, and the pennant race is getting sticky, too.

Charlie has the ace teacher's way about him—a nice, slow, and easy style of talking and making his points. He loves to teach hitting. Technically, he is very sound and takes one point at a time and gets it ingrained through repetition. He is an accomplished psychologist, and, like every good teacher I've known, has the ability to make his protégés respect and believe in him and have real confidence in his teaching ability. For example, as we were talking and dissecting hitting, he introduced me to one of the Royal players, prefacing it by saying that

although this player had the misfortune of not getting very much playing right now, he can certainly hit, and hit to the opposite field in splendid fashion. The player beamed—his day had been made and his mind in the future would be more than open to any suggestion from his hitting coach.

Another Royal hitter sat on the steps of the dugout and asked me if it was all right if he listened to our seminar on hitting, as this would be a refresher course. The player, John Wathan, showed his real major league attitude, and there was no doubt he had mastered hitting. Part of our seminar follows.

Charlie, what is your basic method of teaching hitting?

I am a very strong believer in the proper mechanics of hitting. If these are executed properly—given a normal ability; decent eye-

Charlie Lau, hitting coach, Kansas City Royals.

sight, reflexes, and strength; the ability to overcome the fear of being hit with the ball (which everyone suffers from to some degree); and the desire and dedication to work and work on your hitting—you should be able to hit the baseball with some authority.

What are these mechanics of hitting as you teach them?

First, and most important, is to watch that ball all the way to the bat and keep your head still—work for total concentration on the ball. Next, you must be "balanced" before the swing, during the stride, and after contact with the ball. Balance is a key word. Your weight should be on your toes, waist slightly bent forward, hands comfortable (without tension), and bat leveled off at the back, almost parallel with the ground. A balanced shifting of the weight at the proper time eliminates tension and puts the weight into the swing, allowing you to hit with authority. I

believe very strongly in mechanics because they pay off.

What would you say are the most common hitting faults with Little League and high school hitters?

The main fault I see most often in young hitters is their eyes leaving the ball way too soon. This is usually accompanied by turning the head too soon.

It was interesting later in the evening when Charlie called me out to the batting cage and pointed out the principle his own hitters were working on—trying to see the ball hit the bat. "Total concentration," Lau said, "is all we're working on in batting practice." Instant analysis followed: "He saw that one pretty good"; "No, he did not watch that one very well." "If a hitter sees that ball all the way in batting practice," Lau remarked, "chances are he will do the same thing in the game."

Rod Carew, poised to hit—perfect balance, relaxed bat held back. In the fourth picture, his hands are back, ready to launch the bat as his front foot is set. Notice the swing and the follow-through. As hitting coach Lau would say, "A Perfect Swing."

The second biggest mistake a lot of young hitters make is standing too close to the plate. Then, if a pitch is in close, they have to step away from the pitch, jerking their head out too soon and compounding the problem of trying to keep your head still and your eyes on the ball all the way to the bat. Pulling away may cause you to lose sight of the ball. The other problem, of course, is that any pitch in tight on a hitter standing too close to the plate will increase the fear of getting hit with the ball, and the batter will have a tendency to "open up" too soon or "bail out." I would much rather have a young hitter stand farther from the plate and go into every pitch. In this manner, his shift will be much more easily accomplished and he will have a better chance to follow the pitch all the time.

Why does balance become such a key mechanic?

It is such a key mechanic because you must be balanced before you can begin to shift your weight and do it successfully. With balance you will be quicker, whether it is in baseball, boxing, football, or almost any other sport. If you watch any of the outstanding athletes, you will see they are balanced most of the time. Balance eliminates all tightness and tension in the body and arms, which becomes crucial in a good hitter.

In the past two years I've noticed a predominant trait of almost all the Royal hitters: they level off the bat behind their head, holding it almost parallel with the ground. Is this one of your mechanics of hitting? If so, why?

A lot of hitters in the major leagues and young hitters will have their bat cocked high or hold it way back away from their body. The mistake here is that they do not leave the bat there or start the swing from that position. They must move the bat down to level out the swing. This takes time off your swing. So why not start from this position? You will have less tension and tightness in your arms and hands. You can wait longer for the pitch if your bat is already close to being level. You'll probably meet the ball square and also hit line drives.

How do you go about teaching the stride?

Again, the main thing is that you must be in balance after the stride is completed. As your front foot touches the ground, your hands must be way back near your letters and not have started forward. A while back; we put separate cameras on the pitchers and hitters and found that when a pitcher comes to his release point, the hitter at this same time must start his hands in some type of reaction to get the bat in position to hit.

At this point, Tom Poquette in the Royals' dugout contributed that he thought this fact was amazing. In the pictures of the 1973 All-Star Game (Lau shot all the All-Star hitters at sixty frames per second to analyze and illustrate hitting techniques), every hitter in both leagues, no matter how unorthodox his style or where he started his swing, had this stance in common—when the front foot completed the stride, the hands and bat were back to the letters. "I try to call this the 'hands position,' which means the hands must be back in the 'launching position' as the front foot hits the ground," Charlie added.

What other mechanics do you stress a great deal of the time?

We are great believers in full arm extension. We like to emphasize swinging on top of the ball. (Chopping down on the ball.) I used to think Cesar Cedeno really chopped down on the ball, but when I took super slow motion pictures of his hitting style, I saw that his swing is almost level on the ball, which amazed me after seeing him hit.

Charlie, how do you teach going to the opposite field?

Well, if you're relaxed and there isn't much tension in your arms and hands, it is easy to let the hands lead the bat through the plate area and swing "inside out."

Do you prefer one stance over another?

We like to work from the closed, or parallel, stance, with a bend in the waist for balance and relaxation. If you are not relaxed, you won't be fluid. If a hitter stands up straight, tension results. One of the things you must watch for is a hitter with a very wide stance who has trouble keeping his weight back. If a hitter is having trouble this way, you may have him put his feet close together. This will help him keep his weight back. The Royals' Al Cowens is a great example of this.

How would you correct a hand hitch?

A hitch down may be all right, but a hitch up with your hands is a real detriment to good hitting. You may help the hitter overcome this by having him level out the bat behind him and rest it on his shoulder.

What about the top, or dominant, hand in hitting?

Some hitters have a really dominant or much stronger hand. Usually it is the top hand (right hand for right-handers, left hand for left-handed hitters). This hand will take over after contact and not allow full arm extension or cause too much hand, wrist, and arm roll. We sometimes advocate releasing that hand after contact with the ball. This is why Willie Horton appears to hit so many home runs with one arm. He releases the other hand after driving through and making contact with the ball.

What about the mental aspects of hitting?

Tonight Dennis Eckersley is going for the Indians. He is a power pitcher who deals in smoke with two different types of fast balls. So George Brett [a left-handed hitter] will think about shutting off everything from second base to the right-field line. He will concentrate on hitting every pitch between second base and the left-field foul line. Anything else will be a bonus. Too many hitters try to pull a pitch even if it is on the outside part of the plate. You must think: cover the outside of the plate first, go to the middle second, and the inside part of the plate last. Hit the ball where it is pitched.

Still thinking about the mental aspects, should your thinking be dictated by the size or dimen-

sions of the park in which you are playing?

Some home parks have outfields as large as airports and you are not going to put many into the cheap seats, so your swing should be dictated by this factor. Pitchers generally make a living by pitching hitters away on the major league level.

What hitting drills do you use?

The batting tee is excellent for developing your stroke and seeing where the ball should be hit. Tossing the ball underhanded and hitting it is another good drill. Through this drill, fear is eliminated and your stroke groove is improved. The greatest hitting drill I've ever found (I noticed a large number of the Royal hitters doing it) is to have the hitter go into the batting cage and stand and swing through a couple of times, like a pendulum. As the pitcher starts to wind, the batter brings the bat back freely to the launching position and goes immediately into the swing. This removes all tension and the hitter can do what he is supposed to do with the bat.

Another way of working with a hitter in the batting cage is to help him determine just when he should make his move to shift his weight and whether he is a front-foot or back-foot hitter. He must be balanced in either case and make his weight shift at the right time, eliminating all possible tension and tightness in his body and arms.

How do you increase bat speed? Also, how much emphasis do you put on keeping that front shoulder closed?

If all of the mechanics are right and you attain the ultimate—a perfect swing—then the above things will take care of themselves. Perfection in hitting is attained with relaxation, elimination of tension and tightness, total concentration, balance at all times in the swing, shifting the weight at the proper time, good position far enough away from the plate so you step toward it, bat leveled off, eyes on the ball, head still, front foot down and, at the same time, the hands are back in the launching position,

John Mayberry, one of Charlie's protégés, in action. John is power personified as he attacks and drives through the ball. Notice the position of the hands and bat in the third photo after the striding foot has been put down. A powerful follow-through and good sweeping action with his arms is also demonstrated.

Pete Rose prepares to hit and looks one over. Notice how Pete gets himself loose. Photos 3 and 4 show the pendulum swing that Charlie Lau calls the finest method to get rid of tension and prepare you to use the bat properly. In photo 5, Rose's eyes are straight ahead and he is completely concentrating on that little white ball. The last picture shows total concentration; even while taking a pitch, his eyes follow the ball all the way into the catcher's mitt.

The perfect Johnny Bench swing. Photo 1 shows pure power, the balanced "L" in the back leg, and driving against a stiff front leg, meeting the ball out in front.

This sequence of George Brett, another Lau protégé, really emphasizes the coach's points on hitting. In the first three photos, we get the pendulum movement; in photo 4 notice the hands in correct position. This is a Lau trademark and a fundamental of hitting. In all the pictures, note the perfect balance at all times and the perfect shifting of the weight from back to front foot as he attacks the ball. Picture 7 is a result of perfect execution of the fundamentals—a classic picture of the perfect hitting stroke.

In this sequence of outstanding hitter Ted Simmons, notice the preparation and relaxation before the pitch is delivered. In the first picture, the top hand appears to be overextended to assure maximum flexibility and snap from that top hand. Photo 6 gives the perfect swing, Simmons style. All the hitting fundamentals are in that picture.

and the arms are fully extended. The hitter is now mentally prepared to know what the pitcher can do and where to hit the deliveries.

How do you approach working with an individual hitter?

I look at a hitter—his build, size, coordination, reaction time, strength, and speed—and then try to get him to use what he's got, to get the most out of his native ability and size. A small man will more often have a better chance of getting a perfect swing than a big man, but when a big man gets a perfect swing and all other factors are equal, he will hit the ball a lot farther than a small man. It is much harder for that big man to get that perfect swing together.

8 | Ralph Kiner on Hitting

Every baseball person knows Ralph Kiner. One of the three or four greatest home-run hitters in history, he is now an outstanding broadcaster who makes the game come alive with his insight and lucidness.

As a youngster, I remember Kiner's short, compact stroke and towering home runs. His ratio of home runs per times at bat is the third best of all time: 14.11 to Babe Ruth's 11.76, and Harmon Killebrew's 13.74. He is the only man ever to lead the league in home runs seven consecutive years.

The image of the home-run hitter is a super-strong athlete who can hunt bears with a switch. Ralph Kiner brought an extra dimension to his craft—he studied hitting deeply and improved on his natural talents. He was the first player to use a golf glove to secure a better grip and eliminate slipping.

Long before television and video tape, Ralph had someone film his swing with an 8-mm. camera at 64 frames per second. He then studied his form frame by frame to check on his mechanics. He also kept a card catalog on every pitcher he faced. Obviously, he was one of the first ardent students of hitting. Kiner has remained contemporary on hitting by serving as hitting instructor with the New York Mets.

The following are Kiner's seven checkpoints to successful hitting. Properly applied, they should help anyone hit well. The neglect of even one can cause trouble.

1. Proper use of the master, or focusing, eye
2. Weight transference to the front leg
3. Up on the back toe
4. Arms fully extended when hitting
5. Front shoulder kept in
6. Two halves (upper body and lower body) coordinating properly
7. Observation of the "L" principle

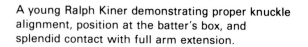

A young Ralph Kiner demonstrating proper knuckle alignment, position at the batter's box, and splendid contact with full arm extension.

Mike Schmidt of the Phillies demonstrates a short, compact hitting stroke with perfect arm extension and follow-through. Schmidt in the third photo has lowered his hands for the low pitch. (You can see the ball in the right part of the picture.) He has slightly lowered his body to zero in on the ball.

Let us explore his principles in depth. First, the master, or focusing, eye principle. It is simple to determine your master eye. Hold your hand fully extended in front of your face, with your index finger and thumb in a circle. Look at the circle with both eyes open. Then close one eye. If the circle does not move, the open eye is your master eye.

For most right-handed hitters, the right eye is the master eye and this eye must be on the ball. The hitter must, however, make sure that he can see the pitcher with both eyes, and that the eyes are on a level plane.

Check the accompanying pictures of Stan Musial. Note his open mouth. Many people thought he smiled when he hit (which he had a right to do!). Actually, he kept his mouth open so that he could see the pitcher better. Try it. Open your mouth and try to blink your eyes at the same time. It isn't that simple. You thus minimize losing sight of the ball for a split second. Incidentally, the open mouth also relaxes the lower face. I asked Kiner the following questions:

Is it possible to watch the ball right up to the point it meets the bat?

No, I don't think there ever was a player who could see the bat hit the ball. By tremendous concentration, you can follow it up to about a foot from the bat or a little closer if it is met on the outside part of the plate. But the speed of the bat and the ball prohibits seeing the actual contact.

What is your theory in regard to shifting the weight from the back foot to the front foot?

Baseball is no different from any other sport. In shooting a basketball you shift the weight from back to front. In hitting a tennis ball, you shift the weight from back foot to front foot. The same principle applies in golf, football passing, shot-putting, etc.

One of the most misunderstood things in hitting is that you stay on your back foot but shift your weight to the front foot. This is the most important thing in hitting.

Why is it so important to get your weight off the back foot?

If you hit with your back heel on the ground, you'll never be able to turn your hips. It is interesting that Tony Oliva injured his back foot a couple of seasons ago and had to get up on his back toe. He then started hitting with a great deal of power.

An excellent way to teach this: put an old baseball under the hitter's back heel and have him take his normal swing. This will make him get up on his back toe and pivot.

Anytime the hitter can shift his weight off the back foot and get his back heel off the ground, his hips will turn. Hitting with the back heel on the ground makes him drop everything underneath the ball and uppercut it.

The hitter who is late transferring his weight forward and getting his heel off the ground is going to get behind the pitch. His hands and his hips won't be able to function properly.

The front arm [left for right-handed hitter] represents another key point in hitting. It must be straight. Anytime a hitter gets caught with his arms bent, it means that he has not put the bat far enough up to the ball.

So the hitter has to work at getting a full extension of the left arm. Look at the picture of Boog Powell, which shows a perfect arm extension. This allows him to make contact with the ball out in front of his body.

The ball must be hit from two to eighteen inches out in front of the hitter. Why such a variance? Because inside pitches must be met farther out in front. Outside pitches can be hit farther back.

Paul Waner's remedy for a hitch was having the hitter reach back as far as he could with his front arm and then swinging from there.

Dick Howser of the Yankees has a great way of teaching this full-arm extension and increasing bat speed. Take your full hard swing with a leaded bat (40 to 70 ounces), allowing the bat to follow through. Hold for a split second, then snap the bat back as fast and hard as you can to the starting position. It is like running a movie projector backward. Repeat this 50 to 150

Stan Musial's unique style stressed cocked stance, relaxed position, knees and body. In photo 2, check the square shoulders and hips, head right in there, step into the plate, relaxed knees, extended front arm, and everything held back for the actual swing. Three excellent points in the next photo to note just after contact: the still head, the arm extension, and the "L" formed at the knee of the back leg. The last picture shows beautifully free arm action and the "L" formed at the knee of the back leg. *Photos by Alfred Fleishman*.

times, without resting or dropping your arms. Although very tiring, it really does the job. It is a great drill for developing bat speed and learning to pop that bat with a full arm extension.

The next key point in hitting is the front shoulder. This should stay in position. Some of the experts thought that Roberto Clemente had a very unorthodox swing. True, he pulled away with his front foot, but basically he had one of the best swings I have ever seen. Clemente would "step in the bucket," but he'd keep the upper part of his body closed.

Many poor hitters turn the front shoulder out. The only pitch this kind of hitter can handle is a fast ball. The curve or off-speed pitch will force him completely out of position.

This brings us to another checkpoint—the body being cut in half at the waist, making two pieces to the swing.

The upper part of the body hardly moves, although it may turn somewhat with the stride. The lower part of the body does the work. You hold the front shoulder as steady as possible and work from the bottom around.

The steady front shoulder also keeps the head in and still, which is essential. So, no matter what the pitch, you will be able to handle it.

The right arm is a very important part of the swing, and the right elbow is the checkpoint. It should be in a hitting position away from the body.

The "L" is the final checkpoint—all the good hitters observe this mechanic, as you have already seen in the illustrations. The L is formed by the back toe, leg, hip, and back as contact with the ball is made.

Mentally, the key to being a good hitter is to get your pitch and hit it. With no strikes, the hitter who swings at a low outside curve or a high inside fast ball is playing right into the pitcher's hands.

Boog Powell illustrates super arm extension after the swing. Also check his head and eyes—they are still trained on the ball.

Perfect bat position a moment after contact. Look at all that power Dick Allen is putting behind his swing, as well as the classic ''L'' in the back leg and the still head. The ball will be met out in front.

9│Keys to Good Hitting

What is the most difficult feat in sports? It has to be hitting a baseball. Hitting requires superlative reflexes and hair-trigger timing. The major league hitter must be able to swing the bat at about 150 miles per hour.

Since it is extremely difficult for the naked eye to focus on the action, hitting hasn't received the same clinical treatment as the golf swing. How many of the great golfers have expressed their theories on swinging? Practically all of them. How many of the great hitters have put their ideas down on paper? A handful.

All the great hitters—Hornsby, Medwick, Williams, Musial, Clemente, Killebrew, Mays, Oliva, and Carew—have an individual style that they wouldn't let anyone tamper with. They do, however, make changes from time to time, and we can all learn from them.

Certain facets of the Gehrig, Musial, Killebrew, and Oliva swings are the same. And at certain critical stages of their swing, even such unorthodox hitters as Dick McAuliffe, Stan Musial, Mel Ott, and Al Simmons emulate the stylists.

Today, with motor-driven stop-action cameras; video-tape machines; better coaching, equipment, and playing fields; superior physiques; and a greater willingness by the experts to share their ideas; there's no reason why an aspiring player cannot improve his hitting. He must be willing to listen and to practice, practice, and practice some more.

One often reads how Ted Williams was such a great hitter because of his outstanding vision. This had to be a contributing factor, of course, as were his quick reflexes and strength. But I also believe that his dedication was just as important. As a youngster, I used to shag balls for Williams. He was then a 19-year-old minor leaguer for Minneapolis. It wasn't unusual for him to hit for hours in a city park and then go to the ball park for batting practice and a double header. (I recall seeing him ignore his bleeding hands.) This dedication to improvement was a prime factor in Ted Williams' ascent to the pantheon of hitters.

How do you find a hitter's natural style? How can you teach him to pull the inside pitch? To hit the low ball? To hit the curve ball? How can a small fellow generate power? How can he develop a quicker bat?

I break the swing down into its basic components and determine where the boy can be helped: preparation, stance, head and eyes, hands, bat speed, leading arm, power arm, front shoulder, rear shoulder, front leg, rear leg, balance, stride, hips, and contact point.

Harmon Killebrew can serve as a model for the young hitter. After one or at the most two preparatory swings, he let the bat rest on his shoulder. He cocked it just as the pitcher started his windup. There is no wasted motion or hurrying the bat back after a practice swing. He took a short, low step toward the pitcher and unloaded with a compact stroke that was a masterpiece from beginning to end.

Let's now put our own hitter into the batter's box and determine his natural style. The only way I've found to do this is to have the hitter stand in a comfortable position and then extend his arms and bat fully (even coming up on tiptoes) toward the pitcher. We then have him quickly pull his bat back to the most comfortable position for him (like running a movie projector in reverse). This will be his natural hitting position.

One of the trademarks of all the great hitters—Williams, Clemente, Mays, Oliva, Frank Robinson, and Killebrew—is a fast bat. This has to start with the proper positioning of the hands. If the hands are not in their natural position, they cannot bring the bat through quickly.

Each hitter has one hand position that enables him to swing the bat with his maximum quickness. You can prove this to any hitter by having him assume his stance and go through his swing while you stand behind him and hold the bat by the barrel.

Now have the hitter change his hand position. Go through it again. Experimenting will show that the boys with a slow bat will hold their hands too high or too far from their body. With practice, the young hitter will actually be able to feel where he's quickest with his hands and bat.

By lowering his hands a little, the hitter will be able to hit the low ball with more authority. If the pitcher is getting him out with high pitches, the hitter can slightly raise his hands.

OTHER MEANS OF DEVELOPING A QUICKER BAT

1. Cock the bat on a more horizontal plane. When not held directly vertical, the bat requires a shorter arc to meet the ball.

2. Move the batter closer to the plate, thus shortening the stroke.

3. Have the hitter hold the bat from four to eight inches away from his body to assure maximum speed.

A slight movement before striding will also help build momentum and give the bat additional speed.

Hitters like Clemente and Williams cock their hips by turning their front knee in and drawing it slightly back toward the catcher as the pitch is about to be delivered. Other hitters draw back as the pitcher rears back in his windup. In short, they provide some movement by drawing their hands back toward the catcher, known as "loading up."

The best drill I've found for increasing bat speed is to position a feeder and a hitter a short distance apart before a wall or a screen. The feeder delivers the ball underhanded and the other player hits it against the screen. We keep increasing the pace of this drill, then have the players switch positions.

This drill can be performed in a very small area outdoors or indoors (by hitting into a net). The coach should make certain that the hitter follows through the same as on any other swing and fires that front arm and bat at the ball.

Harmon Killebrew's swing is perfect: bat out in front of plate, eyes on ball, arms extended, back leg bent and on toe, front leg straight.

The natural hand position: hold bat by the barrel while hitter takes stance and goes through his swing.

Increasing bat speed: feeder and hitter set up short distance apart, and feeder delivers the ball underhand, slowly at first, then faster and faster.

This can develop a good pop in a lazy front arm.

The advantages of a fast bat are numerous. Basically, it enables the hitter to wait longer before committing himself and to hit with more authority and power.

The batter should use a relaxed grip and hold the bat in his fingers, not jammed way back in the palm of the hand, which tends to choke off the wrist action. Generally, the second knuckles of each hand should be lined up, and the wrists kept locked until after contact. A premature wrist roll will cause the hitter to swing over the ball and lose power. Wrist action, as such, is greatly overrated in hitting. (Check Charlie Lau's idea of the dominant hand in his chapter on hitting.)

Never overrated is the importance of keeping the eyes on the ball and having a still head. The eyes must be trained on the ball from the time the pitcher releases it. Some hitters try to pick up the spin—backspin denoting fast ball, over-spin denoting breaking ball, for example. One of the reasons the slider is so effective is that the spin looks like a fast-ball spin approaching the plate. Observe every good hitter and you'll see that his eyes stay trained on the ball up until contact.

The eyes should be kept level rather than slanted or cocked, a fault which prevents many young hitters from seeing the ball properly. In his stance, the hitter should turn his head so as to keep both eyes on the pitcher; he shouldn't have to look around his nose to see him. For a drill, I like my hitters to simply stand in the batter's box and concentrate on the ball all the way from the pitcher's hand until it hits the catcher's mitt.

A still head is a must. Any movement will cause a corresponding movement in the rest of the body. The still head will also keep the eyes steady, preventing the necessity of another adjustment. This will help eliminate many faults, such as overstriding. (Try to take a long stride with someone holding your head; it isn't possible.) It will also help keep the hitter from opening his front shoulder too soon. From Little League to major league, the practice of taking the eye off the ball or jerking the head is a serious detriment to good hitting.

Ask a major league hitter in a slump for the cause of it and he'll probably answer, "I'm taking my eye off the ball or jerking my head or overswinging."

We have two ways of helping hitters with head-pulling problems. We might suggest to Bill, a right-handed batter, "Let me see you hit the ball into right field." This will force him to keep his head and front shoulder in longer. We then have Bill hit three or four more pitches to the opposite field. Before you know it, he'll be making contact with the ball, which is an accomplishment in itself.

For the second aid, we have the hitter swing down. This will require him to take a longer look, and his eyes will automatically look at the ball longer.

The stride is largely a timing device. Most great hitters stride straight toward the plate or toward the pitcher, starting just as the pitcher is about to release the ball. The short, low, easy stride enables them to time the ball. If the pitch is faster than they expect, all they do is accelerate the stride. The hitter who strides too quickly can't hit with power, as he commits himself too soon. Change-of-speed pitches will cause him much trouble.

The length of the stride varies with the hitters, from none (Vern Stephens) to a long stride (Musial). Most hitters take a short or moderate stride of from six to fourteen inches. Since the stride represents your timing device, it's necessary to set that front foot before the pitch gets on top of you.

There is a good drill for overstriders. The hitter stands on a table, with the feeder underneath. Whenever the hitter strides too far, he'll fall off the table.

Why can a hitter who stands 5 feet, 5 inches, and weighs 135 pounds hit a ball 400 feet? Two factors are largely responsible: keeping the weight on the back leg and foot, and hitting against a stiff, well-planted front leg.

Note that all the hitters in the accompanying photos are driving against and actually hitting off their straight front leg. This enables them to deliver a much harder blow.

A hitter can prove this to himself by bending his front knee and then swinging against this

Overstrider's drill: the hitter stands on table while feeder underneath delivers the ball. Whenever the hitter strides too far, he'll fall off the table.

locked front leg. It will be easy to feel the difference in bat speed and power.

Another important aspect of the stride: it must assure you of complete plate coverage. This is the only time such coverage is important. You may have plate coverage before the pitch is delivered but lose it by striding away from the plate.

The back leg is the real key in avoiding uppercutting and overstriding. Keep the back leg comfortable, but don't let it buckle too much. That will force the front shoulder up, and generally cause the head to open up, the rear shoulder to drop, and the front elbow to fly out. By not allowing the back leg to buckle, you can also bring the bat more quickly to the same level as the pitch.

Another key to good hitting is a quick and full extension of the arms. A big help in this respect is a 35-inch bat weighing 55 well-balanced ounces. The bat factories manufacture them on request. Set the feeder behind a screen and have him underhand the ball to the hitter. That extra-heavy bat will force the hitter to extend his arms completely and throw the barrel of the bat at the ball. (Having the arms too close to the body and cramped while swinging is one of the biggest faults of high school hitters.) We like to tell the hitter to throw the barrel of the bat at the ball. We then want him to "belly button" on the ball (turn his belt buckle quickly toward the ball). This will help give him a quick hip action.

Now to summarize what I feel can be taught to any hitter:

Eyes on the ball and a still head.
Grip with the fingers, work to develop a fast bat from a natural stance.
Quick hands.
Pop the front arm (bottom hand).
Weight on the back leg and use of the stride as a timing device.
Hit against a stiff front leg.
Control the amount of buckle in the back leg and throw the barrel of the bat at the ball.

As the batter steps into the box in a game, he must remember that his primary objective is to hit the ball. All other thoughts should be erased from his mind. He should be confident, not uptight.

Our batting drills include the aforementioned speed drill. The batter hits fifty balls into the net or screen, then takes ten swings on the table drill (put a stair tread on the table so he doesn't slip). He then moves to the batting tee for ten or fifteen swings at different pitches to check his plate coverage (low and outside, high and inside, etc.). Next, he stands at the warmup plate for five minutes, just watching the deliveries of our next batting-practice pitcher.

Following the observation drill, he goes to the plate and executes in succession: sacrifice bunting a man to second, the hit-and-run with a runner on first, going to the right side with none out to move a runner on second to third, squeezing in a runner on third with less than two outs, and bringing the runner on third home with a fly ball. After this, he takes five swings and later on ten more swings at another cage, thus getting two chances to bat against live pitching.

We also use a ten to fifteen minute drill in which the hitter gets only one swing. We tell him he has two strikes and must choke up on the bat to protect the plate, or that he has two balls and no strikes and must be ready for his pitch. If he doesn't get it, he must take the pitch; if he does, he must take a good rip.

In another drill designed to help our bunting as well as our hitting game, we tell the hitter to lay down two bunts and a squeeze bunt against hard pitching. If he properly executes all three, he gets three regular swings. If he can't execute all three, he loses a swing for each poor effort. Notice that each hitter swings the bat at least a hundred times a day.

Later in the season, we like to have our pitchers throw full speed in batting practice, as we feel that the hitters don't get too much benefit from half-speed pitching.

We keep a hitting chart on each player, which informs us what he has done in every at bat. It tells where he hit the ball and how (fly ball to left field, line drive, etc.). (See Illustration on Hitting Chart.)

Tony Oliva exhibits perfect form in his stance and step. Note his square shoulders and hips, bat cocked exactly at shoulder level, eyes looking at the pitcher over the front shoulder, and relaxed knees. He steps directly forward without throwing anything off line; power is still back waiting to be unleashed. He will hit the pitch hard somewhere.

Greg Luzinski's driving swing is a real power stroke. Notice in picture 2 how his front arm is fully extended back, with little or no bend. This was Lloyd Waner's way to eliminate a hand hitch. (See Chapter 5.) Photo 5 shows everything going into the ball.

Thurman Munson says, "I hit to score runs." Munson is very quick with his hands. Notice in the second photo the perfect position of his hands and how quick he brings them into the pitch. Notice in the last few photos his quick start for first.

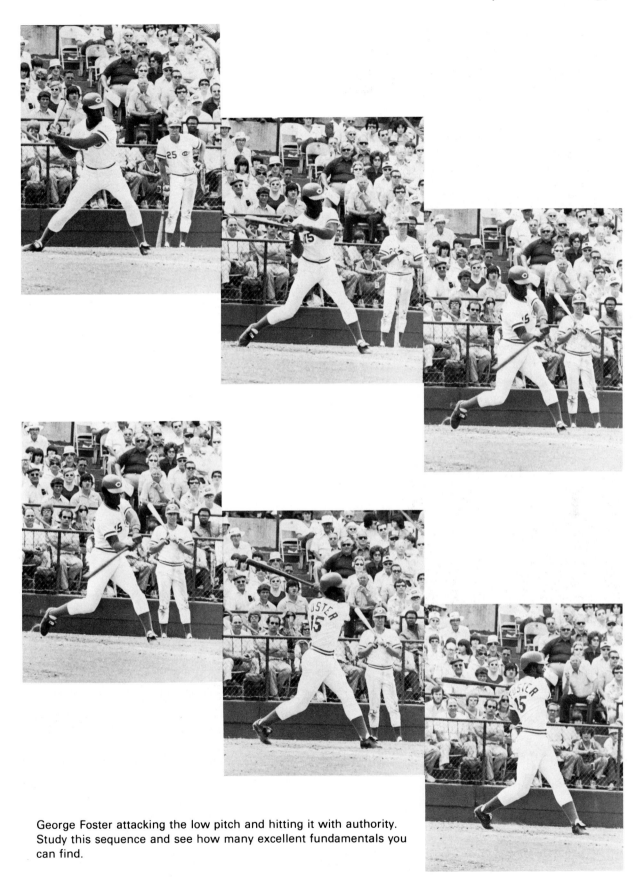

George Foster attacking the low pitch and hitting it with authority. Study this sequence and see how many excellent fundamentals you can find.

Reggie Jackson shows the classic swing in photos 3 and 4, as he swings down on a high pitch. Reggie likes to whip his bat like a fly swatter, handling it in a highly effective manner. He wants to sting the ball out in front of himself.

10 | Third Base Play with Brooks Robinson, Clete Boyer, and Rich Rollins

LET'S TALK WITH BROOKS ROBINSON

The best thing that I can tell a young fellow about fielding is that he should try to keep his glove as low to the ground as possible. Many balls that are hit go underneath a fielder because he is not down with the glove. When I joined the Oriole organization, although I had real good hands, this was the one thing they tried to emphasize to polish up my fielding. They said that this was going to feel awkward, but they worked with me a great deal on trying to keep my glove on the ground. When they hit balls to me, they would almost have me put the glove on the ground and leave it there. It did feel awkward at first, but now I think that it is much easier to get in the habit of fielding balls by getting in front of them with the glove down. It certainly is easier to come up on a ball that takes a bad hop than it is to go down.

I found that the less movement you have in fielding, the better off you're going to be. I think that a lot of boys make the mistake of not carrying the glove in a position to catch the ball. At the last second, they'll try to throw the glove down, which gets themselves in all kinds of trouble. You will be much better off if you tell the boy to keep the glove in the position that he will catch the ball at all times. Probably my toughest play before retiring was going to my right and backhanding the ball. I had a lot of trouble in not getting my glove over there in position to catch it. It's only natural to want to throw the glove down at the last second. Try to get that glove down in position earlier. It makes it much easier to knock the ball down and to see the play better. The glove should also be open. I used to make the mistake of bringing the glove over my head en route to placing it down. This took up unnecessary time. All you have to do is simply bring it across your body.

Brooks Robinson.

I've watched plenty of third basemen, and I think that my preliminary movements before the ball was hit to me were different. Clete Boyer, whom I consider the finest third baseman I have played against, employed a very wide stance. He felt that he could get a better jump on the ball like that. My particular method is to try to be moving a little when the ball is pitched. I seemed to be able to get a better jump on the ball this way. The largest percentage of balls hit to me were to my left, not toward the line. I was always able to go better toward my glove side; I think that most people do. I always tried to be leaning with the pitch, but not committing myself one way or another. During one year, I was having a little trouble and Billy Hunter (then an Oriole coach) thought that I was moving too much. I was committing myself too far to the left. If a ball were hit on the right, I'd have to stop and go back.

Just like in hitting, there is a great deal of concentration that goes into playing third base. I know that if I really concentrated on who was hitting and the things he did every time he took a swing, I would say that 90 percent of the time I anticipated when a hitter was going to bunt. He makes a little different motion up there, like moving his bat in closer; in other words, he gives himself away.

When Mark Belanger was playing shortstop, I was informed of what pitch was next, especially a breaking ball or change. If you really concentrate on the hitter, you can almost tell when he will hit the ball to you by the way he starts his swing. I asked Robinson the following questions:

What can you say about the size of your glove compared to the shortstop's or second baseman's?

On our ball club, there really isn't any difference because of position. Mark Belanger prefers a real small glove. I used a big glove compared to many infielders. Without a whole lot of feel there, I sometimes had to reach two or three times before getting the ball out, especially on slow-hit balls. With a smaller glove, perhaps

I could throw to first base in one grab. I used a medium glove when compared to the outfielders.

In a World Series film, it shows that on the two pickups you made, you came up and threw overhand. Do you specifically work on a scoop with the overhand throw rather than across the body?

Every time I bare-handed the ball like in the Series, I threw overhand. If I made the play with the glove and hand down low, then I'd throw underhand. This is a play that takes a lot of work, too. The whole secret is to field the ball off the left foot, whether the play is made with the bare hand or with the glove. On the very next step, you can throw. If you catch the ball off your right foot, it will take an extra step to throw. I may have had to take a little stutter step to get into position, but I always seemed to end up properly. It's just like when I hold a ball to throw, it always ends up across the seams.

When I messed up that slow roller, most of the time it was because of looking up to see the runner. It is important to concentrate on the ball, pick it up, and throw it. There isn't much time to see the first baseman. You kind of see him out of the corner of your eye. You'd be surprised how accurate you can be by just picking up the ball and throwing.

What do you do with runners on first and second in a sacrifice situation?

In this situation with a bunt in order, you must consider the person who is pitching. I tried to get a little in front of the base line and draw an imaginary line based on how far that pitcher could go. If it was to the right of that mental line, then I just told myself that I had to field the ball. You certainly don't want to end up with the bases loaded and nobody out. If there's any questions, you better get the ball and make the out.

If the ball is bunted back to the pitcher, the catcher then plays a big role by yelling where to throw. Of course, you have to hustle back to third for possible play in this instance. This is messed up an awful lot because of lack of communication. The louder you can holler, the better off you're going to be. Paul Richards always emphasized this.

How do you use your shortstop on cutoff plays when the throw comes in from the outfield for a possible play at third?

I usually didn't say anything unless I wanted him to cut it off. Then I'd yell "cut it off, cut it off," as loud as possible. Most of the time a good shortstop can tell whether he'll have a good shot at the man or not. At home plate, however, Earl Weaver wants the catcher to yell "cut it off" or "let it go," depending upon the throw and position of the runner.

After seeing the Orioles play, I noticed that with men on first and second base and a possible bunt in order, Belanger will break to cover third. How does the timing work on this play?

We work that play. I'm not sure whether we ever got anybody or not. In a sure bunt situation with a man on first and second, we'll work the play as follows: the third baseman breaks for the plate, as will the pitcher. Belanger breaks toward third for a possible play. If the ball is bunted, we'll have an excellent chance of getting the runner at third.

If the batter fouls it off in attempting to bunt or if the pitch is a ball, we may employ the pick-off. The third baseman initiates things by telling the pitcher that the play is on. Everyone else will know as well. After the pitcher comes to the set position and looks to second and home, the third baseman breaks to home and Belanger breaks to third. Immediately following, the pitcher wheels and throws to the second baseman for the attempted pick-off at second. It's a good play, but it must occur in a sure bunt situation.

Do you have a rule regarding who is the cut-off man on balls hit to the left fielder near the line?

I was the cut-off man in that situation.

Should you take all the ground balls that you can get to your left?

I took all the balls I could get. If the shortstop had a better shot at it, he'd call me off.

Sometimes, however, I committed myself so far that I couldn't stop and made the play anyway.

How do you work a rundown?

On a rundown, of course, the object is to get the man out as quickly as possible. We try to run at the man as quickly as we can, with the ball in full view. The fielder not holding the ball will shorten the distance between himself and the runner. We then try to get the runner going as fast as he can so that a properly timed throw will get him. Quickness in catching the man is important because other runners might be attempting to move to the next base. We don't necessarily try to fake with the ball, but it sometimes occurs naturally.

Where do you throw to the second baseman on a double play?

Dave Johnson liked it chest high on the inside of the bag where he could see it.

How did you and the shortstop call for pop flies?

If there was a play that I could get, I'd yell for it. If I couldn't, I let him yell me off. If he didn't say anything, then I just kept going after it. If he called for it, I'd just stop.

Let's assume that you're playing on a fast infield. Is it true that you should never retreat on a ball?

I don't know, but I retreated on many. I not only retreated, but I got out of the way. In fact, I perfected the play to the point where I could really look good getting out of the way. I might even get a standing ovation. Seriously, I tried to stand my ground and knock the ball down. It's much easier going in a little, although if it takes a bad hop, you may back up some.

Should you watch the ball all the way from the pitcher to the plate?

I generally picked it up about halfway in.

If men are on first and third and the runner on first is hung up in a rundown, who is responsible for making the call when the runner on third breaks for the plate?

The third baseman may be hollering, but I

think the men over there will be able to yell more effectively. It's a judgment thing.

On a slow roller directly toward you or a little to your right, should you charge directly at the ball or at an angle?

The best thing that you can probably do is come in at a slight angle and get a better body position for the throw. If the ball is coming to a stop or has stopped, use the bare hand. If the ball is still rolling, use your glove.

How many rounds of infield practice should you take before a ballgame?

We take about two rounds of "one," two rounds of "two," one "long one," and a throw home. I generally liked to take infield every day; it really loosens you up. I also believe that balls should be hit to your right and left, and both hard and soft to provide practice accordingly. Playing third during batting practice gives you all types of balls to field.

DEFENSIVE PLAY AT THIRD BASE: CLETE BOYER, NEW YORK YANKEES

I'll probably surprise you, but I've got different ideas about playing defense than most of the coaches from the old school. I don't go for what everybody says about getting in front of the ball.

First of all, I do believe in a lot of hard work. I think the only way to learn how to play defense is to get out there everyday and catch all the ground balls possible. And I think I had one of the greatest teachers in the world, Frank Crosetti. I was fortunate to be able to work with him for years. And, at the age of 60 or 65, he still studies the game as if he were a player; I know he studied the game when he was a player. But Frank and I had a few differences in our ideas of playing defense. In other words, we both were right. We never argued or anything, but we had different ideas on how to play. We're two different types of ballplayers. Frank Crosetti playing shortstop always had his feet close together. Well, he was quick on his feet. I mean he was like a cat, you know. He could start from anywhere.

My philosophy is to get down as low to the ground as possible and still be comfortable. First of all, that puts the glove right on the ground. You can always come up on the ball, but you can never go down. You never stick your hand back down on the ground and knock the ball down. Your automatic reflexes always come up. By this method your eye level is closer to the ground; in other words, you'll be able to pick the ball up off the bat a lot easier. You won't be bobbing your head so much, and that's why a lot of ballplayers miss so many ground balls. I always spread my legs comfortably as far apart as I can. My idea is to go back and forth to the left and right, rather than going in and coming back. You can always recover and go in, but you can seldom recover and go to your right or left.

I guess the most famous third baseman is Brooks Robinson. I've got a different philosophy than Robinson. He comes over and has his feet almost one in front of the other, ready to come in on the ball too much and to go to the left. This guy's probably as good as you can get at third base, but I've seen him actually dive for balls unnecessarily. If he were to spread his feet apart, he could just turn over and backhand the ball; otherwise, it would be difficult to recover from that right foot. He would have had to dive for and fall over the ball in order to catch it. I'm not knocking him. I think he's the greatest, but I guess it's up to every individual. That's how he learned to play and this is how I learned to play, and I think we're both right. In other words, he probably couldn't play the way I did.

The one thing that I disagreed about with Frank Crosetti is that he teaches the young kids to catch every ball in front. I don't agree with him at all; the hardest ball to catch is the ball right in front of you. It ties your hands up, and you don't have any freedom in your hands. I'm not saying just to get out of the way, but you shouldn't make an extra effort just to get in front of the ball. Some say that if the ball takes a bad hop and bounces off your chest, you can still throw the man out. I don't go along with that idea because I didn't anticipate balls bouncing off my chest and having to pick them up. Anyway, my chest wasn't big enough to do it.

These two pictures show how to pick up a baseball which has stopped rolling. The key is to use your entire hand—pick up the ball as if you are going to screw the ball into the ground. Also notice how he has picked the ball up next to his right foot so that he won't have to take an extra step.

Get out and practice catching the ball wherever it is; don't make an extra effort to get in front of it. I think if you go out and practice and study enough, just common sense will change your mind. In other words, I helped change Frank's mind a little bit on that idea, although he still teaches to catch the ball in front. I think you have to practice both ways.

I'd like to talk just a little bit on playing the position. If there's a left-handed hitter up who can run pretty well and I managed the defense like Eddie Stanky, I'd fine my third baseman if that hitter bunted for a hit toward third. I don't care how far in that third baseman plays—I can't see letting a speedy left-handed hitter with bunting ability get a free hit. It's a lot tougher for him to hit the ball by you down the third-base line than it is for him to bunt. A guy like Maury Wills or Matty Alou may have hit a ball by me for a base hit, but they didn't bunt on me for a hit. I think Eddie Stanky fined his third baseman if a left-hander got a bunt base hit. He's probably the only guy who did this, but it's a pretty good theory.

I don't know if you have played third base, but there's a kind of happy medium out there on where to play: the farther back you go behind the bag, the more ground you've got to cover. I could take you out there and show you where you could stand right in front of the bag, take one quick step to your left, and get a ball. If you were to back up, say ten steps, that same ball might take maybe three or four steps to reach. Many people asked me why I played in. I think it's just a matter of studying the game and practice. If you go out there, you can prove it to yourself. When you play third base too deep or too close to the line, you'll find a lot of balls going between third and short. I always tried to guard the line without overexaggerating it. Some guys really overdo it. I think you should find the proper position so that a ball hit down the line—unless its a shot—is within your reach. Because you can always go much easier to your left than to your right, you can maybe cheat one step toward the line and be in a position to go both ways. It's easier to guard the line that way. If the ball is hit past you to your left into left field, the guy's going to get a single; if he hits it to you on the right, he's got a double and there's no chance for a double play. If you keep the guy off of second base, you won't worry as much about making errors or bobbling the ball.

One play was the toughest for me as a third baseman: when there's a man on second base and a bunt in order, especially with a fast runner who could steal third. You know the bunt situation dictates that the bunt will be coming to you. Well, we make plenty of mistakes up here, but I suppose in high school or college they probably make more because they don't play as many games. It's really just a matter of knowing your pitchers. You've got to learn if they can get off the mound. I played three or four steps in front of the base and had my body face a little bit toward the pitcher. In this position, I could pick the runner up right as the pitcher took his stretch, thus making it easier to tell if he was going to break or not. It's a tough play. In other words, if a fast base runner like Luis Aparicio was on second and the bunt situation was up, I thought he could steal third base anytime he wanted. When a third baseman takes one or two steps in, he can't recover quickly enough to return to third. You kind of have to cheat. You must move in a couple of steps at the beginning and set your mind to go in on the ball after it's bunted. That's a rough play in itself, but you must also recover to get back to third base if the guy decides to steal.

I agree with all your philosophies on the way you play third base. However, what would you suggest when you've got a boy on third base who hasn't got that good gun? How does he fit into your philosophy?

Well, if a third baseman doesn't have a good arm, he's going to have to shorten up a little bit. But, at third base you really don't need that good an arm. I think it's just a matter of getting rid of the ball. I think the biggest thing in playing third base, especially in the major leagues, is knowing your pitcher and your hitters. Of course, in high school and college there's such a big turnover. In four years you don't really get to know your hitters and your pitchers very well. Up here you must know your pitching and have an idea where your pitcher is going to pitch each hitter. I'll give you an example of Whitey Ford pitching against Al Kaline. Now Kaline was a great right-handed hitter, so we would figure to play him more toward the line. However, statistics kept over a period of years proved that Al hit Whitey up the middle all the time, so we started giving him the line and somewhat of a hole between third and short. I don't think a guy has enough time to study that in high school and college.

You fellows see the hitters all season and at the college level you might see the hitters once or, at best, twice a year. It's hard to figure their power. On the college level, are you going to bring the boy in or let him stay back of third?

Well, you're going to have to have an idea about the hitter. If the guy appears to be one of the better hitters on the club, you're going to give him the slow ground ball, the topped ball in other words. You have to play back and guard for the double down the line. If, instead, he's an average hitter who runs pretty well, then you're going to have to play in on him. It's just like I said—you can play too deep. I think there's a happy medium out there. The farther back you get, the more ground you have to cover. The closer you get, the less ground there is to cover. The main thing is to get the jump on the ball.

Is there a definite pattern to follow in retreating to cover third base?

Whenever I knew I had to return to third base, the first thing I did was turn around immediately and go right to the base. You should be able to get back to third, and put your heel on the outside of the bag on the third-base line. Therefore, I think it's pretty important for a ballplayer to learn to put his foot on the outside of the base. I also put my heel on the outside of the base because I tried getting into a squat position where I could go back and forth either way.

Sometimes a third baseman will turn and go back toward third base, put his foot on the corner of the base, and stretch out like a first baseman. A pitcher could make a good throw in such a case that might get by the third baseman. I think that's really an important play. You don't see it done very well in the big leagues.

I frequently made the wrong decision on whether the pitcher might be able to field a ball hit down the line, but it's still the third baseman's decision. When I hollered for the ball the pitcher is supposed to just keep on going and let me have it. Sometimes it just doesn't happen, but you should have enough time to know whether you can get that ball or not. You know that when a ball is hit, everybody scrambles. But, if you look at the ball for just that split second, you can tell whether you can get it or not. You know how long it takes to get back to third. If a guy were to go out there and practice on that play a few times a week, he'd get it. It's just not that difficult.

How do you make the play on a slow roller?

That play should be worked on quite often. Of course, you have to charge the ball. The third baseman must know whether he's got enough time to catch the ball in his glove or not. If he can, it would be better. If he can't, a barehanded pickup is in order. In either case, you just keep running straight toward the ball, never thinking about making any kind of turn toward the first baseman. Just come in, pick up the ball and, with the throwing arm never stopping, get rid of the ball. I don't know off of which foot you throw, although I believe it is the right one. Take that one step and throw it underhanded. That's a play which takes a lot of work. Even Brooks Robinson had trouble. He made that play by coming in to catch the ball and kind of throwing overhand. He couldn't throw the ball underhand, but he made that play as well as I. I just came in, grabbed the ball, and threw, probably off my right foot. I didn't try to make a turn toward first base while coming in; I just headed straight toward the ball, thinking that

I'd keep going in the same direction even after I got rid of the ball.

Where are you looking when a ball is being pitched?

I focused my eyes right on the hitter. I never watched the pitcher when playing third base. Although the shortstop can get a better picture of the pitcher, no one really watches him at all. Just pick a spot in there around that hitter, say right around his waist where he's going to hit.

We had trouble one year with something that I think the Yankee organization executed successfully for many years: the relaying signs to the third baseman. Your shortstop should be able to get the signs from the catcher and pass them along to the man at third. To me, this made my job much easier. If it were any type of off-speed pitch, the shortstop would always holler "heads up, Clete," or something like that. The coach at third is not going to be able to relay that message. I think it's really important in playing the infield to know what pitch is being thrown. If a right-handed hitter is at bat and the pitch is a curve, he's going to get around on that ball more than on a fast ball. Conversely, because he's not going to get around as much on a good fast ball, you won't have to play him as close to the line. I always wanted to know when a change-up was coming, because I knew that I had to lean more toward the line with a right-hander at bat.

Should you try to catch all balls hit to your left?

I took every ball I could reach. There shouldn't be any problem with the shortstop. There are some balls that I knew the shortstop could handle, but because I was going toward first base, it was a lot easier for me to make that play. The shortstop would have had to grab the ball and throw across his shoulder.

Is there an exception to this on a double play?

Yes there is. It occurs once in a while, I don't know how often, when you're playing back for a double play. If you have to catch a ball far to your left, recover, and throw to second base, it's sometimes so time-consuming that the shortstop would have a much faster and easier play.

Did you use a short or long-fingered glove?

I used the biggest glove allowable at third base. Now the shortstop and second baseman usually have short-fingered gloves to get the ball out more easily. But even when I played shortstop, I used a large glove. I used my last glove for five years. It was the loosest one I could get. Third base is more of a reflex position than any other on the field. It requires many reflex plays. Therefore, many times you catch balls with a big, loose glove that you wouldn't be able to handle with a small glove. Bobby Richardson and Tony Kubek always had real short gloves. I couldn't use a small glove even if I played short or second. I think it's a matter of what the ballplayer likes. If he likes a little glove let him play with it, but personally, I used a big glove.

How do you work the rundown play?

There is only one way to make the rundown play and that's to follow the ball. It's just that simple, if you know what I mean. If the runner is between second and third, the pitcher throws the ball to me and follows the ball; he comes right behind me. Then I chase the guy back toward second base and whenever I release the ball, I make sure I get out of the base line. You've got to make sure you get out of the base line and not get hit by the runner. Then I go ahead and follow the ball, taking the position of the second baseman, to whom I just threw. Then the second baseman goes ahead and follows the runner. When he releases the ball toward third base, he goes ahead and follows the ball. It's actually that easy. You won't end up throwing the ball back and forth or as messed up in the base line. You should never have to throw the ball more than twice; many times it's only once. You shouldn't have any problems at all on that play.

In what situations do you as a third baseman act as a cutoff man?

I prefer the Yankee system. I think the Phillies have also used it. I don't know who designed it but the Yankees used it all the time. The Atlanta Braves adopted it after I went there. Anytime that first base was not occupied, I was the cutoff man. If a runner was on second base and a ball was hit to right field, I'm the cutoff man between the right fielder and the catcher. You just have to practice; if you break quickly enough, you should be able to get in position in time to cut the ball off. The idea behind the play is to let the first baseman drift back to first base so that the runner can't make the turn. The play is not really designed to pick men off, but to keep the runner from taking second base. Actually, we do pick off four or five runners a year. When the opposition is aware that you have that play, they know the first baseman is going back to his base and now they can't take a big turn. Lots of times the right fielder even threw a ball over my head, but the runner still couldn't take that extra base because he was concerned about getting back to first base. That's the best cutoff play to use. When a ball is hit to the center fielder, I just went right to the mound; many times right on it. That still left the first baseman free to go back to cover his base. The third baseman must get over there. He'll forget once in a while if you don't remind him.

Who covers third when you are the cutoff man?

No one, actually, although the shortstop will be able to cover once in a while on the play. It really isn't necessary to have a man there. On most hits a man will score anyway from second. If not, he'll take a big turn around third base and then he can freely walk back there, but the idea is to prevent the batter from going to second base.

RICH ROLLINS ON THIRD BASE PLAY

I feel one of the basic fundamentals which is tremendously important for all infielders, not only third basemen, is first to have your glove and bare hands close to the ground and keep them there. After you are in this ready position, you should get into some type of controlled movement—a little step, walk, jump, or something to get your body moving. The reason is that your reflexes are quicker and will be much better if you're moving and you'll get a better jump on the ball.

Fundamentally, you can't stand flat-footed and be a good infielder. The next time you're at the park watch Buddy Bell or Rick Burleson or Dave Concepcion. They all have this little movement as the ball reaches home plate.

What drills do you feel will help a third baseman?

I believe in taking as many ground balls as possible at third base during batting practice, because there is a real difference in fielding balls hit from a fungo bat and ones coming off a hitter's bat. Another good drill is simply have someone roll baseballs to you and you can throw them into a net.

What are some of the teaching points on the 5-4-3 (third to second to first) double play?

On balls hit directly to you or to your left, you must drop your left foot back and open up your body. Never let up on your throw to second —this is a big key.

At what depth would you recommend playing at third base?

Playing deep is very much exaggerated. Seventy percent of the balls hit to the third baseman are topped ones. I would like to see a medium or shallow third-base starting position.

How do you play defense for the bunt with runners on first and second and nobody out?

The key is to get at least one out. You want to know the pitcher and how far he can cover toward the third-base line. Then make an imaginary line between the mound and the foul line; if the ball is hit anywhere on the other side of that line, charge it and field the bunt. How much territory can the pitcher cover? This tells you where your imaginary line will be. This line will vary with your pitcher and his defensive ability. Jim Kaat could cover the line very well. Other pitchers might have more trouble. Try to field bunts with both hands when possible. Come in on the ball from the side so your body is angled and facing first base. Also, before this play or when you have a runner on second, angle your body so you can see second base easily.

How would you teach defending the squeeze play from third base, or when to expect any bunt play?

The hitter will generally give it away when he's in the on-deck circle or as he walks to the plate. With my peripheral vision, I could oftentimes pick up the mannerisms that told me the hitter was going to bunt. He might not go to the pine tar; he may look at you or he may look away from you when he usually looks at you; or he would take a different position in the batter's box. You should also try to find out if the hitter is in a slump and, of course, whether he has the ability to bunt.

11 | Shortstop with Bud Harrelson

When I play shortstop (I'm not very tall), the best thing I like to do is get as close to the ground as possible. I could bend about half an inch and I'm pretty close. I've talked to Clete Boyer and he has the same type of philosophy. I've watched Clete. He spread his legs tremendously. Of course, he's a little bit taller and had to bend over. This is the same thing I like to do. I don't have to spread my feet quite as far as he does. I get up on my toes and try to keep my balance equally distributed so that I am able to go in either direction. On third base you can almost wait until you can see the ball; you don't really need that much of a jump on the ball to still have a chance. You can't knock the ball down at short. You must get to it quickly, keep in front of everything, field it cleanly, and get your momentum going back to first base.

How do you prepare yourself for each pitch?

Once the sign is given, you can't move be-cause you're tipping it off, but you can still think ahead of time. With a certain pitcher on the mound, you know what he throws. I say to myself, "I know every pitch that is coming—gee, it's a slider." He likes to throw the slider away instead of inside. This particular hitter goes with the pitch—he will hit either to right field or wherever it's pitched. I will lean rather than move. I will commit myself; if he pulls it, this is baseball. You have to cheat in certain instances, and if you are wrong then you should be man enough to admit that you are wrong. On the other hand, if you are right, you sometimes can look quite good, and this is what you look for. So I would say, know what's coming, don't move but have an idea of where you think the ball is going to go if the fellow hits the ball.

How do you help the rest of the team know what's coming?

Some of the outfielders like to know what's

Ideal form by Bucky Dent on a bounding ground
ball. Notice his skater's stop with his right foot so
he can get something on the throw. Both hands
are relaxed and together, eyes following the ball.
The body is relaxed and crouched like a tiger, arms
outside and away from the body.

Tito Fuentes illustrates perfect form in getting a jump on a ground ball. His hands are out in front and low, with a slight movement as the ball reaches the plate in photo 2, and then powerful crossover and thrust with back arm as he is off at the crack of the bat.

coming, although it's pretty tough to give signs. I would rather not give signals than to confuse them. On certain instances I have given the open or closed hand. We haven't used this much. But I work mainly with the second baseman. I think the fellows who need to get a good jump on the ball are at second or short. We work together on this using the signs—the mouth indicator for who's covering—like everybody else. We employ them but not as effectively as some of the other clubs.

You were saying that you get up on your toes. What do you mean by that?

Everybody is different. I've found something I like; I've noticed that some do it differently. I know that Bobby Wine used to put one foot in front of the other and take a step forward. This gave him the ability to move. Now he wasn't locked by spreading his legs and standing there. What I do when I'm "up on my toes" is simply fall forward. I spread my legs and get the sign; while in a crouched position, I drop my hands, open. As the pitcher comes to the plate, I get on my toes and actually fall forward. Now I have trouble by doing this; if you do something one way, you're naturally going to be weak in another aspect. I have trouble going back when I do this. Everyone does it differently, so I don't say, "Gee, you shouldn't play shortstop that way; you should do this." I played shortstop approximately two years before I got into professional baseball, and it seemed natural that a lot of this was just going and getting the balls. The only time I had to refer to the fundamentals was, of course, when I made mistakes.

I'm a firm believer in watching the ball. A lot of fellows gaze out and watch the ball until it is about ten or fifteen feet from them. My high school coach used to say, "Show me the button" (the button on my cap). I used to drop my head and show him the button, proving I was watching the ball all the way into my glove. This is an overexaggeration, but if you work on it, gradually you'll be doing it automatically.

Clete was telling me about cutoffs. We always have a man on the cutoffs, but we have a tendency to miss him. It's our biggest problem. At one time we used the double cutoff a lot of times. The Mets liked me to take the ball except when it was down the right-field line. When the ball was hit to right-center field, I would go out in front of the second baseman and he would trail behind me. We used the double cutoff in right center, left center, and also down the lines. When it was down the lines, the first baseman or the third baseman took my place.

Is this with no runners on or do you still do this with a runner on first?

It depends on the situation. If it's a sure double, then we don't mind leaving second open. This calls for the situation which has to be thought of ahead of time. There is a difference, of course, with the coaches and managers each year—they change policies. With a man on first, we use the first baseman, who leaves on a sure double. Nobody is going to be on first anyway. The third baseman stays and I would trail out behind the second baseman.

What are your thoughts on the double-play situation?

I overcheat on a double play. Bill Mazeroski waited for the ball on second base. This is good; when a second baseman can come and plant

Right: Willie Randolph illustrates Bud Harrelson's idea of showing the button on his cap to the coach. Rich Rollins' idea of moving as the ball is being pitched is illustrated by Willie in sequences 1 and 2. You can't be flat-footed and be a good infielder. Sequence 5 shows perfect form to field the ball; notice the glove flat on the ground, knees bent, hands out in front—the perfect position. Sequences 7, 8, and 9 show the shuffle, cross-hop, and the throw to nail the runner.

As the pitch is about to be delivered, notice the infielders in excellent starting position. Photo 1 shows the hands starting to be lowered. Then, in photos 2 and 3, knees are bent, the bodies lowered. In the last picture, they are both very low with their gloves almost on the ground.

Notice how Bert Campaneris has the weight forward on the balls of his feet in the first picture, and his unique way of getting his hands back to give him a little starting movement for a quick jump on the ball in photo 2. In photo 3, he surrounds the ball and gets his body low. Notice in picture 5 how he drops his left foot back to open up his body so the second baseman can see the ball clearly. Another reason Campy does this is to get rid of the ball quickly to start another easy double play.

instead of being in motion, it's much easier to throw. I have had five second basemen in two years. I throw differently to each one. I have to adjust my throw to each second baseman. I would rather take a little bit more time and make sure that he has his body under control. I used to pick up the ball and get rid of it—if the guy was still running, that was tough; now I take a little bit more time on the double play. It's always a better throw, even if it's a little softer, and the ball gets there a little later, when the second baseman is under control. Now he can make a better throw. It may be a little slower, but it's certainly more accurate. I can't really say because I don't know of one certain second baseman that I can work with each day. Bob Johnson played deep on a double play and liked to run over, so I just gave him the ball. Jerry Buchek liked to stop and throw—he had a stronger arm.

The ball is hit to second—do you like the ball before you get to the bag or right on the bag?

Just before I get to the bag, so I can pick out whether to stop, or go on across. There is less chance of a shortstop being taken out of a play when he stays back, because the runner isn't willing to slide hard into the bag. I'd rather stay at the back, get the ball, and slow down before I get to the bag. A lot of times I'll come eight to ten feet across the bag.

The shortstop is your most important infielder. He is the key to the double play, cutoff, base hits in the hole, and defense against the double steal.

The double play, one of the greatest plays in baseball and the most beautiful, is also among the hardest to execute. One of the most important things in turning the double play is seldom discussed. The player must ask himself, "Do I have the stomach to make the double play? With a 6 foot, 4 inch, 200-pound guy barreling into second base, do I have the courage to stay in there and make the play and get wiped out?" This happens sometimes. The reason some double-play combinations don't make the play even on the major league level is that the player doesn't have the guts for the play. It takes courage to make the double play consistently.

SHORTSTOP REMINDERS

1. Anticipate at all times what you will do with the ball before it is hit to you.

2. Stay on top (overhand) with most throws.

3. On a ball hit to your right, throw out the right leg and slide along the top of dirt when going for the ball. As the ball is fielded, plant the foot and throw against it.

4. When the double play is in order, don't play too deep and cheat towards the bag. Cut down the angle by coming in.

5. Find out which is your strong and which is your weak side; then set this in your mind. Cheat towards your weak side.

6. Use the crossover step initially more than any other infielder, because of the greater area you cover.

7. Charge that ball aggressively, especially on topped or slow-hit balls past the pitcher. You must be able to charge the ball more than any other infielder.

8. Cover second base when a bunt is on.

9. Work on holding runners close. Don't let them get big leads.

10. Let the second baseman cover second base when the double steal is being made, unless a left-handed pull hitter is up—then you take the bag. When the second baseman takes the bag, yell when the runner on third base breaks for home so that he can come toward home plate to make the throw.

12 | Second Base Skills

All of the fundamentals of second base play are so important:

1. Knock the ball down at all times; yours is a short throw.

2. On a hard hit ground ball with the bases empty, don't be afraid to drop to one knee or dive and get your uniform dirty. (One of the plays which still sticks in my memory is of Bobby Richardson, one of the great second basemen, going down to the ground on one knee in the World Series to make sure he blocked an important ground ball.)

3. Establish the range of the first baseman and run him off most balls to your left.

4. Your throw will generally be a three-quarters type. However, when acting as a relay man, as well as when firing to the plate, stay up on top of the ball for better accuracy and distance.

5. Don't get in the habit of flipping the ball. Arm strength cannot be developed this way.

6. Communicate with the shortstop on who is covering the bag. Let the shortstop determine this by the hiding mouth with glove method. Use closed mouth (me) and open mouth (you).

7. Anticipate at all times what you are going to do with the ball before it is hit to you.

8. On a ball hit to your right, throw out your right leg and slide along the top of dirt as you are going to the ball. As the ball is fielded, plant the right foot and throw against it.

9. Cover first when a bunt is in order.

10. Make every effort to get to pop flies down the right-field line that the first baseman can't reach.

11. Go back on all pop flies until an outfielder runs you off.

12. Do not play too deep; you must cheat on double plays as well as covering the bag for steals.

13. You must get to that bag quickly to turn the double play.

14. When covering first base on a bunt, go to the bag and play it as the first baseman would. Don't time it to just get there—be there early to give a target.

15. The second baseman should cover the bag when a double steal is in order, unless a real left-handed pull hitter is up.

16. When covering the bag for the double steal, listen for the verbal command from the shortstop. If the runner on third base is going home, you then will have to come up from the bag and make your throw to home. If the runner stays, then you must lay back and tag the runner out coming in. Catch the ball on the edge of the grass.

MAKING THE DOUBLE PLAY: THE GREATEST DEFENSIVE WEAPON IN BASEBALL

Before anything else, be there on time so you will not have to throw on the run. Other important factors, are:

1. The key to getting something on your throw is turning your right foot toward first base as you set it across and in front of the bag toward the grass.

2. Use a small pancake glove so you can get rid of the ball quickly.

3. The biggest mistake young players make at the keystone spot is not having both hands together to get rid of the ball. This saves precious time.

4. Do not feel that every ball hit with a man on first is a double-play ball. The speed and direction of the batted ball determines this.

5. Always get the lead man. Your job is first to catch the ball, then give the shortstop a good throw. The shortstop will execute the double play.

6. The shortstop covers all balls hit back to the pitcher unless a real right-handed pull hitter is at the plate. It will then be your responsibility.

7. Point 6 may be changed, however, if it is established that the shortstop has a very weak arm. In that case, the second baseman will make this play.

8. When going to the bag to execute the double play, charge the bag hard, then have a slight hesitation or shuffle to see what direction the throw is coming from. (The closer the

The second baseman has started the double play with a splendid feed to shortstop Fred Patek. Notice in picture 1 that both hands are together, so that Fred can get rid of the ball quicker. He then shuffles across to the outfield side to avoid the sliding runner, plants his front leg, and gets something on the throw. Note the total concentration in the last three photos—concentration on where the ball is being thrown.

shortstop is to you, the more you can anticipate a good throw that you can handle. The further he is from you, the more chance of a harder throw to handle.)

9. When you receive a poor throw on your glove side, it may be necessary at times to throw your left leg to the left and tag the bag with your right foot, throwing as the right foot touches the bag.

10. When possible, come across the bag to get out of the way of the runner.

11. Use the bag (corners and side so you don't trip or stumble on the high part of the base) as a pushing-off point.

12. Try to determine your distance from the bag. When you come up with the ball, decide between a throw or an underhand toss to get the runner.

13. When using the underhand shovel, give it to the shortstop firmly, with no spin. A stiff wrist increases accuracy.

14. When a ground ball is hit close enough to the bag, tag the bag yourself. When it is not necessary, don't handle the ball twice. Stay in back of the bag if you can on this play.

15. Don't hide your throws. There is only one time you will turn completely around and that is on a ball hit deep in the hole to your left. (It is very difficult to turn this into a double play.)

16. There is no need to jump or make a full pivot on a double play. Catch the ball, turn your hips and upper part of your body, bring your hands and ball back, and throw.

17. In finding the amount of ground you can cover, during practice draw a line in the infield; on one side of the line you must throw from, the other side you can shovel the ball.

SHORTSTOP AND SECOND BASEMAN CUTOFFS AND RELAYS

Balls in the left-field and left-center area are the responsibility of the shortstop, and he is the lead relay man.

Balls hit to right field and right center are the second baseman's responsibility and he is the lead relay man.

1. Get into position as soon as possible, hold your hands high in a "U" shape, and holler "hit me." Let the outfielder know where you are.

Perfect tag at second base. In the first picture, the bag is straddled, knees bent, and both hands are together awaiting the ball. In the second photo, he has lowered his hips and put the back of his glove hand down well in front of the bag. Now he can slide the glove laterally depending on which way the runner slides, letting the runner tag himself out. In the last picture, he gets his glove hand out of the way as quickly as possible after the tag.

This sequence at second base shows several key teaching points in turning the double play. In picture 1, the approach is controlled running. In photo 2, he has both hands together which allows for a quick release and throw—no wasted time. Notice the right foot is set and pointing toward first base. This permits the second baseman to get something on his throw. By pointing the right foot toward first, he will get his body momentum going toward first, as he starts across the bag in the last picture.

Dick Howser's second baseman's drill—learning to get rid of the ball on the double play. The key here is that both hands are together. Notice how he has his hand on the back of the glove.

2. Take throws from the outfielder from the side position, not with your back facing the infield. This keeps your hips out of the way and makes it easier to get off a quick, more accurate throw. Set your back foot so you can get some mustard on the throw. Don't throw off balance.

3. When acting as a back-up or second man in the relay, let the other infielder know where to throw the ball. A loud verbal command is needed. Be awake for a poor throw when acting as a back-up man.

4. When backing up another infielder, be ready for a poor throw, then make the play.

5. How far out you go is determined by the strength of your arm and the outfielder's arm.

6. When your defense calls for the third baseman to set as a cutoff man, your shortstop covers third base.

7. When lining up the throw from the outfield, glance back to see that you have positioned yourself properly with the base you will be throwing towards.

13 | First Base— The Big League Way

First basemen at the highest level come in all shapes and sizes: Steve Garvey, John Mayberry, George Scott—they are all different. It helps to be tall, rangy, and left-handed. (The big advantage to being left-handed comes on the first-to-second-to-first (3-6-3) double play, because you do not have to turn for a throw after fielding the ball, in a sacrifice bunt, or in throws to third base.)

The one outstanding trait a real fine first baseman must have is a good pair of sure hands. He must not be, as they say in the trade, a "cement hands." Through hard work and practice, you can improve your fielding and ability to handle all types of balls, to the point where you're an outstanding fielding first baseman. The first baseman today must be able to hit and be an important part of the team's arsenal. It also helps to be a powerful hitter.

What do we mean by a good pair of hands?

Once that ball gets into his hands, he never bobbles it. Examples today are Garvey, Mayberry, and Scott, all splendid defensive first basemen who make their infielders look great by digging numerous throws out of the dirt, coming down the line on wide throws and making the tag, soaring high in the air and spearing high throws, and covering the far right side of the infield like a blanket.

The second important asset in a first baseman is agility. At first base there are a lot of plays where you must shift your position; if you have good agility, you can become as smooth as cream in your execution.

The first baseman has four basic positions: deep, half-way, in, and holding a runner on first. The position he takes is dictated by the situation, inning, score, outs, the hitter, and the manager or coach's instruction. Let's look at each of these positions.

DEEP POSITION

Back on the edge of the grass (on a dirt infield) you must be able to guard the foul line when an extra base hit will allow a runner to score. This should also be done in the late innings of a close game. Doing this also allows the outfielders in left and right to play closer to the center fielder and cut down the real estate in the gap areas. This deep position rules out the slow, heavy set first baseman. He can't play this deep position properly.

HALF-WAY POSITION

In this position, you are over and to the right with a right-handed hitter at the plate, a "Punch and Judy" type hitter, or a hitter who can drag or push bunt.

IN POSITION

The in position is on the infield grass with your weight on the back foot to drive off toward the plate.

HOLDING A RUNNER ON FIRST POSITION

You are facing directly toward the pitcher, knees bent, body slightly crouched in balance with the mitt, giving the pitcher a good target, about waist high. Your right foot is on the closest corner and facing the pitcher, and you are not spread out too much. Your feet are about shoulder width apart (if you spread out too wide you can't make a move quickly and have locked yourself in position). Your left foot is almost in fair territory. This position is one in which you can face the pitcher squarely, and if he makes a bad throw over to the right or left, you are in a position to go either way. Now if the pitcher throws over, you know the runner has a number of different ways of getting back to first. You are now in a position to tag any part of that base or any part of the slider's body who is coming in. Now, if the pitcher delivers to the plate, you use a crossover step, jump, soar, sail, and come down with both feet in a parallel position with the glove open and close to the ground, facing the hitter. By doing this, you

cover a maximum amount of fair territory and cut down the distance between you and the second baseman.

Let's put you back twenty to twenty-five feet. The first thing you do when the ball is hit to the shortstop, second baseman, or third baseman is to come over and find the bag. Don't even step right on it—you can have your foot against it and do your shifting from there.

It is the worst thing in the world for the first baseman to come over and not find the bag. Catching the ball and coming back looks nice from the grandstand, but sometimes it takes time to get into that position and you could possibly miss the bag. When you are playing back as far as you should you haven't time to come back. You are doing a better job defensively by staying back farther and getting over to the bag quickly. Then you should put your foot on the bag to get the longest reach. You can have some fun with this by tagging the bag with whichever foot gives you the longest stretch. Right or left, it varies, of course, if you're left- or right-handed. There is a definite advantage in the length of stretch depending on which foot is on the bag. Take a tape measure and find out which one gives you the most distance.

One of the most important plays in playing defensive first base is the sacrifice bunt. As you break from the grass to field the bunt, you have more weight on the back foot. When the pitcher delivers, launch off that back foot toward the plate. In case the ball is bunted, keep right on going with the idea of making the play at second base. You should always have in mind the play at second base. In order to make that play, you must keep the ball to your right. You may have to run at a slight angle, but you get the ball by almost going toward second base and throwing it for a quick play. Never pick up the ball in front of you or on the left side because that takes time. The idea is to field the ball in such a position that you can make the quickest throw to second base. If you come in fast enough, almost any ball bunted toward first base can be fielded and you will have a chance to get the man at second base.

If a bunt goes down the line, get the ball and

make an underhand throw. That is a left-handed first baseman's advantage over a right-hander. If the ball is bunted harder and comes on a line, get set and make a harder throw, but it will have to be overhand to get there quickly.

With a sacrifice in order and men on first and second, the first baseman plays off the bag and in from the line. If there is a big, strong left-handed hitter like Willie Stargell in there, you are not going to run in unless you have your health insurance paid up, but if you don't expect the hitter to swing away, play in closer. As the pitcher releases the ball, watch the batter to determine if he is going to bunt. If he is not going to bunt, then stop; if he is, keep going in with the idea of making that play to third base. You may field the ball but find the base runner is too close to third—therefore, stop and throw to first. Have in mind that you are going to throw to third base, and you will be more ready in case the runner has not gotten there quickly.

I used to try to make a play where I picked up a bunted ball on the third-base side of the pitcher. So many first basemen do not think of that. They only have in mind going to third if everything is all right. On this play, you must tell your pitcher beforehand to go toward first and cover the base. It is a question of getting there fast and releasing the ball quickly to get the lead runner. You have to make the throw to third base on the run. I am not a bare-handed first baseman. Once in a while, a first baseman can do that. Often they don't get it, but if they do, the crowd goes wild. (In baseball we call that playing with your head in the grandstands.) Go in there hard and get that bunt —practice a little bit and you can get the ball with both hands. The idea is to field the ball with two hands and throw to third base. I believe that if first basemen would have that in mind—forcing the runners at second or third—they would help break up a lot of rallies.

When fielding balls hit at you, always turn to your right and have the bag behind you, because if you get behind the bag you won't be in position to tag the man. On all plays, the first baseman should have the runner in front of him. A right-handed first baseman making plays to

second base should always turn to the right for the same reason, to get the ball away. Besides, you have the base runner in front of you. There are some plays, of course, where the ball might be hit down the line. You can't turn the opposite way.

On the 3-6-3 double play, your throws to second base should be about letter high and accurate. Work with your shortstop in practice so that balls fielded in front of first base or on the infield grass can be thrown at a target on the back side of second and toward the infield grass, so you don't bounce your throw off the runner's back and out into the outfield. If you field the ball even with the bag or behind it, have your shortstop give a target on the back part of second toward the outfield and holler "outside," so you don't bounce your throw off the runner. This play takes a lot of practice to execute. It doesn't make much difference how you throw—the idea is to get the ball away quickly and get your man.

Form-conscious first basemen who don't accomplish anything are just a detriment to the team. The idea is to get the ball away fast and get the first man, but whenever you throw, try to make it as accurate as possible and give the shortstop a ball he can handle. You don't have time to get set, because in that case you can't make the double play.

TIPS FOR FIRST BASEMEN

1. When stretching—always pushing off the back leg (left-handed thrower, left leg; right-handed thrower, right leg)—you will always get the maximum amount of reach.

2. Get in the habit of using one hand, except for poor throws in the dirt.

3. Block all bad throws.

4. Remind the pitcher when the runner is taking too big of a lead.

5. When tagging the runner coming down the line on a bad throw, do not jab at the runner. Close the glove tight around the ball, but let the glove and hand give and follow through after the tag. Let the runner tag himself out.

A splendid pick-off attempt at first base. Notice George Scott's perfect position in the first picture: knees bent, arms relaxed, foot on the inside front corner of the bag. Picture 2 shows the perfect target with the glove hand. In last two pictures, notice how Scott has bent his knee right to the ground to get his body closer to the bag for a quick tag. The base runner, Buddy Bell, for his part, has stayed low and quickly dived back, head first, to the back of the bag, giving the first baseman only one hand to tag. Excellent defense and offense.

6. When practicing to improve one-handed plays, put the throwing hand in the back pocket and use only the glove hand. You will build confidence this way.

7. To learn to come up with balls in the dirt, have someone throw you short-hop balls in the dirt, medium hops, and long hops. Don't slap at balls in the dirt. Short hops can be handled by just leaving your mitt wide open and stationary. Close the mitt immediately after the ball hits. The medium and long hops should be handled with a short give toward your body, with the hands like you're handling eggs. This takes a tremendous amount of practice, but it marks a really class first baseman when he can come up time and again with the throws in the dirt.

8. Knock down all ground balls—lie in front of them or fall on your knees if necessary. First base is close by, so a play can always be made. Your pitcher should be there to cover. This is another play you should practice a great deal.

9. Get in the habit of taking every throw as far out as you can. Don't catch the ball at your chest—stretch at all times. Don't let the throw ride in.

10. Give your pitcher a good target for a pick-off play.

11. Don't be afraid to come off the bag to make a play. This is a judgment play and you will have to determine if you can get back in time.

12. Determine the range left of your second baseman.

13. Get any ball you can that is hit to your right.

14. Yield to the second baseman if the play is easier for him; the pitcher will cover.

15. Call the pitcher and catcher off of all pop flies which are easier for you to take. Go to the fence, railing, or screens, then come back to make the catch.

16. When acting as a cutoff man, hold your hands high giving the thrower good target.

17. As cutoff man, get sideways to your target to make a quicker relay to the plate or third.

18. When acting as a cutoff man on a throw from center field, get in front of the mound so that the throw won't hit the mound or rubber and take a crazy hop.

19. Always hustle to get yourself in the cutoff position early.

20. There is no value in being too close to home plate as a cutoff man.

21. Listen for the catcher's command when acting as cutoff man.

22. When it is necessary for the pitcher to cover first base, get the ball to him as soon as possible.

23. Give the pitcher a firm underhand throw; a stiff wrist will aid accuracy.

24. You should follow the flight of the ball to the pitcher. If he drops the ball, you will then be near to make the play.

25. Advise the pitcher of other runners on base when they try to advance.

26. Follow a runner to second base (with the sacks empty) on the sure double—then the second baseman and shortstop may act as a double cutoff team.

27. Guard the foul line when an extra-base hit means an important run.

28. Run pitchers off topped balls or push bunts when it is easier for you to make the play.

29. Shout to catcher "There he goes" when base runner is stealing.

30. Make as many unassisted putouts as possible when fielding ground balls when it is not necessary to make a throw to the pitcher. Don't take the chance of having to handle the ball twice.

There is a common misconception in baseball that just about anyone can become a qualified first baseman. This is an untruth! To be an outstanding first baseman takes a lot of time, effort, and good hard practice—be the best!

14 | Catching: The Center of the Defense

The catcher must be a take-charge guy. It's his show and he must run and orchestrate the game and his club correctly. It takes guts to catch, plus a good knowledgeable head!

THE FUNDAMENTALS OF CATCHING

THE CATCHER MUST REMIND THE PITCHER

A. When fielding bunts, where to throw
B. When starting a double play, who's covering second
C. Balls hit to your left, break toward first
D. Get off the mound and back up third and home plate when throws are coming to these bases
E. The score, and the number and importance of outs
F. Pick up the target
G. Concentrate
H. Keep all motion deceptive
I. Pitch low—keep that ball in the basement
J. Follow through and bend your back
K. Shove off of back leg and drive toward home plate
L. What base to cover
M. Change speeds—take something off or put something on the pitch
N. When to cover first base and other bases

THE CATCHER MUST REMIND THE FIRST BASEMAN

A. Speed of runner
B. When the bunt is in order
C. When base runners may be stealing
D. When to act as the cutoff and where to stand
E. Importance of tying and winning runs
F. The amount of room any first baseman may have when going for pop flies

139

Blocking the plate. Notice in photo 1 the catcher sets his shin guard and leg facing down into the runner to help protect himself. He makes the tag gripping the ball with all fingers so the ball does not jar loose.

Catching perfectly on a
low target. Notice the
bare hand out of the way
with no runners on base.

Coming up throwing in
the perfect position.
Notice the hand right by
the ear, the body going
forward to get something
on the throw.

CATCHER MUST REMIND THE THIRD BASEMAN

A. Speed of runner
B. Bunts when in order
C. When to be a cutoff man
D. Going for double play and letting one run score
E. Amount of room the third baseman has when going for any pop flies
F. Give an inside target to the third baseman when a man is trying to score, so the third baseman will not hit him with the throw

CATCHER REMINDERS

In giving signs, use the squat position: right knee pointed at the pitcher, right wrist close to the groin. The glove hand is extended over the left knee, with the pocket facing the plate.

1. The position of your glove blocks the vision of the coaches
2. Hold the glove in the same position, whether the pitch will be a fast ball or a curve
3. Think about the situation and what is needed
4. *When in a tough spot, call for the pitcher's pitch*
5. Don't be afraid to pitchout when you think the runner may be going or when you want to attempt to pick someone off
6. Don't be in too big of a hurry to give your signs—*think out the situation*
7. Don't give your signs too low so that the on-deck hitter can see them below your bottom or between your legs
8. Finger signs are 1-2-3-4; wiggle fingers for off speed
9. Flap sign up—curve ball; down—fast ball and slider; wiggle—off speed
10. Some catchers give their sign outside (Thurman Munson does this a great deal): touch your mask, hips, chest protector, glove, etc.—these are real signs, not the fingers or flap signs.

Carlton Fisk giving the signs and a splendid low target. In the first picture, Fisk has his knees closed and the glove over his left knee so the coaches can't pick up his signs. The arms and hands are outside of his legs so he can move quickly on a pitch and not be tied up. He is sitting on his haunches so as to lower his body and give a fine knee-high target, even though he is a big man. Notice in the last photo how close he is to the hitter. This is a mark of an outstanding catcher who will get more strikes for his pitcher. From this sequence, how can you tell there isn't a base runner on first base?

Johnny Bench explodes in front of the plate and, with his Howitzer arm, throws out another would-be base runner. Notice in photo 2 the perfect overhand throw and Bench pointing at his throwing target with his front foot. In picture 3, he has followed through with his arm completely.

15 | The Outer Gardens

Like the infielder, every outfielder must say to himself, "Every ball that is hit is going to be hit to me. If I must go to my left for the ball, I am going to throw it here; if I must go to my right, I am going to throw it here." Prepare yourself mentally for every pitch, and in that way you will never be caught unprepared.

HOW TO BECOME A GREAT OUTFIELDER

1. Your basic stance should have one foot slightly in front of the other, because you can start quicker in this way. Your hands should be off your knees, and your body should have a little forward motion as the ball approaches the plate.

2. If you are fooled on line drives, learn to count "one thousand and one" before you break. Develop your hearing so you can tell by the crack of the bat how well the ball is hit. Know your pitcher and what he's throwing. Many times this will get you that extra jump on the ball.

3. During batting practice, shag balls at your own position. Balls act differently coming off the bat in left field and right field, as opposed to center field.

4. Charge all ground balls during the game, as well as in batting practice.

5. Charge all ground balls hit directly at an infielder. You never know what might happen, even though it looks like a sure out. Get in the habit of backing up your infielders.

6. Take only one step after catching the ball. Too many steps allow runners to advance and poor throws are usually made after running with the ball.

7. When throwing, follow through at all times as would a pitcher. Overemphasize this while warming up and during infield practice.

Ken Griffey gets the most out of his arm and body on this throw from the outfield. In the first photo, he throws from over the top with everything going into the throw. Look at the cords in his neck. Photo 2 shows how he puts his whole body behind the throw.

You will find this will strengthen your arm as well as make it more accurate. Warm up from 150 to 200 feet apart when playing catch with a partner. This is the type of throw you are going to have to make.

8. By charging the ball, you will be able to get more on your throw.

9. Keep all throws low so that the cutoff man can handle them.

10. Take one or two steps back from normal position; then, as the pitcher is about to release the ball, start creeping just like an infielder. This will make you more alert and you can get a jump on the ball quicker.

11. Stay on the balls of your feet while running. Running on your heels will cause your head and eyes to jar and bounce and will also cut down your running speed.

12. Know the game score, inning, outs, and what the wind is doing.

13. Don't throw behind a runner. Know what base you're going to throw to before the ball is hit.

14. If possible, don't allow the tying or winning run to get into scoring position.

15. Know the weaknesses and strengths of outfielders playing along side of you.

16. Shade yourself to your weakest side.

17. Back up the other outfielders.

18. Help other outfielders verbally—constantly tell them what to do.

19. Run infielders off all pop flies you can catch as soon as possible. The infielder will keep coming until the outfielder calls him off.

20. If possible, when going for a ball near an outfield fence, go to the fence first and then come in. This avoids collisions. Also, put your body sideways against the fence for maximum jumping.

21. All ball parks and outfield fences are constructed and textured differently. Before the game starts, check how the ball comes off the fence as well as how balls react and kick around in the corners.

22. Depending upon the game situation, score, outs, and how deep the ball is hit, outfielders must decide when or when not to catch a foul fly ball.

SOME ADDITIONAL TIPS FOR OUTFIELDERS:

1. Try to catch all fly balls with two hands.

2. Catch fly balls with the back of your glove toward your face when the ball is above the chest.

3. Catch the fly ball with the glove pocket facing the sky when the ball is below the chest.

4. Be relaxed, especially your hands. Don't be a cement hands—let your hands give and let the ball fall into your glove. Don't jar it.

5. *All* balls hit to the opposite field have a tendency to slice toward the foul lines. Be careful in shagging the ball off of opposite-field hitters.

6. Your position in the outfield will depend upon the sun, wind, and other physical factors. Check these things out before the game starts.

7. Play as shallow as possible. More hits will fall in front of you than behind you.

8. When at all possible, outfielders should try catching the ball on their throwing side. This enables them to get rid of the ball much quicker.

9. Hands can be resting on knees with weight on the balls of your feet, until the pitch is about ready to be made. Then start a creeping *controlled* movement and bring your hands off your knees.

10. Run another outfielder off if you are in a better position to make a throw.

OUTFIELD DRILLS

1. Throw overhand and follow through like a pitcher. Slap yourself in back with the follow-through hand.

2. Get as many ground balls as possible; if possible, shag grounders in the infield but do it as a drill, not as a play period.

3. Pepper games, when played properly, are good for agility.

4. Practice the cross-over even though you may not be shagging a ball.

5. Throw at extended distances to strengthen your arm.

6. Line up with other outfielder about thirty feet away and toss the ball over each other's head. This will help determine proper ways to go back on the ball.

7. Practice gripping the ball across the seams. Get into the habit of feeling the ball correctly when making your throws.

8. *Charge Ground Balls—Charge Ground Balls—Charge Ground Balls.*

9. Run pitchers and all others out of your position during batting practice. This is the way you will learn to play—play it alone.

10. Practice catching the ball off the throw-ing foot. This saves a step. If the ball is high enough, it can be done.

11. Practice one short step when catching both ground balls and fly balls. You can't throw anyone out if you run with the ball.

12. Get yourself a good, big glove, but put it on your hand—don't let it hang loosely.

13. *Run, run, run*—an outfielder is only as good as his legs.

Below and right: Ken Griffey making a difficult catch a sure one. In the first picture, he has both hands together as he watches the ball all the way into the glove. Notice in this sequence how his hands give as he catches the ball. This action lessens the impact. Cesar Geronimo is in perfect position, backing up the play.

16 | Base Running with Whitey Herzog

Any time you talk about base running, the first thing you think about is speed. Speed is a baseball player's best asset, mainly because he can use it both defensively and offensively. However you can be the best runner on the ball club or in the league and not necessarily be a good base runner. But speed will take care of many mistakes. Now Lou Brock stole seventy-four some bases one year for the Cardinals. If you watch Brock carefully on the bases, you will note that he does not have good base-running fundamentals. He could be a better base runner.

Now you always say that some ballplayers have instinct and some don't. Well I don't know what instinct is, but some people say it's a sixth sense. I know Willie Mays had more instinct than anybody I've ever seen on a ball field. He didn't need any coaches when he was running the bases; he just seemed to know what to do all the time. Ken Boyer was also a good base

runner. He wasn't fast, but he was always able to take the extra base. I think instinct is more the anticipation of what is going to happen next and being ready to do it when it arises. Today in the big leagues, colleges, and everyplace else, the runner returning to first base talks to the first baseman rather than thinking or remembering what is going on. This is what I'm trying to stop in our organization because I think today that baseball is changing rapidly. Pitching is dominating more and more, the defenses are getting better, and every new ball park built today is bigger. The long ball now is not going to be hit as often as before. We have more than two hundred ballplayers in our organization; in this group I'd say we have three kids who can hit twenty-five home runs—the rest of them can't. So we're going to have to learn to run the bases, learn to take the extra base. We're going to have to scratch for runs.

The one thing that I think that we fall down

Whitey Herzog, manager,
Kansas City Royals.

on in baseball compared to football is in teaching the boys to be quick. Football has agility drills. I put these drills into our spring-training program because we get kids 6 feet 2 inches and 220 pounds who can't run. Your first two steps are the most important in stealing a base, getting out of the batter's box, and chasing a ball. If I can take the kids who fall in this category and give them agility drills like in football, then I can make some of these boys a little quicker. Consequently, they'll be better base runners.

The hardest thing to teach the kids is to be aggressive. Why this is I don't know, but every ballplayer is afraid that he's going to make a mistake; they won't get any leads off first until they have confidence in their ability to do something. It's hard to make them do these things. When I was managing a ball club in the Florida Instructional League, I laid out this set of rules: if a man on first base didn't go to third

on a single to center or right, it was an automatic fine. I didn't care what the score was, how many outs, or anything, because I was just trying to teach my boys to know that they were capable of going from first to third. After a while, they started doing these things. We had a lot of guys thrown out, but we also won quite a few ball games.

I believe that any time you want a kid to get confidence in anything he's trying to do, you must make him try it first to prove he can do it. I know that our ball club came along pretty well. In teaching base running, the first thing we've got to remember is to stress that base running starts in the dugout. Too many players in the dugout are shooting the bull, talking about something else besides what is taking place on the field. They have to watch. You should know that if a left-handed left fielder has to go to the line, he can't throw to second very well. If a right hander in right field has to go to the line, he can't throw to second very well either. It's harder for these outfielders to do this. You should have these things in mind before becoming a hitter and a runner. It might mean taking some extra bases. A player should think about this all the time. Kids today don't even watch the other teams take infield practice—they don't know where the good arms are, let alone which pitchers have good moves.

Good base runners and good ballplayers don't need coaches. Really, if you think about the good base runners, they always pick up the ball. Anytime the coach holds them up, right away they pick up the ball. This is the basic fundamental you must acquire to become a good base runner.

I drill every day in the spring. The first one is to let the batters hit a lob pitch and then run to first. I want my boys to glance at the ball when they hit—to know where the ball goes and where it is at all times. They have to be taught that they can run just as fast by watching or glancing at the ball as they can by running with their heads down. Now the old-timers won't agree with this—they'll say get to first base as quickly as you can—but I'm saying you can get there just as fast by glancing at the ball.

The worst thing that a lot of hitters do is to run to first base about seventy-five feet, angle out, and make the big swing. When running to first base and planning to round the bag, he should instead pick out a point about three feet outside the line, run directly to it, and then start the cut. I think a runner who did it very well was Matty Alou. Professional ballplayers, and I know I've seen it at the college level, don't consider base running important. Professionals don't think it's important because the only thing the general manager talks to them about at contract time is batting average, RBI's and home runs.

I don't care what foot a runner touches to the bag in rounding. Anybody who tells me that every ballplayer rounds the bag and touches it with his left foot is incorrect, because there is nobody who can continuously touch the bag with his left foot. When you come to the bag, touch it with either foot, but touch the bag on the inside corner so you can push off and make your turn. This takes practice. Instead of having my players run ten to fifteen sprints after they're through working out, I generally have them run two doubles, two triples, two home runs, and make them round the bases. Keep a stopwatch on them and get their times. If they can do all that, they're doing pretty well.

Casey Stengel told me that there are only three things you have to know as a base runner: first, where the ball is; second, the number of outs; and third, the defense. You can do this rather easily. As you return to a base, glance to right field, center field, and left field, then pick up the pitcher and the coach. You can do it all with one look—it just takes a second. By that time, you're ready to become a base runner and prepared to go on the next pitch. Most ballplayers, as I said, come back to first base, shoot the bull with the first baseman, and don't know what is going on. They haven't picked up the sign and don't know what the pitcher is going to do. A good many don't even know the number of outs. I believe that we've really neglected this aspect of baseball. The first-base coach tells any man on first to pick up the defense and the ball, and how many outs. The runner should look around and see where the defense is playing. On a bloop hit, for example, this can mean an extra base.

In my opinion, there's a right way and a wrong way to lead off at first base. (I say to the kids, we're going to do it the Royals way—I know Stengel used to tell me we're going to do it the Yankee way.) Get them to take a lead, even though they're scared. I put down a line and make them go that far. I don't care if they get picked off once in a while. I'd rather have them get picked off or be aggressive. If they can get back, take some more. I think a ballplayer can get a ten-foot lead against any right-handed pitcher, but they won't do it. Watch them—they won't get off that far. Some get off more than that, but I'm talking about most everybody. So, over-all, I make all my kids get off at least ten feet.

The only thing I say in taking a lead at first base is never cross your left foot over in front of your right foot. I don't care if you cross your left foot behind your right, because you can still get back to first base. Most kids like to shuffle off the bag and I like that, too. That's all right. I don't care how they get back to first, as long as they get back. They can dive back, jump back, any way at all. I don't like a feet-first slide, however. I think they lose something there. They're better off standing up than coming back that way.

When leading off of first base and you're not going on a hit-and-run or a steal, you just shuffle up the line about two steps with the pitch. So many kids want to crossover. You don't cross over if you're not going. The only time you crossover and pivot on the ball of your right foot is when you're going on a steal or a hit-and-run.

On a steal or hit-and-run, I teach my kids to glance to home plate on the second step. Some organizations in professional baseball don't teach glancing on a steal. If you practice it enough, you can teach your kids to run just as fast. By glancing on the second step, they'll always know where the ball is and what to do; they're not going to be decoyed by a second baseman or shortstop acting like a ground ball

This is the perfect way to steal home, but be sure the hitter and the base runner receive the sign and acknowledge it, or the runner coming in from third could have a big headache if the hitter swings away.

has been hit. Also, they won't look like a fool if a pop up is hit and they don't know where it is. By stealing a glance, they can run just as fast. I do this every day in batting practice. On a player's last swing, he comes to first base, rounds the bag, and takes a lead. Then he takes off on the first pitch. I have my hitter hit-and-run so the runner can get in the habit of glancing. Once they get it down, they'll have it for the rest of their lives. It's real easy to teach, but you've got to harp on this continuously.

When you're on first base and a right-handed pitcher is on the mound, try to detect something in his delivery that might indicate if he's coming to first or not. About nine out of ten times, right-handed pitchers will raise their right heel—that's the only way they can pivot off the rubber. Some guys now are getting a little better; they take their stretch and do it all in one motion, one jump. But 90 percent in the big leagues and the minor leagues today still raise the right heel. It's the first thing they do when they're coming to first. If you can't detect this in the pitcher, he might tip it off with his shoulder. Many will take their stretch with their shoulder open and, when they want to go to home, you'll see their shoulder go that way. Now others will be just the opposite. Some take their stance with a closed shoulder and, when they're coming to first, their shoulder starts moving a little bit. Many pitchers in throwing home make the initial move with their head, dropping their chin. I don't know whether they feel this is a way to get more on the pitch. Believe it or not, some pitchers in the major leagues today look one time to first or to second base and that's all. Then they go to home. If you study these pitchers and get to know them, it really can pay off.

Whitey Ford probably had one of the best moves in baseball to first base. He balked every time. Some pitchers do that and they call balk, but Ford balked all his life and got away with it. On left-handed pitchers, especially mediocre ones who do not have a good move to first base, just watch their head. When they look at first they're going home; when they look at home

they're going to first. Really watch and study them. Ninety percent of them will do it every time. At the high school, college, minor league, and major league levels they all do it. And that's all you have to do—just watch that left-hander's head. Now you couldn't do it on Ford because, like I said, he balked. He stepped to home and went to first or stepped to first and went home. It was different, but the umpires let him do it.

When you get to second base, the size of the lead is not very important. You can walk off or get off second any way you wish. I might say that a good lead off second is twelve to fifteen feet. The runner really doesn't have to listen to the third-base coach, because if he keeps his eyes trained on the pitcher, he should be able to get back to second base by himself. The most important thing at second base occurs when the pitcher goes to home plate. Once again, the runner shuffles the line about two steps, ready to go on the pitch. If his momentum is going in the right direction, he will get a good jump when the batter makes contact. There's no reason for a ballplayer, any ballplayer, no matter how fast he is (unless he's a catcher who can't run at all) not to score from second base on any base hit, unless it's a line drive on one hop directly to an outfielder. Any ground ball hit to either side of an outfielder should enable a runner on second to score easily if he has a proper lead. And there's no reason why anyone can't, but you have to take some of them out there, run reaction plays, and teach them how to do it. You've got to show them and you've got to make them do it. I think that some of our kids have learned. Before spring training is over, I hope that we instruct and harp enough on this that all of our kids in the organization can do it.

I feel that the most important offensive play in baseball is at third base. I teach my kids in batting practice to stay on third after reaching on a hit-and-run, and practice a walking lead for the entire time the next hitter is in the batter's box. This is a very important play. There's no reason why a ballplayer cannot score on a ground ball to the infield, even if the infield is in, unless it's a one-hopper right at someone. If I'm coaching third base and there's one out and men on first and third, the runner is always going to run on a ground ball. I'm talking now about a man on third base and no one else on. If that boy can learn to get the walking lead and a good jump, that infielder has to make a great play to home plate if the ball is not hit directly at him. And the way hitting is today, your chances of scoring with two outs are less than 25 percent anyway, so you might as well tell them to get the good jump and go ahead on the ground ball.

I continuously have my kids take a walking lead. When I talk about a walking lead, it sounds simple, but it must be practiced every day. First of all, you step outside the base line and take your lead approximately the same length off of third base as the third baseman is playing. Walk down the line slowly—do not run. Glance at the pitcher all the time you're walking and try to time this play so that your right foot will be coming down on the ground at the time the hitter makes contact with the ball. Like I said, you ask your kids, "Can you do this?" and they say "yes," but they can't. It's an instinctive play. It may take a ballplayer two or three months to learn it. I harp on this and I make my kids do this every day. If I see they can't do it, I keep them over there for eighty pitches once in a while. I get two or three of them over there and push them down the line. I think today that you can win more ball games by having the proper jump off third base than in any other situation in baseball. Now you can wait for a home run and you might get one, but you may get three guys over to third base who fail or don't even attempt to score on a ground ball. If you teach your kids to get this jump, you're going to win more ball games than by sitting around waiting for a long ball.

Would you advise moving outside the base line when leading off of second base?

I don't care if you get three or four feet outside the base line. It's all right if you think you can cut around third to home better, but the shortest distance between two points is a straight line. I think that's perfectly all right.

What's your feeling on the walking lead at first base?

Well, we're working more on moves today than ever at the major and minor league levels. Anytime we see a guy taking a walking lead now, the first thing the pitcher does is stand there holding the ball. He has to make him stop. Once he's stopped, he's got him. He can't take a walking lead. I like a walking lead if you've got a pitcher out there who just looks once and fires. Then you just take a short lead and get going. But I definitely feel that to get the jump a little larger lead and the crossover step is better. Today, the higher you go in baseball, the less you'll be able to take the walking lead.

Do you work on getting a batter to move more quickly out of the box to first?

Well, I've heard them talk about getting a jump out of the box, and I try to make a lot of kids get a little faster jump out of the box. But, once you get it in their mind to get out of the box in a hurry, I feel you may take something away from their hitting. They may stop following through with the bat and think more about running. That's all right for a Bud Harrelson or a Matty Alou, but the big hitter must take a good swing at the ball and follow through before dropping his bat and running.

When you lead off at first, do you usually have a direct line or do you lead off in front of the bag?

No, I want a direct line.

17 | Hot-Box Situations

There's nothing like a well-executed pick-off or cutoff play to give a team a lift. It's the kind of play that can kill a potentially big inning or rally and save or turn around a ball game.

Conversely, there's nothing more discouraging than to catch a runner and then botch the play, permitting the trapped man to get back safely or, worse, advance a base through a dropped throw, being hit by the ball, or a fielder's obstruction. One major league manager once spent a great deal of spring training time teaching runners in hot-box situations to deliberately run into an infielder as soon as he made a throw.

We begin our hot-box practice early in the year and continue working on it throughout the season. We have our entire squad work on the play so everybody will know how to handle it both offensively and defensively.

In executing the play, we observe the following rules·

1. Try to get the runner with as few throws as possible.

2. When you get the ball, grip it bare-handed in an overhand position, ready to throw.

3. In preparing to receive a throw, stand in the infield side of the base line to reduce the possibility of the throw hitting the runner.

4. Immediately after throwing, veer out of the base line in order to prevent obstruction. Then back up the man you threw to.

5. Don't use voice signals. When you want the ball and can make the tag, take 2 steps toward the runner. This should be the signal for your teammate to throw to you.

6. In making the tag—with either hand —give with the runner in the direction in which

Craig Kusick starts the play by catching a runner between first and second. He gives a short toss to Roy Smalley and veers to the outside so the base runner can't run into him and get an interference call. Smalley sets off at full speed and tries to make the tag without another throw. Seeing he won't catch the runner in time (photo 4), he raises the ball high so it is easy to see. Also notice no faking action with his wrist or forearm, just a nice soft toss which is easy for the pitcher to handle and make the tag.

he's moving. This helps eliminate the possibility of his knocking the ball out of your hand.

7. When there's more than one base runner, go after one and make the tag as quickly as possible to prevent the other runner(s) from advancing.

8. If you feel that an overhand throw will hit the runner, step to the side and throw sidearm.

9. Remember, you cannot block the base path without the ball (this is obstruction), and that if two runners are on the same base, it belongs to the lead runner.

10. If you're the front man in the hot box and have the ball, run hard at the runner to force him back toward his original base.

11. After a successful pick-off at first, the short stop, who's moving toward the runner in a direct line with the first baseman, should be the lead man. The second baseman should cover second, backing up the shortstop.

Whenever possible, we want our players to stand about three or four feet in front of the bag. This is an advantage on a late throw. If the tag must be made at the base, our man will still have a chance to make the play. If he were farther away, the late throw would cost him the putout. It's vital to stay out of the runner's way when someone else has the ball.

We don't go for excessive arm-and-ball faking. It can fool the other infielders just as readily as the runner. If you must fake, we suggest using only one motion, to let the receiver know that he'll get the ball on the next motion. The throw should, incidentally, be soft.

The following plays are excellent for setting up hot-box situations:

1. Runners on first and third—pitcher bluffs a pick-off move to third, wheels, and fires to first to trap the runner.

2. In an obvious bunt situation (runners on first and second) or with the runner on first representing an important run, call for a curve ball on the first-base side of the plate. The first baseman charges hard and the second baseman sneaks in behind the runner at first for a pick-off throw from the catcher.

3. With the pick-off in order at second, the catcher comes out in front of the plate and raises his hand or talks it up. This initiates the play. When the catcher squats for his signs, he touches his left shin guard with his bare hand to inform the shortstop to cover. The pitcher checks the runner and looks in to the catcher. When the catcher feels the runner is vulnerable, he throws both hands open quickly and the pitcher turns and fires to second.

18 | Conditioning and Training: Larry Starr, Cincinnati Reds Trainer

How would a youngster train for prevention of injuries?

Well, first of all, I think, Starr replies, there is not just one program or one particular tool or one mechanical apparatus that can do it. It has to be a comprehensive program of a number of things. A baseball player's main concern should be flexibility. To get flexibility, it is necessary to do stretching-type exercises for the entire body. We recommend that all our players go through a series of exercises to increase their flexibility in their shoulders and hips, hamstrings, calf muscles, and so forth. The second area of concern is strength. You should include some type of weight training in your program. We at the Cincinnati Reds follow the Nautilus program. The Universal Gym or barbells are also useful. The third area pertains to the throwing arm. It is important that you keep

that arm loose, stretched out, and flexible, so we have all our people throw year-round. The fourth area is your heart and lungs—try to develop your cardiorespiratory endurance and so forth. We would ask that you do long-distance and sprint running. The long-distance running builds endurance; the sprints are important for muscular strength and running skill. Therefore it takes a comprehensive program of flexibility exercises, strength training, throwing, and running. This combination will get you as an individual into the type of physical condition needed to play the game the way it should be played.

What kind of exercises would a person do for the various positions—such as catching, pitching, infield or outfield—or are there any differences?

Yes, I think there are some differences. One thing to remember is that strength and conditioning are general and skill is specific, so it is important that you work on your entire body. Just because you're a pitcher doesn't mean that you don't need strong legs. If you're a hitter, it doesn't mean that you shouldn't have a good, strong arm. Now one thing that is important to me is that a youngster should not worry too much about specializing in different positions. I don't think a youngster should concentrate all his time on baseball.

What about youngsters at the age of 15 or 16 years, or even 19 years old?

Not even at that age. It is still a game at that time—you should experiment with different things. But, at that age, if you really want a complete comprehensive conditioning program, there is not one area that you should leave out or do more. As you get older, if you're an outfielder, you will probably concentrate a little more on your strength. If you're a pitcher, you are going to concentrate a little more on your flexibility. That is all important, but the main objective is to do everything.

What things should a youngster avoid to prevent permanent injury or the shortening of a career before it even starts?

Once he is in top physical condition, there are a number of things during the season or at other times that he should do to protect himself and prevent injuries. Of course, the first is proper warm-up. You should never walk on that field without being loose and without being properly warmed-up. You should never pick up a baseball to pitch a game or whatever without gradually loosening and building up your arm. A pitcher should definitely go out on the mound fifteen or twenty minutes before game time and practice his entire repertoire of pitches. He should throw as hard in the bullpen as he is going to throw during the game. He shouldn't just go half-way in the bullpen, then go out on the mound and pitch as hard as possible.

Another important thing is to always keep the arm warm. On cool or windy days, or even in your room, try to avoid drafts. We always suggest to all our pitchers that they wear a jacket during the game when they are not pitching, of course, and when they are sitting on the bench after the game. If they are back in their room, we ask them to wear a shirt. Keep that arm covered and avoid drafts on the arm, including air-conditioning.

Proper intake of fluids also prevents injury. We always allow our players to drink fluids as they desire. When working out and playing, you sweat—your system loses fluids and salts that must be replaced. So drink as much fluid as you can, and salt your food to replace the salt you lose when you perspire.

Those three areas—proper warm-up, keeping the arm covered, and proper fluid and salt intake—are all-important to a pitcher.

What is your thinking about pitching curve balls, knuckle balls, etc.?

I think that is a very individual question because every person matures at a different age. It depends on the different individual—how quickly he has matured, how his muscular structure has developed, and so forth. But I would say that I advise avoiding curve balls until a youngster is 16 or 17 years old. At that time he can work on curves. In the meantime, he can practice his control, velocity, and proper throwing mechanics. At 16 or 17 years of age, he is usually physically and mentally mature enough to capably handle something like a curve ball. If he does it too soon and injures the arm, it could be a permanent thing. It could even progress to the point where he could never be able to throw like he used to again. So it is important to protect the young pitcher and not ask him to throw all the breaking pitches until he is physically mature.

How would a person train to avoid injuries such as groin muscle pulls, hamstrings, and so forth?

Again, you get back to the same basic question—getting into proper physical condition to make sure your body is flexible. There are certain individuals who have very tight muscular systems and tight joints. If you are that particular type of individual, then you might have to work harder to increase your flexibility.

Another particular individual might have good flexibility but lack good strength. He should work on his strength. It is very important that an individual is strong in his complete system, not just in one particular area. Total body conditioning, with concentration in your particular specialized area, is the desired training program to help master the art of playing baseball.

CINCINNATI REDS BASEBALL STRENGTH-TRAINING PROGRAM

Many misconceptions and fallacies have been established concerning weight-training principles and objectives. Often weight training is solely related to the muscle-bound individual who is unable to perform naturally. This is not the case with this program and is definitely not the objective of a baseball strength-training program. On the contrary, besides increasing muscular strength and endurance, you will also show increased joint flexibility and range of motion.

If all other aspects are equal—body proportions, neurological efficiency, cardiovascular ability, and skill—the stronger athlete will win. Absolutely nothing can be done to improve either body proportions or neurological efficiency; however, we can do something about the other three factors. Skill is improved by the various drills, as well as the actual playing of the game. Cardiovascular ability is increased through the conditioning program, running, and playing. Muscular strength can also be increased through a conscientious, properly executed strength-training program.

Strength is important in every sport, including baseball. Although some sports may require higher levels, all baseball activities require some degree of strength. Strength is important to the baseball player because it increases the prevention of injury; muscular

Below and next page: Running with a purpose, stretching exercises for flexibility, and getting loose are well illustrated here. Note the different methods—one Twins player is using a bat. Rod Carew in the middle has splendid flexibility.

Conditioning and training.

endurance, thus enabling the player to compete for a longer duration without fatigue; the length of a player's career.

Knowing these important and necessary aspects of muscular strength in baseball, you then must decide on the best method of producing the desired results. You actually have four alternatives, listed in order of best productivity:

1. *Nautilus time machine:* best method for producing full-range, high-intensity, short-duration strength-training exercise. Nautilus is the only rotary form of automatic prestretching and full muscular contraction.

2. *Barbells and dumbbells:* limited in full-range exercise but can be beneficial in producing increased strength.

3. *Universal gym machine:* less productive than Nautilus or barbells, but can give some results for strength training.

4. *Iso-kinetic (Mini-Gym, Exergenie, etc.):* does not provide a full-range exercise. This type of exercise equipment should be totally avoided.

Based on a review of the available literature, personal communication with leading sports-medicine people, and actual strength-training programs, we have concluded that Nautilus is the best method for developing strength, endurance, and increased flexibility.

When establishing a strength-training program, it must be remembered that strength is general, not specific. You should work all joints throughout their complete line of action. It must also be remembered that many injuries are caused by an improper balance between agonist (muscles which move a body part) and antagonists (muscles which oppose that movement). For example, when strengthening the thigh muscles, if we devoted all our time to the quadriceps and ignored the hamstrings, the ultimate result would be numerous injuries to the hamstrings. This would be true for hips, back, shoulders, elbow, and ankles. Keeping in mind these principles and the specific actions and activities necessary in the game of baseball, the following programs should be instituted:

Muscle Exercised	Nautilus Time Machines	Barbells and Dumbbells	Universal Gym Station
Lower back, hips buttocks	Hip and Back Buo-Poly Contractile Machine	Hip flexor, using high bar	Leg press and hip flexor
Quads	Leg extension	Squats, knee extension	Thigh and knee station
Hamstring	Leg curl	Squats, knee flexion	Knee station
Calves	Calf raises (Multi-exerciser)	Calf raises—barbell on shoulders	Calf raises, shoulder-press station on shoulder
Upper torso	Super pullover	Bench pullover	High lat. station
Latissimus	Behind the neck	Bench pullover	High lat. station
Pectoral muscles	Double chest	Bench press and pectoral lift—on back, arm extended, and lift	Chest-press station
Deltoids Supraspin	Double shoulder	Abduction lift—arm straight at side, lift to shoulder level, and return	Shoulder-press station
Rhomboids Rotators	Rowing machine	Rhomboid lift—lying on stomach, arm straight, lift up, and return	Rowing station
Biceps	Bicep curls	Bicep curls	Bicep curl station
Triceps	Tricep curls	Tricep extension—barbell behind head, arm bent, straighten, and return	Negative dips on dip station
Wrists & Forearms	Wrist curls (Multi-exerciser)	Wrist curls	Wrist curls (bicep st.), wrist developer station

When doing the program, start out with a relatively light weight, so that you are sure to properly execute the exercise. Lifting a weight is not enough, regardless of the amount of weight. How you lift a weight is a factor of far greater importance. You should be able to do at least eight good repetitions—if you cannot, the weight is too heavy. If you can do twelve or more, the weight is too light and you should add another plate of five or ten more pounds. The program should stress complete range of motion, attempting to obtain a stretch before executing the movement.

Your off-season conditioning program should start two to five weeks after the season ends. During this period, concentrate on individual weaknesses and developing strength throughout the entire body. Depending on the type of equipment, you should be working on all twelve muscular areas as listed previously. Do your strength training on an every-other-day basis, thus allowing your muscles enough time to recover from the work. You should be able to complete the program in approximately one hour or less. Concentrate on form, gradually increasing the resistance as the repetitions become easier. Base your increases on the eight to twelve system as explained previously.

The objectives of the strength-training program are to increase muscular strength and endurance, joint flexibility, muscular speed.

With these objectives in mind, you should keep the following fundamentals when completing *each* repetition:

1. Do all repetitions throughout complete range of motion.
2. Do all repetitions by raising on a 1-2 count, and lowering on a 1-2-3-4 count.
3. Do all repetitions slowly, making sure to pause briefly at the fully contracted and starting positions.
4. Do all repetitions concentrating on form; weight increases will follow accordingly.

19|Getting It All Together in Practice

Baseball practice must be fun, interesting, and challenging in order to develop a high degree of excellence. It must also simulate game conditions as much as possible, be fast-paced, varied, and give each player an opportunity to sharpen his skills to the best of his ability. Constant repetition of the correct techniques will enable the player to do the right thing instinctively.

Practices can be adapted to whatever aspect of the game the coach wishes to emphasize—offensive, defensive, a combination, or simply fun time (after an especially tough loss or letdown following examinations or a heavy emotional experience).

Although it is impossible to include all drills every day, we pick the ones that the team needs most at that particular stage of the season. A typical early-season practice has the players warm up with some running and each man doing some stretching exercises to loosen all of his muscles. Our thinking here was influenced by Percy Cerutty and the European soccer players who warm up almost entirely by stretching.

We then do some catching and pepper to warm up the throwing arms. A typical early-season practice would go as follows:

2:00–2:15: Individual drills

2:15–2:20: Burma Road (explained later), a conditioning or base-running drill.

2:20–2:35: Team defensive drill—double cutoff (against first-and-third attempted double steal) and defensing the squeeze play.

2:35–3:40: Hitting drills—eight swings and two bunts: (1) 0-2 count (choke up on the bat, shorten stroke, and widen strike zone); (2) move runner over to third from second with nobody out; and (3) squeeze play.

3:40–3:50: Timed baserunning, touching all bases (13.2 to 14.5 seconds is excellent).

3:50–4:05: Infield or situation drills

4:05–4:10: Burma Road.

Organization par excellence at the City College of New York: unit work on individual drills includes the third baseman charging slow-hit balls, catchers blocking pitches in the dirt, pitchers working with first baseman on balls hit to his left, and outfielders working on fly balls over their heads. This keeps the squad busy and interested while making the most out of the available area and time.

Let us take a closer look at each component of the practice. We generally like to start practice with individual position drills, but this varies from time to time. We want to create as many game situations as possible and work on them every day. We also do a lot of small-group work at the same time. In fact, we bring the squad together only when everyone is needed. This gives each player many more chances to improve a certain technique. For example, in eight minutes an individual can get twenty double-play opportunities. The following are some individual drills we work on.

THIRD BASEMEN

1. A string of fifteen balls is laid down between third and home (parallel with the foul line), and each third baseman charges in and scoops up the balls—one at a time—and throws to first.

Once the players become adept, we have someone roll the balls very slowly at them to give them practice at scooping up the topped ball or bunt.

2. Pop flies near third and home.
3. Protecting the foul line in late innings.
4. Fielding hard-hit ground balls to the left.
5. Backhanding balls hit to the right.
6. Holding runner on third.
7. Following runner in on squeeze play.
8. Charging bunt with runners on first and second (force play at third with shortstop covering third).
9. Cutting in front of shortstop to take any ball he can reach.
10. Putting the tag on runners.
11. Playing deep with a force situation at third.
12. Double plays from third to second to first.
13. Hot-box situations with catcher. (Also with shortstop and second baseman.)
14. Taking throws from outfielders and putting the tag on.
15. Cutoff situations.

SECOND BASEMEN AND SHORTSTOPS

1. Double plays on balls hit in the hole at short, right at the shortstop, and to his left on medium and soft ground balls.
2. Roll a wooden barrel over second base to simulate a runner trying to break up a double play. You will be surprised at how much quicker your keystone pair will learn to get rid of the ball. They will develop a feel for getting out of the way of the runner.
3. Double plays from second to short to first on balls hit to second baseman's right, left, and directly at him.
4. Stretching on force plays at second.
5. Pop flies back of second baseman and shortstop (work with outfielders).
6. Pick-off plays at second working with pitchers.
7. Keeping runners close to second.
8. Double cutoff situations (both men out on extra-base hits in the alleys).
9. Cutoff positioning and relay throws.
10. Charging topped balls from a deep position.
11. Hot-box situations.
12. Comeback double plays—pitcher to shortstop (or second basemen) to first.

FIRST BASEMEN

1. Stretching drills on throws (opposite leg from glove hand to assure maximum stretch).
2. Shifting on bad throws, left and right.
3. Throwing the ball in the dirt to each other—short hops, long hops, and inbetween hops.
4. Jumping for high throws and making a slap tag (bending both knees before throw arrives).
5. Throws inside and down the line.
6. Pop flies from behind first to the plate.
7. Working on balls hit to his right and feeding the pitcher (overhand and underhand).
8. Double plays on ball hit behind and in front of first, with shortstop covering second.
9. Charging and fielding bunts.

This drill for a pivoting infielder is one of the finest for developing quick hands and getting rid of the ball. A feeder will have about twenty balls in front of him on the ground and start feeding them one at a time to the pivot man, who will throw into a screen or backstop. As he gets better, you increase the speed with which you feed him. When he really becomes adroit around the bag, have him fold his glove fingers in and catch the ball with the back of his glove. His bare hand is always working to develop surer and quicker hands with a fast release. Another ball will be on the way to him as he releases the ball in the last photo.

In this sequence, the young ballplayer has a lead baseball (same size as a regular baseball but weighing between five and eight pounds) in his pitching hand. In photo 2, he stands on his tiptoes and extends his arm as far as possible. In the final picture, he is gripping the lead ball with his fingertips and then turning it in his hand and on his fingertips, just as if he were screwing a light bulb in a socket. Begin with 5 repetitions and gradually build up to 150. This is one of the best drills to build up your arm and the ligaments and tendons in your pitching elbow.

These two pitching sequences illustrate an excellent way to teach a young pitcher how to get his body into the pitch. One youngster holds the other's back ankle loose enough so he can pivot and go to the plate. Notice how the body comes completely through and behind the pitch in the last two photos. It is not necessary to have a baseball in this drill, but by doing this dry run 50 to 100 times every day, from the stretch and windup, you will soon have the feel of what it is like to pitch and use your whole body, not just your arm. Your pitching form will become second nature and much easier on your arm. The second photo sequence shows the same drill from the left side.

This sequence shows an excellent individual drill practice session. In the background, first basemen are working on digging the ball out of the dirt. In the middle, pitchers are stretching and charging bunts on the first base line. Catchers are working on throws to second, and third basemen will work on slow-hit topped baseballs off the plate.

The start of the Burma Road, everybody's favorite conditioning drill. On this leg, the young men sprint to first, as the second group waits its turn. Notice the all-out effort and keen competition among the teammates. A splendid conditioner and a great way to finish up practice on an upbeat. Burma Road also improves base running.

Another drill with the lead baseball which will help the flexibility and strength of your throwing hand. Notice that he is supporting his throwing arm with his other hand as he slowly moves his wrist, fingers, and hand forward and then backward through the full range of movement. Start with 10 and gradually increase until you can do 200 each day.

10. Protecting the foul line on balls hit to his left (late innings).

11. Cutoff situations.

12. Work with catcher on dropped third strikes.

CATCHERS

1. Blocking balls thrown in the dirt.

2. Shifting for throw to second, stepping with right foot first.

3. Shifting and throwing to third with right-handed hitter at bat.

4. Blocking the plate and making tags.

5. Taking throws from outfielder at plate—short, medium, and long hops.

6. Feeding pitcher covering the plate on wild pitches or passed balls with runner on third.

7. Pop fouls back of and in front of plate.

8. Fielding bunts in front of plate.

9. Dropped third strike.

10. Pick-off at first base.

OUTFIELDERS

1. Charging ground balls and throwing to a relay man.

2. Blocking ground balls.

3. Going for balls hit over head (crossover step and go).

4. Handling ball lost in the sun (step to one side or the other). Work with sunglasses also.

5. Call drills with all three outfielders.

6. Call drills between center fielder and right fielder.

7. Call drill between left fielder and center fielder.

8. Backing up on a fly ball, then coming in to make a throw after the catch.

9. Line-drive drill.

10. Picking up a ball by the fence and hitting relay man.

11. Diving catches.

PITCHERS

1. Covering first on anything hit to his left.

2. Backing up first on 6-4-3 double play.

3. Covering home on a tag play.

4. Backing up third and home (forty-five feet back, if possible).

5. Comeback double plays with shortstop and second baseman covering.

6. Force plays at second and third in bunt situations.

7. Squeeze play.

8. Throws to all bases.

9. Fielding ground balls and line drives near the mound.

TEAM OFFENSIVE DRILLS

If space is available, we will break up into several groups. Pitchers will work on sacrifice and squeeze bunts in one area. Infielders may be simulating batters where the next two pitchers are warming up. Certain individuals may be working on a specific drill for correcting hitting faults.

Once the hitter has his swing grooved, we use live pitching with our pitchers throwing from three-quarters to full speed and mixing their pitches. We like the hitter to see the type of pitching he is going to face in a game. Very little is accomplished by lobbing the ball over to a hitter standing there with his shirt unbuttoned who swings all-out at pitching that he will never see in a game.

Intrasquad games are fun. You can have them whenever feasible, with two players doing the managing. There are several ways to control the scrimmage. We have one which we call "one pitch." The pitcher delivers; if the batter hits a fair ball, he runs it out just as in a game. If the batter takes the pitch and it is a strike or if he foul tips it, he is out. If the pitch is a ball, he gets a walk. This makes for a speedy game and helps the players who like to take a lot of pitches. You can also specify three balls as a walk and two strikes for a strike-out.

Each team gets nine outs before changing sides. This saves time and makes for a fast-paced scrimmage.

Other team drills we like are three bunts (against a live defense)—two sacrifice and one squeeze. If the hitter executes all three properly, he gets three additional cuts after bunting. If

Coach Dick Howser of the New York Yankees demonstrating his bat-speed drill. This is one of the finest ways to increase your bat speed, especially if you do this with a 55- or 60-ounce lead bat. A college or pro hitter will have a hard time doing this drill all-out, 150 times. Start your swing in the first four photos, launching the bat through as quickly as possible. You take your full swing and follow through, as in photos 6 and 7. Your follow-through is held for a split second in photo 7, then, as you see in the next picture, start your swing backwards and fire the bat as hard and quick as you can—like running a movie film camera backwards. In the last two photos, the bat returns all the way along the same path to your original starting position, as in photo 1. Repeat the drill immediately. Young players start with about 20 repetitions, then add 5 to 10 each time until you reach 100 or more. The key to this drill is to go all-out when swinging through and bringing the bat backwards. You will be amazed after a month or two of doing this how much faster you become with your hands and bat.

The bench drill is a real winner for agility and leg development. This drill should be done for about six minutes. (You will have to gradually work up to this—start with three minutes.) The bench can be up to knee height. After a few minutes, you should face the other way and use the opposite leg to hop up to the bench. This is a great conditioner for pitchers' legs and helps pitchers develop the muscles in the leg which give the push off the rubber.

Pitcher flexibility test for curve-ball pitchers. If you can't bend
your hand straight down from the wrist as shown in this
picture, you are going to have trouble developing an
outstanding curve ball. Some young players don't even realize
this and wonder why they never develop the great curve ball.
If you lack this flexibility, work with the leaded baseball. If it
doesn't improve, you should seriously think about developing a
slider, fast curve, or another type of breaking ball.

he misses all three, he gets no swings. If he misses one, he gets two swings. If he fails two, he gets only one swing. This drill has helped improve our bunting.

The following routine is recommended as once-a-week drill, as it is too time-consuming to run every day. The hitter must execute the following facing a live defense and pitching: sacrifice bunt, hit-and-run, moving runner on second over to third by hitting ball on right side, squeeze bunt, and getting ball out of infield.

If the hitter executes these five skills, he gets ten swings. For each of the five he does not execute, he loses two swings. This helps our hitters concentrate hard on each task.

Our one-swing drills also provide fun and benefit. They are all done against a pitcher and defense, with the hitter staying up as long as he produces what is expected:

1. Chokes up and protects the plate with 0-2 count, swinging at anything close.
2. Swings only if he gets pitch in his "joy" zone with 2-0 count.
3. Gets a base hit with one swing.
4. Tries to hit ball on the ground.
5. Squeeze drill—suicide and safety squeeze.

BASE RUNNING DRILLS

1. Each man is timed around the bases, starting with one foot on the plate. Five seconds are added for each base missed, and the bases must be rerun. An excellent time is between 13.2 and 14.5 seconds. The competitiveness of this drill extracts a maximum effort from every player. They enjoy the challenge and the comparisons of times.
2. Going from first to third on balls hit to the outfield.
3. Scoring from second on a hit to the outfield.
4. Getting a big lead at first and watching left and right-handed pick-off moves to first.
5. Scoring from third on any ground ball not hit back to the pitcher.

6. Stealing home. We feel that a runner on third should be able to steal home on any pitcher who takes four seconds or longer to deliver the ball to the plate from the start of the windup.
7. Line-drive drill: restrain the natural reaction to go forward.
8. Drawing throws from the outfielders by rounding first hard on base hits to the outfield, tagging up on fly balls, and bluffing to draw throw.
9. Sliding, with emphasis on throws which draw the first baseman off the bag, and slides at the plate.

TEAM DEFENSIVE DRILLS

1. Bunt defense with runner on first, runners on first and second, and squeeze defense.
2. Double cutoffs on balls hit into the outfield alleys.
3. First and third drill: delayed steal, runner on first breaks as catcher cocks arm to return ball to pitcher; bush steal, runner on first breaks as pitcher comes set; and straight steal.
4. Situation drill: any situation can be set up and the ball then fungoed to the desired spot.
5. Call drill: emphasis on pop ups between infield and outfield.

CONDITIONING DRILLS

1. Burma Road—one of the best conditioning drills. The players sprint to first, then form a single line and walk around the bases. When the first man in the line touches home, the players sprint to second and walk home. At the next touch of the plate, they sprint to third and then walk home. At the next touch they sprint around all the bases twice. The teams can be broken up into groups by position to inject more competitiveness into the drill.
2. Foul-line to foul-line: the players sprint one way and walk the other thirty times.

There is an old saying that "Practice makes perfect." But it works only if you practice the right thing.

This is a drill which helps an infielder learn to get rid of the ball fast by using the back of his glove as a deflector. In picture 3, he deflects the ball with his glove to his bare hand and, in photo 4, throws into the backstop. Another ball will be fed immediately. As you get quicker with your hands, have the feeder increase the speed with which he feeds the balls. Twenty balls at one time is enough. Go all out with your hands.

20 | Baseball, Japanese Style

I had the pleasure of playing baseball in Japan and also teaching and coaching there. The Japanese have a deep love for the game and work tremendously hard to improve themselves as players. At the high school level, they have a national playoff for all schools in the country. A high school game can draw 50,000 fans. I've seen people playing baseball in two feet of snow. In the major cities, streets are closed at lunch hour and pick-up games or catch are standard fare.

Here are some of the methods and ideas used in Japan for mastering baseball. You might find something to help you.

First, on the professional level, the Japanese like to have a hard four-hour pregame workout, the idea being that they keep you in shape. Three team meetings a day are generally held to go over the opposing team, its pitcher, and the mistakes made that day. Jim Lefebvre, a former

Los Angeles Dodger, played in Japan and expressed his experience:

On the road on the day of a night game, for example, the players eat breakfast together, take a group walk, and have a meeting. In the afternoon they have lunch together and another meeting before the game. After the game, they eat a late supper together and have a final meeting just before they go to bed. The managers and the coaches are with the players all the time, of course.

Before the game, for instance, they'll talk about the opposing pitcher they're going to face, as well as the strengths and weaknesses of all other players they'll take the field against. In the final meeting late at night, they'll discuss the game in detail, especially any mistakes they made.

Americans tend to criticize Japanese baseball tactics, but maybe we can learn something from them, particularly about things like togetherness. You won't find too many feuds among players on the same team over there. They believe the strength of the team lies in togetherness and that's the key to their idea of what makes a winning team. You'll even see the players taking their exercises together in the outfield before the game. And you'll hardly ever see a fat or out-of-shape player in Japan.

When I retire from playing, I want to coach baseball in the United States, and I certainly want to apply some of the principles I've learned in Japan.

Most of their professional teams each have about ten coaches plus the manager. Their Little League teams practice like the big leagues; seven-hour daily sessions with identical routines. They have a Fighting Spirit Award for each game.

A typical spring practice is a 7-hour day with 20 minutes for lunch on the field. They run 5 miles; 2½ miles at the start of practice, 2½ miles at the end. Some teams start the morning with a 5-mile run. Their calisthenics are 200 sit-ups, ten 100-yard sprints, the back arch (you hang upside down on someone's back while another holds you by the leg), 100 pushups, and a one-hour intrasquad game.

The Japanese practice sliding and defensive drills. There are four separate batting cages to accommodate a right-handed pitcher, a left-handed pitcher, a pitching machine, and one for a breaking-ball pitcher or another machine. There is group groundball practice, and one hour of special practice for problems such as hitting slumps or poor breaking pitches. They have group defensive drills including infield double plays, outfield fly balls, catchers practicing with wild pitches, and pop-ups.

Some players will run steps with a fifty-pound pack on their back. They use the step drill running the stadium steps, three hundred up and down, several times a day. Hitters will get up and take five hundred shadow swings to start off the day and another four hundred swings in the various batting cages during the day.

Pitchers will train by throwing three hundred

pitches a day; this, they believe, makes their control razor sharp. A batter or a pitcher never quits working on his form.

The pitchers hang a cork on a line strung between two poles for practicing the low strike and control. I like this idea.

The fungo drill will include a guy hitting fungoes right and left, possibly 350 times or until he drops from exhaustion. One hundred fly balls follow the same pattern as above, only this is for the outfielders.

The infield drill includes practice for those who like to get out of the way of wicked line drives. The players line up on a foul line twenty feet away, and they are hit bullets. This drill ends thirty minutes later, with fingers and hands bloody, black and blue, and bent.

The team meeting includes a chalk talk before practice at 10:30 a.m. Practice is over at 5:30 p.m.

A pitcher will sometimes warm up twice—once one hour or so before the game, then again just before the game. The manager keeps his lineup a secret until just before game time.

Japanese baseball puts tremendous emphasis on scoring the first run. About 80 percent of all teams who score the first run win the game.

Japanese players try to develop a calm mind for pressure-type games. Through Zen, meditation, retreats to the mountains, and nature retreats, they refresh and regenerate their spirits.

In Japanese baseball, it is felt that an average player with "fighting spirit" can become a good player. And a good player can become a great player. If he has a will to win and spiritual strength, this will enable him to perform at top level, regardless of his physical condition. The Japanese Fighting Spirit Award was won one year by a player playing a series on a broken ankle. A pitcher with fighting spirit will finish a game and get the people out. Pitchers in Japan's major leagues may start the opening game of a series and come in and relieve in the next day or two.

"The good Japanese team is like a beautiful Japanese garden"—the Japanese team philosophy and morale follows that thinking. They feel that every tree, every rock, every blade of grass has its place. The smallest part ever so slightly out of place destroys the beauty of the whole. The rocks and the grass and the trees viewed separately might be pleasing to look at, but when properly organized, the garden becomes more than just the sum of its parts—*it becomes a work of art. It becomes perfection.*

While in Japan I received a carving in wood of a bear representing the Fighting Spirit trophy. It is called "Hokkaido Pitching Bear."

21 | Major Leaguers Help You Become a Baseball Star

HARRY WALKER ON HITTING

Hitting today is something where much improvement can take place. For years it has been neglected. It was as if you couldn't help a hitter. This is entirely wrong in my book, because if that were true, then we are very poor teachers.

What we are trying to do is teach contact. If a fellow can make contact with the ball often enough and do the right things, then he has a chance to become a pretty good hitter. Power will come if he develops and gets stronger. The young boys that you have will show a certain amount of power, but this can be very dangerous. Most young ballplayers think they are going to hit sixty or seventy home runs, and they wind up ruining their whole career as a result. Only five or possibly ten percent of the major leaguers are good power hitters.

A big fault and our biggest trouble in professional ball is the fact that most hitters continue trying to hit the ball too hard and to pull the ball too much. They develop bad habits, starting at a very young age. After we get them, it's a real big job to stop and change them.

If a fellow can learn to hit, he has an excellent chance to play in the big leagues. When I first worked out with Detroit, Hank Greenberg told me that if I would learn to swing the bat, they would find a place for me to play. Nobody had better advice to give than this fellow, and they played him in the outfield and at first base. I never saw anybody work any harder at being a good ballplayer than Greenberg. He never was a graceful fielder, but he got by and did a pretty good job. His bat was the big answer. Say we sign about one hundred ballplayers. Out of that one hundred, only four to six percent will make it to the big leagues, including pitchers. Now what happens? The answer is the bat! We can't scout throughout America and find five out-

197

standing hitters in one year who are a cinch to make it. They develop later on. While some players develop, others fall by the wayside, because of the bat more than anything else.

Hitting problems occur more and more because of Little League ball. Little League baseball so far has hurt professional baseball. It's great for the community, the kids, and the family, and I never knock it for these areas. I consider it very worthwhile, but I never knew what a strikeout was, other than swinging a bat three times, until I was 14 or 15 years old. I never knew what an umpire was until I was about that age, and I never had a uniform until then. I just went out and played ball in the back yard or a pasture or on the big diamond when the big boys weren't using it. I took a bat and a ball and swung all day. We played in every back yard we could find. The only way we struck out was by swinging three times, and we never walked. If you watch the Little League World Series, you see them walking. In every game the coaches say, "Son, you're little, don't swing the bat." Well, if I had followed that advice, I never would have played; when I was growing up, everybody said I was too little and I weighed only 100 pounds. If I had gone through Little League instruction from age 9 through 14, I would have never developed as a hitter. I swung the bat everywhere I went. I hung the glove on my belt, and I would hit the ball on the way to the park. I swung the bat all day.

When Ted Williams was growing up he played in the back yard. He would say to himself, "I'm in the Polo Grounds, it's 3–2, and I'm going to hit this ball right out of here." He told me that he would swing that bat a hundred times a day, developing strong, quick hands—the secret of hitting.

We need to swing the bat. Little Leaguers are lucky if they swing ten times a day. They won't even play unless the coach is there and they have a whole ball club. We used to play if five guys showed up. We played One Old Cat, chose up sides, and had a game. We were constantly swinging the bat. Hitting is something that requires practice.

In teaching, attitude is number one. If a fellow has the right attitude, you can approach him and work with him. If he doesn't have the proper attitude, you try to find a way to reach him. Forcing something on him is the least effective method; then he tries to prove in every way that he is right and you are wrong. I have seen that in professional ball. The guy who can hit .230 in Triple A winds up in Class D batting .240. They will bring him up because he can run and field, thinking that he'd have a chance if he could learn to hit. He comes up to Triple A and you start trying to tell him something. He will say, "I've been doing this for three years." For three years he's been hitting .220, .240, and .250.

To me that just won't cut it. And yet he's going to argue with you day in and day out about that's the only way he can do it. If that's the only way he can do it, he'd better quit unless he's the greatest glove man you ever saw at shortstop, second base, or behind the plate. Then the rest of the ballclub would have to do the hitting. If you are going to be a winner, you must have enough men who can swing a bat. Look at the World Series. Those teams have players who can hit the good pitchers. It takes a combination of hitting and pitching.

Attitude is the key in your work with your ballplayers. Find a way to reach them, to get them to want to learn to be a better hitter. Approach each player as an individual. There is no set pattern in handling people. The toughest job is to get a ballplayer to want to learn. Once you get a boy to say, "Please, coach, let me work on this and work on that," you are on your way. Timing is important. Pick a time when a ballplayer begins to get a little disgusted and is willing to talk and cry on somebody's shoulder. At that moment you might get him to listen. You might be better off by not worrying him or changing him during the game. Tell him to go on and hit in his natural way.

I know from experience. My brother, Dixie, was a fine teacher, one of the best. When Dixie worked with me, I had always hit pretty well; in fact, the first year in "D" ball, I played in about sixty or seventy games and had a ruptured appendix. Although I hit .370, I got released at the end of the year. I was skinny and weighed 145 pounds, and they said I would never throw. Eventually, I could stand by the hitting cage in Philadelphia and throw a ball almost on the left-field roof, about four hundred feet away. I went out every day and stretched my arm for distance just by throwing. If my arm hurt, I just kept throwing, as long as I got good and loose. In time, I overcame my arm weakness. I hit .300 right on up into the big leagues. Then I went into the army and tried to become a power hitter. I came back and I wasn't hitting at all.

In my first year in the majors, I hit .315 and the next year I hit .296; then I found myself hitting .230, .240, and .250, while playing a little here and there. Dixie talked to me and said, "Harry, you're trying to pull every ball and hit it out of the ball park, jerking your head. You're doing things poorly and you better change or you won't be here." He and I fought every time we got together. I argued with him and told him, "I can't do it that way!" Then we'd wind up in a big free-for-all until we got where we'd have to stop talking about hitting. Finally, he approached me from another angle: "Harry, why don't you go out in batting practice and get somebody to throw to you, even if you have to pay him to do it. Then see how long you can wait, just trying to hit every ball through the middle or to the opposite field, keeping the ball on the ground. But, if it's in a game, forget about it." So I did that in practice for three weeks, day in and day out. You must have patience with your ballplayer and work with him so that it doesn't affect him while he's playing the game. I finally decided to follow Dixie's advice, and after three weeks I was in the World Series. I hit .412, led the team in RBI's, and drove in the winning run in the final game.

That was a battle I went through, but it taught me to understand my ballplayers a little bit better. Hitting has to be a habit. It is tough for us in pro ball to correct a person's faults, which have often been performed in high school, college, and then in lower leagues. When I get

him in the major leagues, he's got that real bad habit and eight or nine years behind him. It's really tough to make a change. There are only three or four out of a hundred who make it as hitters. I can't believe that the scouts are that bad. Part of it is our fault for allowing mistakes to continue so long.

Power is something that a fellow either has or doesn't have. He can develop a little of it, but most of it is natural. Too many try to hit the long ball at the expense of making contact. If a fly ball can win the ball game and the batter cannot make contact, he is useless.

The first and second place hitters in the batting order should be bat-control men, who can run and get on the base with a base-on-balls. Your third man should be a pretty good base runner who can hit average and with power, stay away from the double play, and be a good RBI man. The fourth man should be the same type of hitter, who is generally slower. The fifth man is much the same. Then come the sixth, seventh, eighth, and ninth men. There are three men in the middle of that lineup who can really hurt you. The ideal situation is to have speed and bat control in front of the order.

In gripping the bat, I like the knuckles to be lined up rather than wrapped way around where the wrists are too tight. If you have a boy who can successfully hit in a particular manner, I wouldn't care if he stood on his head. If he can do the job, don't bother him! If he has troubles, you look for them.

As a hitting instructor, I've watched hitters over a period of time and checked their records and background to see what they've done and how well they've hit. Everybody will go through a streak where for two or three weeks they might not hit. If a person has a good hitting background, you must let him work things out.

I asked Hank Aaron what he did when he got into a slump. He said, "If I hit four or five home runs in a period of a week or ten days, I had to be careful that I didn't get into trouble by jerking my head, pulling my body, and not going after the ball." He did that for the last two or three years of his career, and his average really dropped. Then Hank Aaron, who was the greatest hitter I ever saw, was the person who hit that ball into right-center field, center field, and left field. With the short fences in Atlanta, he could just flick the ball in there. He said, "When I got into bad habits, I practiced a few days hitting the ball through the middle and to the opposite field." This is what the great hitters will do. All hitters have problems.

As a golfer, Arnold Palmer would go back to his father for advice. He respected his dad and listened to him because he knew his style. He could be his eyes for him. As a hitting instructor, that's what you are. You watch the guy and you see when he's right. In your mind, you form a picture that everything is coordinated and put together. When that picture changes, you have to watch it closely enough to know it. Sometimes I take pictures when a person is going right; then there is something to check back on. I compare those pictures to others taken when he's going bad to see if he's doing anything differently.

The first step to being a good hitter is to assume a good, comfortable position. There are all sorts of styles, but you shouldn't try to copy the style of a Musial or somebody else with an unusual stance. For example, Mel Ott had the craziest batting style in the world, but he did everything right after he got ready.

The hands should be comfortable and not too far away. If you get too far out, you are going to get tied up. Don't get those hands too far forward either. Choke up on the bat slightly.

Your stance and grip should be almost the same as when you play pepper. You must have the same rhythm and balance to be a good hitter as to be a good fielder. Everything in baseball is balance and body control, including fielding, throwing, running, and hitting. In hitting, if you ever get your weight too far back, you are dead. You can't adjust. Hitting in plain words is nothing in the world but getting in a good set position where you can control the bat.

To good hitters such as Ted Williams, the secret of batting is waiting. The stride starts with the pitcher's arm. Time the arm, but keep your hands and hips back—they are like a set of triggers. If you commit yourself too quickly, you will be in trouble because of a failure to adjust to the ball. A good hitter strides to get into position, waits, and adjusts to what the ball does.

Everybody can't be a good hitter. However, everybody can wait for the ball as long as Williams did, except most people don't hit it at the same spot as Williams. They hit it further back in the strike zone than Williams. I could wait just as long as Williams and I could see that spin just like Williams. However, I hit the ball in the middle of the plate and Williams hit it two feet out front. Now, I was just as quick as Williams, except I couldn't pull the ball. That's simply it!

If your weight is not too far forward, you can adjust to the breaking ball. It's automatic.

Suppose you have two cars on a 120-mile track. If one car goes 60 miles per hour and the other goes 40, the latter would have to start one hour sooner for both of them to hit the finish line at exactly the same time. That's the best example I can give to compare two hitters. Suppose that thirty minutes after the first car started, it was learned that the track wasn't ready. There goes one car. Meanwhile, the other car is sitting back waiting. That's the hitter. The first one is thirty minutes down the road and that ball isn't what it originally looked like. The batter is just like that car—torn up. He's committed himself and he's in trouble. Make both of them wait just a little bit. Let that first car have an extra hour, and they both get there. To be a good hitter, you have to wait and let the ball get into the right position and your finish line is one hour shorter. I set 80 miles instead of 120 miles as my goal. Now I can start both of them at the same time and neither one will get into any more trouble than the other.

Pitchers thrive on people who will go up there and try to guess. They'll tell you right quick that they'd rather have a power hitter up with a man on third base than a guy like Dick Groat. Pitchers would much rather face someone who strikes out 150 times than a guy who strikes out 30 or 40 times.

When you are working with hitters, have them break the knees slightly. That puts the balls of the feet into a position where they control the body. If you get back on your heels, you have no control. My knees and my back are like an elevator—they can come up and go down. They helped me get the bat to the ball. Then I could maneuver my hands and arms to where I could throw the bat at the ball.

Those hands and hips, once again, are back. Once the hips come around, then your hands have to do all the work. Bringing that belly button around has to come right with the hands.

Today, everybody tries to hit the ball out of the ball park. The high ball gives them a lot of trouble, especially those who lift everything. There are very few hitters in the major leagues who uppercut and are good hitters. Ted Williams had one of the strongest, quickest pair of hands in baseball. He came up over the ball. Most hitters come under it, and they sky it or miss the ball completely, especially anything above the waist. Good hard stuff gives them trouble. The slow stuff they can handle.

Fifty percent of your boys have the habit of locking that back leg. If they do that, they will be doing nothing but swinging with their hands. When I first started, they said to get the hands high, keep them away from you, and keep your weight on the back foot. Well, I don't teach any of that. Keep your hands in a comfortable position above shoulder height. If they are too high, you have to bring them back down anyway. Your most natural position is shoulder high.

Eighty percent of the hitters in baseball overstride in an attempt to get more leverage and to hit the ball hard. You need a short stride. I've seen rubber bands, chairs, etc., put up in front to stop this overstriding, but the minute you take them away, they're back at it again. So I've found a way to cut down on the problem. Keep

the back leg comfortable, but do not let it buckle. If the back leg buckles, the shoulder comes up and the elbow comes up. This makes it tough to hit the baseball.

As soon as you can, get the bat and the ball on the same plane. Bill "Moose" Skowron used to hit balls off of his ear to the opposite field like bullets. He wouldn't get around on it quickly enough, but bat and ball were on the same level when contact was made. If he's uppercutting, there is only one spot where he can really make contact. On the other hand, you have nearly the entire length of the bat with which to operate if you get the ball and bat on the identical plane.

Step up and into the ball when you hit. Now you don't want to hit off the front foot, although that's what a lot of people might think you are doing. Just hit off the back foot into the front foot. That front leg is stiff or slightly bent when that back leg comes through. Rather than hit and fall back, hit and follow through. When you throw a baseball, the weight begins on the back foot. As you stride forward, you throw into the front foot and push against that stiff front leg. Hitting follows the same theory. That front leg is slightly bent, and you hit into it.

If my shoulder drops under the ball, then the high pitch will give me a little trouble. Remember to pick up the low ball and hit down on the high one.

Teach your boys to hit to various fields. The secret in hitting to the opposite field is to let the ball come to you.

Never "snap" the bat over. Many people say that the way to hit is to roll the wrist over. Well, I'll show you a hundred films that disprove that idea, unless the ball is away from the hitter.

Once again, if you are going to hit that high ball, you have to feel like you are hitting down, but you'll still be hitting level. The minute the hitter buckles that back leg under him, his front shoulder comes up. Then he will have a tendency for the head to open up. Teach the hitter to go to the opposite field. That makes him wait and allows him to watch the ball and to keep his hands in there. That's why you stress going through the middle when a guy's in trouble. It is even important for your good power hitters to follow this idea. Sacrifice the power for a while and get that timing back.

If the hitter has two balls and no strikes, he can gamble by looking for the fast ball. If he gets the ball he's waiting for, he can hit it out. In a tough situation, however, they're going to change speeds. You have to know the pitcher. If he doesn't have a good change-up or breaking ball, you don't have to wait as long. Each pitcher is a different challenge. The big secret is learning to wait.

The next step is to put the bat on the same plane as the ball as quickly as possible and keep it there as long as you can. I find that the back hip controls this more than anything else. On the low ball you go right on down, pick it up, and just follow through. Whatever happens will happen. However, to bring that bat over on the high ball, you must stress that you are "chopping that top limb." Let that hip roll over. It's really nothing but a follow through. Paul Waner talked about the importance of the "belly button." That's all right, but there are other things that have to happen before the belly button gets there. That's nothing but a follow through.

If you want to hit to the opposite field, the "belly button" doesn't open up as much. To hit to the opposite field, you must keep the hips somewhat closed. Pulling the ball requires a snap of the hips.

Where do you stand in the box?

The position in the box is something that

varies. When the hitter strides, that front foot controls it. He should be about a foot off the plate and stride straight to the pitcher or slightly in. He should at least give himself a chance to keep those hips closed—you hit with your hips. Your power comes out of coordinating your hips and your hands. Keep your eyes on the ball and watch it meet the bat. Then the head comes through a little.

I heard Paul Waner talk about hitting down on the low pitch. What is your thinking on this?

He may have said that, but I have movies of Paul Waner hitting the low ball by picking it up instead of hitting down. In my book, the secret of hitting is putting that ball and bat together where they can meet. Many hitters have difficulty because they don't give the bat and the ball this chance.

Hitting doesn't mean that you must be strong. Matty Alou hit .340 or .345 and used a 36-inch, 36-ounce bat. He choked way up and just hit sharp line drives. The ball just has to travel about a hundred and twenty feet and bounce a little bit or skip between the shortstop and third baseman. Everybody wants to drive it out of the park. You are lucky if you average ten home runs per man on a ballclub a year. Get your ballplayers to make contact and go with the pitch.

How do you get wrist action?

You're not going to get much wrist action other than throwing the bat. We love to see our opponents try to pull the outside pitch. The secret of hitting, once again, is striding and getting into a comfortable position where the bat can be snapped best. Hitters should wait long

Matty Alou at bat.

enough to see the ball move. When it moves, he must go with the pitch. If I reach way out and try to pull the outside pitch, then I'm losing my power by trying to hit something I'm pulling away from. The big end of the bat must go to the ball. That's why you teach a batter to hit the ball straight away if he can't pull with success. He must develop according to his ability. I couldn't be a Ted Williams. I made my money by getting on base and learning to use my legs which, by the way, were no good to me if I were on the bench everytime, striking out or popping up. I had to get on base to become a threat. Then the big guys scored me. I could steal, tag up, and do a lot of things to win.

Do you have any feelings about adjustment when the batter falls behind on an 0-2 or 1-2 count, for example?

Frankly, I'd say to hit the same way. Have you ever tried to hit a golf ball when you had the wind behind you? Your timing and rhythm get fouled up because you throw your body into a panic by trying to hit too hard. I say hit the same way!

I've seen too many games get messed up because the ballplayers are going to win it "right now" in the ninth inning. "Coach, I'll win it for you, don't worry." The hitter has batted three times and struck out or popped up three times. Then he says, "I should have hit it out." Well, there's a guy on the mound and he's going to try something to keep you from hitting it out.

I learned another thing from Dixie. He said, "Harry, if you go to bat and get base hits the first two times up, for God's sake, don't go acting foolish and start trying to drive the ball out of the park. You'll go 0 for 3 the next three times at bat." Continue the same stroke, try going to center with the ball, and have a good 4 for 4 day. It's a shame to see somebody hit well the first time up, then go 0 for 4 because he's trying to jerk the ball.

The hitter should use what he has; if it's power, let him hit with it; if he doesn't have power he should take what he's got and develop

it. He should make himself the toughest man in the league to get out with two outs or with a man on third base.

Do you prefer an open stance or closed stance?

I wouldn't care if he stood on his head, if he can hit. After the stride, however, he should be able to have plate coverage.

Once a hitter disciplines himself to wait, what can he do to improve bat velocity?

One of the things we're talking about is drilling holes at the top and bottom of the bat and filling the bat with lead. Make it five or six ounces heavier than one you would normally use. Strengthen your arms by just standing there swinging, over and over. Quick, strong arms are essential, and you might develop them this way. However, you don't want to get muscle-bound. You should have long, flexible muscles in our game, not stout, tight muscles—that's why football players are strong. Give them the right pitch and they can kill you; get it in tight and they can't get their arms in there to manipulate the bat. Hitting is adjusting to the pitch. The body helps you get into position. Then you must be smart enough to know what you can and can't do.

Do you teach anything about where to put the bat in the palm of the hand?

Yes. You don't like the bat jammed back in the palm; that locks your wrists. The bat should be up in the fingers. This allows the hand to be loose and relaxed. Don't tighten the wrists because that will stop the wrist action. The wrists have to be just like the other joints, so they can be manipulated and snapped.

I have pictures of Mickey Mantle and Willie Stargell gliding into the ball. Their hands and wrists were strong enough to do this—I couldn't. My wrists are small. I had to hit with bat control and use the good legs. Eddie Stanky rode me. He used to say, "If they ever take those legs away from you, Walker, you'd starve to death." I couldn't be a home-run hitter. Today I can still walk out and hit the ball sharply. We've played seven or eight old-timer games and I have eight straight hits.

If you have a lefthander who can run, have him hit the ball on the ground to the left side. When that shortstop goes to his right, he's in trouble. If he hits the same ball to second base, it's a routine out.

What about the split grip?

I really don't know. I've never liked it, but some people have used it. Ty Cobb used it. That's something you don't teach. You would not teach somebody to hit like Stan Musial or Ted Williams. You take a normal stride and grip and try to teach the typical way of doing it. The percentages are that it's the easiest way. There's an exception to anything, but not when you are talking about the great majority of hitters.

When I was hitting the ball well, I found that if I aimed at the shortstop I'd hit in the hole between short and third. If I aimed right at the third baseman, I'd foul the ball in the seats. The pitcher will help determine this. If he's real fast, then I'll have to aim more to the middle because I'm going to be a little late. If he's a little slow, I can aim more to my target. Too many hit-and-run men try to place the ball past the first baseman, and they hit the ball foul into the seats.

Glide forward and hit the ball right at the second baseman. Keep the bat over that ball. The quicker that ball is moving when it hits the ground, the sooner you are going to get that base hit. It might take a hop or skid off. The pop fly or the easy fly ball won't drop very often. Make the other ball club handle the ball. Make it tough on them.

What about bunting for a base hit?

Well, that's an act you have to practice. Your first move is to wait. Too many guys break and run. Get the ball down first and then go. That's a matter of practice.

For a sacrifice, I teach them to hold the bat high, knees apart, and the bat over the top of the ball at the top of the strike zone. Reach out and just push the ball. Bunt hard to third base and soft to first.

TED WILLIAMS ON HITTING

Coaches and teachers are always special to me because I certainly respect these professions. I envy them because they are sometimes a greater influence on a boy than his parents. Coaches know basically the things that I have found to be correct in baseball. In principle, the stance that is completely closed with the front foot parallel to the front of home plate and the back foot about two feet straight back (Joe Rudi uses this stance) helps the batter in two ways: It gives him a little more time by turning around and getting away from the plate, and he hits the ball at 90 degrees away from the direction in which he's pitched as against trying to hit it at 45 degrees and lessening his hitting area by 60 to 70 percent.

The correct stance is only part of the game. I think more should be said about the mental aspect, because I think the mental side of hitting—the correct way to think of hitting—is just as important as the physical part.

I know that Joe Torre aligns his fingers. Well, I could never line my fingers up. I always felt that my grip was just right and then I'd look down and say, "Well, my knuckles are not lined up just the way they're supposed to be." But, I had good success my way so I left it alone. I was very fortunate as a young boy to learn early how to get out of a rut. Everybody knows that if they had to pick the ideal way to hit, it would be with the ability to pull the ball 350, 360, or 370 feet. Hit the ball into the air, and I guess you've got a million-dollar ballplayer. I don't know, but that's the ideal way to hit a ball because you hit home runs. Of course, everybody's trying to hit home runs and, of course, everybody can't hit home runs and still be a good consistent hitter. It's too bad that more fellows don't realize this because they're making themselves .230, .240, or .250 hitters when they could very well be .310, .320, .330, or .340 hitters.

The statistics prove that there are more

Roger Hornsby.

strikeouts today than ever in the history of baseball—almost twenty-five fellows strike out more than a hundred times a season. In the big leagues, more home runs certainly are being hit than ever. During the first 100 years of baseball there were five players who hit 500 home runs, and I guess in the next 50 years there will be 25. I don't know for certain but there is a pretty good chance. So you see that today the ills of hitting probably have increased because of this attitude more than any other single reason. I get a little discouraged when I watch television. As a young boy, I used to ask all the hitters whom I thought qualified for advice on hitting. I would ask them, "What's the single most important thing I have to do to become a good hitter?" I heard answers ranging from feet to everything else. The only thing that ever registered with me was something that Rogers Hornsby told me at spring training in Daytona Beach. I remember him down there as one of the greatest authorities on hitting I ever talked to. He said that the most important thing in hitting is getting a good ball to hit. Now that has to be the right answer. I'm convinced in my own mind it is. You can take two fellows with equal bats, strength, eyes, and reactions. The batter who's thinking properly, who makes fewer mistakes against hitting the pitcher's offering all the time instead of hitting a bad ball when he doesn't have to, is the better hitter. If a hitter has two balls and no strikes or three balls and one strike, then hitting that questionable pitch, or tough pitch, or pitch that fooled him a little bit is certainly a mistake. With everything being equal, the fellow who makes fewer mistakes that way is going to end up much better than the other. That's just the difference between a real good hitter and an ordinary hitter, or maybe a good hitter and a great one.

Sometimes perfect timing comes awfully tough, but a fellow can help himself to a great degree. If I don't have flexibility of hand action or the ability to get the meat of the bat on the ball, I strongly suggest pepper games. I'm thoroughly convinced that there's not enough pepper being played and certainly not the way it should be played, with a hitter and two fielders in a good snappy game. It helps the pitcher and the hitter, and it's the best way to work on hitting without actually having batting practice. I didn't hit too much pepper after the season started, but certainly in spring training there was no one who hit pepper more than me. Being left-handed, I used to personally like left-handers throwing pepper at me because I felt that just seeing that left hand would help me a little bit more in hitting. Again, this all goes back to the thinking part of hitting.

Everybody wants to know how you hit a curve ball. There is certainly no physical change to employ. If there were, it might only be to close yourself up, but you'd have the same swing and batting stance. There may be other things you could do. Depending upon how the curve ball is bothering you, you might move up toward the pitcher.

But why can't batters hit the curve ball? Number one, everybody looks for the fast ball. We're ready for the fast ball. Number two, batters don't swing at the curve ball; they take it and wait for that fast ball. Number three, they don't practice hitting the curve ball. Probably the biggest reason they don't hit the curve ball is because they're not thinking properly and anticipating it at the right time. Now I admit you can be looking for a curve ball and the guy will bust one in low and outside. Well, in such a case, kind of salute him and say, "Gee, that's a hell of a pitch. I wouldn't have hit that if I'd swung at it." So let him have that pitch, because even the best pitchers don't consistently have that good control. Now the best pitchers, of course, have that little better control.

How did your thinking alter when the count changed?

That's a very good question. As a matter of fact, my thinking changed practically on every pitch. I might be up there and think, well, I'm going to look for a fast ball on the first pitch, and he starts out with a curve ball for a strike. I'm fooled by it a little bit or I foul it off, so right away my thinking changes. It might change or very likely could change depending upon the weather conditions, the type of pitcher I'm facing, who is catching, or whether the guy's going with that one pitch all the time. Some pitchers throw in a pattern; most good pitchers don't. Anyway, my thinking would modify. I have a boys' camp on Cape Cod and we get these questions all the time. Ninety percent of the kids will tell you that a curve ball is harder to hit than a fast ball. Then I say, "Well, how many of you fellows look for the fast ball?" Everybody's hand goes up. It's quite obvious that they don't anticipate the curve; they don't lay for it enough or watch for it, especially at the right times.

Once someone asked Whitey Ford if I ever had him in a hole where I thought that I had a little edge. I had him three and one, bases loaded, and I knew he had to throw a strike. But because Ford was a particular type of pitcher (I told him this and he agrees), he never conceded to the real good hitter in the tough spot. He said to heck with it; I'm not going to let this guy beat me. With that 3-1 count, I had him and I was still debating in my mind what I should wait for, when a fast ball came in, the prettiest thing you ever saw. I hit into a double play. Because he pitched that way to me all the time, I couldn't get set in my thinking up there on that particular ball. I'm sure that if I had been a little bit more ready for that fast ball, I'd have hit it.

In looking at two different types of hitting, if it can be called two types, your name is mentioned along side Henry Aaron's. How do you determine which method to teach a particular boy?

Well, it really amounts to this: it would be silly, for example, for Whitey Ford to try to tell some big guy like Jim Palmer of Baltimore to learn how to pitch like Whitey Ford. And it would be silly for some fellow who has the physical attributes of Richie Ashburn to try to learn how to hit and swing like Ted Williams or anybody you might mention. It would have been just as silly for Paul Waner to try and hit like Lou Gehrig—two different animals. Now there's the point I'm trying to bring about: the sooner a coach—whether college, high school, or professional, and particularly at the lower levels—gets across the idea to a fellow to adopt a style that conforms with his capabilities early, the better off the player will be. If I don't pull or feel good trying to pull the ball, then I should not be encouraged to go the home-run route. Certainly, if a man is successful going one way, you leave him alone.

Have the breaking pitches such as the slider or the knuckle ball changed hitting?

I would say that in 1948 and 1949—certainly '49—that most of the good pitchers in our league had a slider. I'm talking about Eddie Lopat, Vic Raschi, Allie Reynolds, Virgil Trucks, all of them. I don't know why Whitey Ford, for example, couldn't throw a slider, but I'm glad. I'm thankful to God that he didn't throw it earlier because I think a slider is an awful tough pitch. A slider is a quick enough pitch that you pretty much have to be on guard and be ready for it. Most of the good hitters that I've talked to in private say they agree, but don't talk too much about it. But this isn't something that's been around just the last five or ten years. The slider has been pitched since the 1940s. I know that Bob Feller threw one to me in 1946 or 1947 and struck me out, the year he broke the strikeout record. Whatever year that was, he threw me a high, inside slider and struck me out. I know he started to throw them that year. Yes, I think sliders have changed the thinking in hitting a little bit.

A guess hitter will be correct almost 50 percent of the time. Now I think a batter could benefit being a 50 percent guess hitter. The good smart hitter will even be better than that, even with the third pitch now being thrown, but the third pitch has made guess hitting a little bit tougher. Now in my particular case, it didn't make it tougher because I practically eliminated one pitch right off the bat: the fast ball. I felt that pitchers were a little bit worried about throwing me the fast ball, but they would just use it from time to time as an "effect" pitch.

So getting the ball to hit isn't that difficult, providing you start deducting things like the count, what he did last time, how they pitched to you, what they did last series, and what you hit last year. You're not going to hit the same stuff all the time. The beautiful part about hitting and the hitters' only real break is certainly not hitting a round ball with a round bat with the ball coming at you from all angles from some guy out there who might not even like you. It's the pitcher who knows less about the game, as a rule, than the other players. I'm not talking about a Bob Feller. I never had a chance to talk with Bob about it, but I want to tell you with all the great stuff that he had as a kid, he was still a good pitcher when he lost his stuff. My thinking certainly changed about this guy's ability as a pitcher. He had good control, worked the ball, learned how to throw a slider, and didn't rely on his fast ball so much. The good ones are still pretty smart, but there aren't that many good pitchers.

When you're holding the bat, are you holding it with your fingers or with the back of the palm?

I think it's better to hold it out toward your fingers because then you get your wrists more flexible. You get it up too high in your hand and you kind of lock it. You know that you can't move your wrists as well. If you hold it tightly at right angles from your arm, it's really pretty hard to throw that clubhead out in front. But if you can hold it in the fingers and flick that bat down, you've got better movement, probably quicker, too.

What about Hornsby's stance, so far away from the plate?

I used to have little games with Hornsby, and I could hardly understand how he could reach that ball. Hornsby had a style that was completely perfected, and he certainly was one of the smartest men I ever talked to about hitting. He had that great advantage, so many things going for him. I think that with any great record, you must have this. For example, he was a right-handed hitter who stood far away from the plate, but he hit to right center, so the opposition was in real trouble. Here's a great hitter. You don't dare pitch him outside too much because he's just going to flick that ball out there, so you pitch him inside, which I still think was where

he wanted the pitch. That's a style that you're talking about, but he certainly had complete control of it. The big thing about him was that he didn't try to pull the ball because he knew that he wasn't a pull hitter. He was hitting almost every ball 90 degrees from the direction of the pitch.

What about the boys who have trouble hitting from a closed stance. What do you suggest?

Well, you kind of surprise me when you say that you have a percentage of boys who are closed. Far and away, most hitters don't close. I admit that this is a pretty hard thing to correct.

Some fellows have the ability to just open their hips better than others. You've got to fool those fellows to a point. I think that the less ability a boy has to open his hips, certainly the further away from the plate he's going to stand. And the less ability he has to open his hips, the less he's going to try or even be able to pull the ball. So the two go hand in hand. You have to make up your mind whether this type of boy is going to be a pull hitter or not. Analyze him again and ask how many balls he is hitting on the fist and how many on the end. That's the only way I can tell you, and there's nothing better than just swinging the bat. You can't get enough of it, and pepper is a great way to do it. Of course, pepper doesn't help you open your hips at all. It's hand action.

How do you recommend a boy hold a bat in pepper—on the end or more toward the middle?

He shouldn't be in the middle of the bat, but he should choke up a little bit. He should be holding the bat loosely and think about nothing but getting the meat part of the bat on the ball with every pitch. That gives you flexibility of hand action.

In pepper do you take a regular batter's stance?

Not necessarily. No, I think I probably open up a little bit. You don't want a big stroke, just enough to hit the ball nice and sharp. It's a very important thing and I think it should be practiced a lot more than it is.

What about a young fellow who is a good hitter but has trouble pulling the ball?

Well, if he's a good hitter you'd just better leave him alone. I wouldn't encourage him to pull the ball because I'm sure if such were the case he wouldn't hit as many balls consistently well. There have been plenty of good hitters, in fact the ones with the highest batting average, who have not been pull hitters. I don't see that much advantage to pulling the ball.

In the Red Sox organization, what do you fellows do with your hitters to strengthen their arms and other muscles? In addition to natural body exercises, do you do anything extra to strengthen hitters?

No, and it's pretty hard to do that because one guy will say you're full of baloney, so he doesn't go along with the program. But you can't beat swinging a heavier bat than you would use during the season—six, eight, or ten ounces heavier—real hard. That will get you all the extra strength needed as far as developing. I used to do pushups, chinups, and all that kind of stuff. Being quick with the bat, getting a bat you can handle, or using a lighter bat are the things that count.

What changes accounted for Carl Yastrzemski's great year?

Well, I knew that was going to come up. Here's what I think. Yastrzemski really made the changes on his own. I know what he did. He moved back in the box a little bit. Everybody crowds him with the ball. He got farther back in the box. He's dealing with pitchers who I mentioned before. It takes them a year to wake up. I don't want to go too much farther into it than that—he made a change and the opposition didn't.

What about picking up the ball?

Of course, I tried to pick up the ball as soon as I could. Now that's the reason why a change in delivery is good, because you get in a groove watching this guy and, before you know it, you're picking up the ball a little better all the time. Then all of a sudden he throws from underneath. Right away you're hesitating while he gets the ball in there. That's the reason why a pitcher coming in with a different delivery should try for a strike. Why waste that delivery? Why waste that deception on a ball that isn't a strike?

You must try to pick up the ball as soon as you can. I'm thoroughly convinced, just as convinced as anything, that eyesight is not the secret either. I've come to the ball park ever since I was a kid, and I've said this a million times: I've had trouble with my right eye. Sometimes my vision is extremely sharp and the next day my right eye bothers me. I got hit with a walnut when I was pitching to my brother, and he hit me with one of those black walnuts right back in my eye. I almost lost my eye. It's too easy to give credit to eyesight and strength. That isn't it. *The secret rests with desire, the opportunity to play, and the player's ability to think in the game that he's playing.* I know a lot of guys who were faster than Whitey Ford. But he had a curve and great control. There's a lot more than physical attributes.

You say the good hitters wait for a certain pitch, even though they might have to sweat out the pitcher. Wouldn't it be more sensible to teach them to hit where it's pitched, especially young hitters?

I would eliminate waiting for a certain pitch, but I would never eliminate trying to get a good ball. Anything that doesn't fool you, whack at it. Now if they take a pitch that fools them, that's great. I call that a plus on your side, don't you? Get a good ball to hit. But if the ball fools you, take it. Anytime you start getting too anxious to swing, you start getting the pitcher's tough pitches. If it is a tough pitch and you swing, nobody can hit it. We tell a kid in spring training who swings at such a ball that Babe Ruth, Lou Gehrig, Joe DiMaggio, Hank Greenberg, and Jimmie Foxx would not have been able to hit that one. But that kid is swinging like hell at it. Nobody can hit that type of pitch, including Houdini.

Did you hit differently in the various parks, also taking into consideration such factors as weather?

Well, I think that the good hitter makes corrections. I know that I did this more toward the latter part of my career than I did earlier. When I first went to Fenway Park, I hit those long 380-foot flies. They were big outs and I'd come back hitting first base and the dugout, swearing and angry at everything. Then with a gale-type wind on the next day, they were again letting me hit them as hard as I could and they're still 380-foot outs. Again, I'm knocking Fenway Park. Well, as I played longer, I tried to take advantage of the park. When the wind was blowing in, I'd try to just hit the ball through the middle that day, but boy, if I got a day where the wind was blowing out or I got a short right field, I certainly tried to pull it. You hit according to conditions, the pitcher, the count, the weather—everything.

What do you tell a boy who feels uncomfortable when trying some change in his batting style?

I want to tell you that I've heard this all the time, the guy saying, "If I close, I can't see" or "I don't feel good." Well, I want to tell you that there were plenty of times when I didn't feel particularly good up there because of the pitcher's delivery, but there are certain things that you've got to fight for yourself. The old expression, "you've got to fight to hang in there all the time," is certainly true in hitting, and it's something that you've got to practice. The best way to practice anything in baseball is to overemphasize what you're trying to correct. If you overcorrect something you are trying to improve, I think you're far and away better off.

What are your ideas on weight distribution?

Your weight really should be pretty much evenly distributed all the time. But, on a high ball your weight should be slightly more on your back foot. Now why is that? On what ball do you think you have to be the quickest, a high ball or low ball? A high ball is the right answer, because it's closer to your hands and you've got

to be farther in front. Now look what happens. The farther I go out on my front foot, the farther I go in front of the plate to hit the ball. In other words, I am giving myself less time. That's the reason it's no good to lunge. You're shortening that distance from the pitcher to the batter's box. Now suppose that on the same pitch I stay back and wait for the ball. I still must be very quick with my swing, but I have a better chance of meeting the ball properly. As a result, the quick hitter, the good hitter, has a greater tendency to lay back on the ball than he would with the low ball. On the low ball you have to stay down, but the weight will be more evenly distributed.

At impact, what is the position of your hands?

I would say that probably 25 per cent of you here, I could be wrong, will probably give the wrong answer. Your hands are level. Hitting a baseball is not like hitting a golf ball. In baseball your hands go in flat. You have more resistance than in golf.

In conclusion, I want to emphasize that the big thing about not trying hard to pull the ball is that you have less chance of taking your eyes off it, keeping your front shoulder in. That is, if you go into the pitch and your head and shoulders stay down, this is fine. As soon as you start to open your shoulder, generally your head tends to follow, and this is wrong. This will be less likely to occur on a straight-away swing. A lot of things fall in line when you don't try to pull the ball. The bat angle gets better, you wait on the pitch longer, you've got more time, and your head stays down.

RUNNING THE BASES WITH BILLY HUNTER, MANAGER, TEXAS RANGERS

I personally had a great deal of trouble running from home to first base. I was considered a good base runner once I got to first base, but I didn't get there enough. I'm sure you have fellows on your club in the same boat. I think you can help a boy running the bases by helping him to get away from home plate. Many fellows take the big swing and are all tied up. Their time to first base may be 4.2 or 4.3 seconds, but getting away from home plate itself might be four more seconds. If you can help the boy drive off after his swing and head straight to that base, it certainly will get a few base hits and more runs for you.

The first-base line is controlled by a rule. If in the umpire's opinion you interfere with a play at first base being made on you while in fair territory, the umpire can call you out. The ball does not have to hit you. If in the umpire's opinion you interfered with the play, you are out. If any of you remember the 1969 World Series, you saw Pete Richert pick up the ball in front of home plate and hit J. C. Martin in the back. You also saw the umpire standing right there taking it in, but you didn't see any call. The next thing you saw was the runner coming across home plate and the ball game was over. We expect our runners to run to the outside of the line and make a little turn just before they get to first base. This will allow the runner to drive off the bag and head as much as possible in a straight line for second base.

I originally signed with the Dodger organization, and Branch Rickey was a stickler for fundamentals. I might add that I spent five years in the Dodger organization and I would not trade that experience for the $100,000 paid to me by the St. Louis Browns. Mr. Rickey suggested that when you round first base, hit the bag on the inside with your left foot, swing your right foot around, and head in a straight line for second base. Now, as you know, it is rather difficult to determine what foot will hit the bag when you are running full speed to first base. In the Oriole organization, we instructed our players to hit the inside of the bag and kick off in as much as a straight line toward second as possible. We had one guy on our team who was pretty quick as a runner and a pretty good player, but after he hit the bag, he just about touched the outfield grass in making his turn to second base. I'll tell you one thing, if the ball goes between the outfielders all the way to the fence, he really does have a straight shot into third; straight from the right-field fence. Speak-

ing of Dave Johnson, and Dave does run pretty well, we called him "crazy legs" because his legs go every which way.

On a ball hit through the infield to the outfield, a fly ball, or line drive, we instruct our runners to leave home plate with the thought that they are going at least to second base. As you well know, on any base hit to the left or right of the outfielder, a runner can go almost halfway down to second base and still get back to first, even if the ball is fielded cleanly and thrown back into the infield immediately. On the other hand, the runner who hits the base, takes a step, and decides that is all the farther he is going, then that is just how far he'll get. If an outfielder bobbles the ball, that runner can't do a thing about it. If the outfielder makes a bad relay coming back into the infield, that base runner still can't do a thing. But, the runner who has left home plate and gone down about halfway can do something—he can be standing on second base instead of first.

We try to impress upon our base runners not to take anything for granted. Take as much as you can; if they want to give you a little bit more, take that too. Assuming now that we are on first base, we have a regular ritual. When on first base, how many outs are there? Our first-base coach tells the man the number of outs; in fact, he gets an answer from him about the number of outs. There are a few occasions, even in the big leagues, where the base runner will say "two outs," then on a subsequent fly ball to the center fielder, you will see that same man halfway down to second, waiting for the outfielder to catch it. Instead, the base runner should be standing on third when it is caught. That runner may have just garnered another base hit, putting him 3 for 10 for the week and raising his average to .258. Add that to what he is going to get next week, and who cares how many outs there are? What I am trying to say is that you've got to remind them. "How many outs are there?" All the time. Look around and see where the outfielders are playing; look around and see where the infielders are playing. Check your third-base coach and see what is going on. Now you've got the number of outs, you know where the outfielders and infielders are playing, and you know what sign is on. Now pick up the ball. Don't step off that bag until you know where that ball is. One thing I tell our base runners is that you can't be tagged out without the ball. If you know where the ball is at all times, you are in pretty good shape.

Now you get into game situations. You get to know your opposition and also your own abilities or disabilities. In other words, let's assume that there's a Ford on the mound. I'm not going to get quite as much lead as if there were a right-hander on the mound. I say this first of all because Whitey Ford was a left-hander with a good move, as opposed to the right-hander with a poor move. So naturally, I'm going to take advantage of that and I'm going to get twice as much lead against the right-hander as I would against Ford. These little things naturally come from experience, and you can go over these things before the ball game ever starts. I'm sure that you do. We suggest a two-and-a-half step lead to a rookie. When I say two-and-a-half steps, I mean just that. A runner should get off the bag and get ready as the pitcher gets ready to pitch. When he comes up to pitch, the runner gets on the balls of his feet. He's not spread out where its going to take too long to get moving. We like a two-and-a-half step lead with the feet about shoulder width, or maybe a little bit farther. His first move is a pivot on the right foot and crossover with the left in a direct line to second base. I say this because when you take your lead and use that pivot and crossover as your first move, you have gone a full step. If you have a lead and your first move, instead of the crossover, is a push off the left foot, you have gone about half a step. After a left-foot push, your next move has to be a shift of weight on the right foot and a crossover anyway. What we try to use is the crossover step followed by a push off the right foot in a direct line to second base.

How many runners are out by a short distance, either sliding into second, on an attempted steal, or sliding into third on a throw from the outfield? If you can shorten the distance at the very start, then you might as well take this advantage. These are just little things

that really make a difference in athletics, whether in football, baseball, basketball, or whatever. *It is the fundamentals that win ball games;* it is the lack of execution that loses ball games. Generally, you don't win too many games—the other team loses most of them. If your ball club executes the fundamentals better than the other team, most of the time you are going to win—assuming, of course, that you have an equal amount of talent. Use the crossover step on a hit-and-run play and on a steal. It is important to get a jump on the hit-and-run play and a steal. After you take a step and a half or two, just take a little glance at the home-plate area. Many times you can pick up the ball and learn if and where it is hit without interfering with your running.

How many times have you said or heard, "Don't look at the ball when you are running down to first base?" Well, I know that I have said it myself and that it has been said to me a hundred times. When you get right down to it, how much does it slow you down to look over your shoulder when you are running down to first base? Naturally, when you hit a high fly ball to left field and you're loafing to first, that slows you down. I'm talking about a ground ball to the shortstop where you are running hard, but you glance to locate the ball. Many times, knowing where the ball is will give you the opportunity to slide and avoid a bad-throw tag at first base. There are little things that help you win ball games, and if that little glance doesn't slow you down that much, it might be worthwhile.

Let's assume that we have a first-and-third situation with one man out. One of the cardinal sins in baseball is to cause a tag play on a ground ball hit to the second baseman, then allow a throw to first for a double play, thereby ending the inning and eliminating that run. Now, there are two ways to break up this play. One is to stop between first and second to make the second baseman throw to first, then during the ensuing run-down at least one run will score.

In sliding into any base, the man receiving the ball will pretty much tell you which way to

slide. For example, if the second baseman has the bag between his feet and the throw is to his left, then it is to the runner's advantage to slide in on his right, is it not? And if he is to the right to receive the ball, then it is to my advantage to slide left. So many times the runner doesn't pay any attention to this, and he'll slide right into the tag. This is one of the little things that can help you in running the bases. Look at the man catching the ball. Some runners will look to the next base; some will look up in the air. If you are stealing second base, look!

There are many different types of slides, and I'm not going into all of them. We use what we call the bent-leg slide, primarily to stay away from injury. You tuck one leg underneath and just ride in on it. The other leg is up in the air, and you are on your backside. It is easy to execute. You will see some runner hook the bag or slide on past it with his feet and then catch it with his hand. That is advanced sliding. A bent-leg slide should be taught to runners who are basically having difficulty sliding. Just tell him as he leaves his feet to tuck one foot underneath, fall back, and go straight into the bag.

If you get to second base on a base hit, take a little look at third and see what's available. If you make too big a turn, the outfielder is going to throw behind and pick you off at second. When a runner is on first and a ball is hit to the outfield, he should glance to see if he can make it to third. He should not glance at the third-base coach about three quarters of the way down to second base. The base runner himself should be able to determine if he can take only one base or if he can go to third. Immediately after crossing second base, the runner should look for the third-base coach. If he goes too far and is told to stop, he will probably be caught in a rundown and be unable to return to second. In seeking help as a runner, the time to look is immediately after crossing second base. The coach will wave you on, hold you up, or tell you to go back to the bag. In professional ball, the best arm in the outfield is usually in right field. Therefore, as a base runner, you don't take many chances on the right-fielder's arm. The reason that the better

arm is in right field is because he has a longer throw to make. He not only has to throw home, but he also has the long throw to third base. The left fielder has to throw home occasionally, but he only has a short throw to second and third.

One of the toughest plays for a runner at second base is on the sacrifice bunt when the batter misses the ball and the runner wants to make it to third base. I'm talking about a first-and-second situation and nobody out, and you're trying to avoid a force play at third. What so often happens is either the batter misses the bunt and the catcher throws to second base, getting the runner in a rundown, or the ball is bunted and the runner doesn't know whether to go or not because it is bunted in the air. Many things enter into this situation as a base runner at second base.

If you are a runner at second with nobody or one man out, and no one on first base, and a ball is hit to the shortstop, how many times will you see a runner thrown out at third base? I know it happens every spring in the big league camps. I made a point of this play and Frank Robinson was keeping count. We got down to the final day one April and nobody had been thrown out on that particular play, but it happened the last day. Robinson said, "We didn't make it through another spring. You were right again." To help the runner on second base, I tell him that after he gets a couple of steps from the bag, keep the ball in sight. If a ball is hit with average speed at or to the left of a typical runner (keeping in mind that the pitcher may be able to field the ball), he can go to third base. But if the ball is hit at him or to his right with better than average speed, then he will be out at third, if the play is executed properly. Once again, the base runner has decided for himself. If he has great instincts, then you don't have to be much of a coach. You are out to help the player without great instincts.

I want all of the runners to round third base until I stop them. Many times as a coach I would allow a runner to come almost halfway, giving him every opportunity to score. I have, on occasion, stopped a runner about halfway when the ball has been cutoff, only to have him thrown out trying to get back to third. This is the coach's fault, not the runner's. I want my base runners to run hard until I stop them. If they do that, they will get a run or two once in a while. We had a play at Baltimore that is no longer a secret because other teams in the major leagues use it. It takes a good runner—by a good runner I am speaking of men like Paul Blair or Don Buford—on first base. Suppose Robinson singles to right-center field. The base runner rounds second and heads for third. Frank will round first and head for second to draw a throw. If the lead runner runs hard around third, he can score if the throw goes to second. I know we did this half a dozen times in a three-year period. It was a natural thing because Frank was kind of a daring runner and could sometimes draw the relay throw into second base. A lot of times the ball isn't even caught in the infield, allowing the lead runner to score easily. I want the runner to run hard until the third-base coach stops him. On many occasions you can pick up another run. Every year, most big league teams win or lose fifty or sixty ball games by one run. *Did you think fundamentals are not important?*

If a man has to slide into third base, I, as a third base coach, would get down and let him know what I wanted. Plenty of times I gave him the down sign. I don't want him to start to slide and then stand up. That's when most legs are broken. A lot of times when I gave the down sign, I would even try to tell him more if I could get into position. The down sign can indicate either right or left. I frequently held him up with one hand and pointed to the bag with the other hand, meaning that I wanted him to stay on the bag. You will often see the runner come in, touch the bag, and take another step, only to have the third baseman catch the ball and tag him out because of that one step. You, as a third base coach, can help the runner.

Once a man gets to third, there are many situations where I'll have him running on any ground ball. In other words, he takes what we call a walking lead at third base. It is the only base where we don't use the crossover when starting to run. We get our lead depending on whether the pitcher is in a windup or a set position. Then, as the pitcher delivers the ball, we take three more steps, trying to time the delivery so that the third step is down when the ball is at home plate. As the pitch is delivered, the runner comes down on that third step as the ball is either being hit or missed. It takes a lot of practice. Do this during normal daily batting-practice routines, spring training, and all season. I think that this might be the most important phase of base running in all of the things we have discussed. I say this once again because so many ball games are decided by one run, and this is one place where you can certainly pick up a run. If the runner has average speed or better and the ball gets away from the catcher, or it is a ground ball to the infield, or even if it is a one-hopper to the shortstop, a good runner with a good lead and break can score. This right then has to be a runner's decision. If he waits, he's not going to make it. I can yell encouragement, but by the time that happens it's too late. This type of lead is taken in foul territory. The return to the base is made in fair territory. We do this so that if a catcher throws to third, there is at least a chance that the runner will be in the path of the throw and perhaps will be hit by the ball, sometimes allowing you to pick up a run.

With runners on first and third, a double steal might be in order. If the runner on third gets a pretty good lead and stands quite close to the line, many times the catcher, in coming up to defend this play, will take the ball from the pitcher, look down to third base, and be lulled into a false sense of security. This is already predetermined by the runners. The reason the runner on third moves in toward the line is to deceive the catcher on how far his lead really is. In this way another run can occasionally score.

Another situation occurs with a runner on third base and none or one out. The runner's first move whenever a ball is hit into the air is to go back to third base. I am particularly speaking of a line drive to left field, one that everybody in the park knows is a base hit. Somehow, every once in a while, one of those gets caught.

The runner thinks it's a base hit, goes halfway home, and then returns and tags up. Gentlemen, by then it is too late. I saw a World Series game lost that way. Whitey Ford was the runner on third base. There was a line drive hit to left field, and he started for home. All of a sudden the left fielder came up with the ball, and here comes Ford, tagging up, still trying to score. He was out. The Yankees lost by one run. A lot of games are lost or won by one run.

I would like to reiterate that most games are lost; very few of them are won. *Don't lose them by not executing the fundamentals.*

How about tagging up from second or from first?

Many times you can do these things. We have our fellows tag up on second base with nobody out on any fly ball, medium depth or deeper. As a coach, I would yell out whether or not I wanted them to come down on a particular play. But with nobody out and the fly ball medium depth or beyond, we want them tagging up. With one out, we want them halfway. With a first-and-third situation, we want the fellow tagging up on first because if there is a play at the plate, he can go into second unmolested. On the deep fly ball, the good runner, even with nobody else on base, will tag up and take an extra base. This is especially true on a hit to the left fielder, who has the worst arm of anyone out there. If every hitter will go out and try to advance a runner every time he gets up to the plate, you will score a lot of runs.

How much do you emphasize the turn while running bases?

We practice running in a straight line and then making a last-minute move. Each individual has his own way of running. If it is acceptable, then we don't try to have him do it in a particular way. We tried to get Dave Johnson to change his particular method for about eight years, and he still did it his way. We tell them to make the turn so that they are running in a direct line to the next base.

With a runner on third tagging up on a fly ball, do you instruct him to leave the base in any

particular way? Do you have him watch the ball, or do you have a coach yelling at him when to go?

I have found that it is much better for the runner himself to watch the ball and judge when to go. If you have the coach instructing him when to leave, then you have the umpire judging from two different factors. He will judge when the runner left, as far as his sight is concerned, but he will also respond to hearing because he heard the coach say "OK." Maybe it wasn't OK when the coach said it, but perhaps the base runner left when it was OK. You don't want to upset these umpires.

Have you done any research on timing as to the best way to make the turn at the bases?

It is an individual thing and, as I said, the only people that we try to change are those who are having difficulty.

You have men on first and third, one man out. What are your instructions to your runner on third when a ground ball is hit to any of the infielders or the pitcher?

You go on any ground ball, unless you will be the only out. In other words, I am talking about a ball in front of the plate, where the catcher or pitcher may be able to make a play to a runner coming in home, but where he can't throw the man out at first or any other base.

What about a short fly, where the catch is doubtful? Should the runner on third tag or go halfway?

Here again the situation enters into it an awful lot. We have tried to score some fellows on balls by tagging up, but maybe the ball isn't twelve feet on the outfield grass. For example, the outfielder might have to make a tough run for the ball, or maybe it's the infielder going away from the plate. The inning and the score are both factors. Each play is too different to tell you what to do.

You have a man on third base and a ground ball is hit. Do you have the runner going in with no one out or with only one out?

Many times the situation varies. We have

them challenging home plate with nobody out, especially if you are in the tail end of the batting order. The pitcher, the score, and the inning have a great deal to do with it. We try to gamble once in a while when going after one run. *I found out that if you force the other club to make plays, if you make them throw the ball, even if it is in the major leagues, they make mistakes and you score some runs.*

I notice in a bunt situation with runners on first and second, that Baltimore has their shortstop go to third, the first baseman temporarily hold the bag, and the third baseman charging.

This is on a given play. It is put in by the manager from the bench to the third baseman. It is a sequence play in that defensively we have the first baseman coming in and the second baseman covering first, behind the runner for a pick-off play. It worked on three occasions for us one year, so it is worthwhile.

RICH ROLLINS ON HITTING

What are your ideas on the mechanics of hitting?

I like the analogy of giving a hitter a long-handled weed cutter and telling him to clear an area. What does he do? First he takes the weed cutter and muscles up and hacks away as hard as he can. He furnishes all the power and work. Pretty soon, after he tires out, he smartens up and lets the weed cutter do the work. That's what you want to do in hitting. Let the bat do the work for you. It's kind of a pendulum motion. I used to love to watch the Yankee hitters of 1962, 1963, and 1964—Berra, Maris, Mantle—take batting practice because they had this great pendulum action and let the bat work for them.

Fundamentally, I think most baseball players are good fast-ball hitters. As a hitter, you should be an outstanding "cripple hitter." By "cripple hitter," I mean you look for your pitch—the one you can really hit—and when you get it, smash it. Hitters generally give pitchers too much credit for great control. A lot of great hitters gear their stride to hit a pitch in their cripple zone. I don't buy hitting the pitch

where it is, but I do buy getting a cripple pitch and creaming it. (Rusty Staub and some other hitters today refer to this as "zone hitting.")

Where you hit the ball is determined by the upper part of your body. Sometimes, in professional baseball, the hitters will get hypnotized by the pitcher or his motion; they call it getting the stares. Sometimes you will see a major league hitter swing at a pitch way out of the strike zone. When this happens, chances are he is getting the stares. He can't be picking up the ball and really concentrating on watching the release point. This will sometimes be the cause of a slump.

Another fundamental fact often overlooked in hitting is that all good hitters are strong. Notice next time you go to a major league park how big the arms and shoulders are on most of the real hitters. The big advantage of being strong as a hitter is that you can wait longer on the ball and swing the bat quicker.

Your hands should be relaxed as you start your swing, so you're not tight. Relaxed hands mean quick, magic hands. Once you're in the ready position for hitting, your first move is back with the bat head, flattening your bat out

Rich Rollins, former third baseman, Minnesota Twins.

or bringing it parallel. (Earl Averill used to call this the "recoil action" like that of a cannon. When the pitcher starts his motion you must recoil.) The whole secret is getting that bathead on the ball out in front of yourself. The recoil doesn't do this, but a fluid swing will. With an 0-2 strike count, I like to see the hitter choke up on the bat. Al Kaline and Rocky Colavito did it their whole careers and they both could hit with power also.

What about some of the mental aspects of hitting?

When you're hitting well, the only thing you see is that little white ball; you see it very clearly and you know you're going to hit it. You're even so confident sometimes you can actually visualize where the flight of the ball will go before you hit it. You have to learn to analyze your hitting style and change it if you're consistently making outs to a certain area of the park. As an example, if you're consistently hitting fly balls to the outfielders but can't hit it over their heads, you better change your swing so you're hitting line drives and ground balls. Joe Rudi is a great example of this. When he first came into baseball, he had problems with his hitting form. But he analyzed it and made changes himself.

Mentally, when you are in a slump, you are thinking about everything visual at the plate. How's my stride, the position of my hands and bat, etc.? But you're not totally focusing on that little white ball, which is a must.

What about beginning in professional baseball? If a young man is signed as a pro prospect and is just starting out, what advice would you give him as a hitter?

If he has enough ability and has mastered hitting to the extent that he's a pro prospect, don't be in too big a hurry to change anything, if you have gotten results to this stage. It is disastrous for a coach to start tinkering with a young man's hitting when he first starts out. It might be the boy's first time away from home, and he'll be making all kinds of other adjustments.

Tony Oliva on Hitting

Tony, what are your views on hitting?

I like to look at and study the pitcher, and once I get his form and velocity in my mind, I go over there and hit the ball hard. I don't try to pull the ball or anything. What is in my mind is that I will come up to the plate and try to hit the ball hard, because if that pitch is inside, I am going to pull the ball anyway. I try to get a hold of the bat, a bat I can swing—not a bat that has somebody's name I admire, but a bat that I can feel comfortable with.

In other words, you like a bat that feels good to you, rather than a bat that is a Joe DiMaggio or something like that. It is important that a bat feels good in your hands.

Yes, that is very important. In the big leagues, you see some guys use a 32-ounce bat, another uses 33 ounces, and still another 37 ounces or 38 ounces. They could be 36, 35, or 34 inches long. Every hitter has his own model, but a lot of guys have two or three models. I remember I used to have two or three models, and the bat that feels comfortable is the bat I use that day. Sometimes the bat is really comfortable and I use it continually. After a while something happens to the bat. But the important thing is to hit with the bat you feel is most comfortable.

Another thing I would like to add, as a hitter you have to listen closely to what the coaches have to say, and you have to listen to other players a lot of times, because everybody at one time or another gets into a slump. When you get into a slump, it is because you are doing something different with the bat. Sometimes you drop your hands a little bit, or you're dropping your arm a little, or dropping the bat, or you're hitting the ball too far in front of you. It could be the least little thing. And sometimes you don't know what you're doing wrong. All you know is that you are in a slump. You know that you're not hitting the ball the way you want to, but you don't know the mistake. Use another's eyesight, like another ballplayer or a coach—they can see your mistake. And when this happens, the best thing you can do is to find somebody who can pitch to you in practice. After you find your stroke again and feel comfortable, you will again hit the ball hard.

Tony, do you feel that a lot of practice is important, getting your stroke down?

You can have a lot of practice, but not be really working on anything. You go out and say "I need practice." You have to work hard and concentrate in your practice sessions if you want to achieve anything worthwhile. If you don't hit the ball the way you want to hit it, come in after hitting for ten or fifteen minutes and analyze your stroke. Look for a possible way you could hit the ball better. When the correction is made and you're hitting the ball with authority, this is the way you want to keep the swing.

How can you teach somebody to hit? Is there a way to teach hitting?

Well, I don't think you can teach a guy to hit the ball, but you can help him a little bit with hitting. A lot of guys go over to a player, and they don't have any idea what they are doing with the bat themselves. I think you just have to play and have some idea who is pitching. The one thing that we like to tell a hitter is to keep his eyes on the ball all the way. This is very important. Hitters go to the plate and try not to do anything wrong. Rather, they should just try to hit the ball hard.

You're just trying to meet the ball, rather than hit it with power?

Right. Not exactly meet the ball—hit the ball hard. If you go to the plate and one thing goes wrong, you might not hit it very hard; but, if you go to the plate and try to hit the ball hard, no matter who is pitching, then you have a chance to hit the ball hard plus maybe get some lucky hits (Texas leaguers, end of bat, etc.).

I would like to teach someone to hit, but it is not that easy. If it were, you could take any strong guy and make a ballplayer out of him. All these guys who play football could play baseball and hit a lot of home runs, if you could teach them to hit the ball.

There was a guy who played football who tried to make it in the major leagues and never could. His name was Candy Carroll, who played for the Indians a long time ago.

There is a great deal of difference between baseball and football. Many guys in high school play in summer leagues, and in college play baseball and basketball or football. It is all the same. This same "big" guy can't make it in the majors because in baseball everything is timing.

Are there any exercises you can use to improve hitting?

Well, every day we do exercises. We do leg exercises. The best exercise you can do is running. We first stretch the muscles. After that we run and get loose. This is the best exercise you can do.

That's something kids don't realize—that having a lot of wind and loose muscles is important to everything.

You know, if you come to a ball park and get loose first, like stretching your muscles and running some, then your legs will get stronger. The stronger your legs, the better shape you are in and the better chance you have of having a good year, because you won't get tired. Suppose you are at the plate and hit a double. By the time you get to second base, you're a little tired. You can't be tired for the rest of the game. So it is very important that you do some exercises. The better shape you're in, the better your whole body performs. All this happens when you are hitting.

How would you teach hitting to the opposite field?

Myself, I would hit to all fields. I hit the ball to left field or to right field. For me, when I go to the plate, I say to myself, "I am going to hit the ball to left field," and then I do it. The only thing I do differently is change my foot a little bit and change my hands a little. I turn my body more toward left field, instead of toward the pitcher. With concentration, I can hit the ball to left field.

In teaching pulling, if I start to pull the ball, the only thing I try to do is open my step a little bit more toward first base. Also, I will get a little closer to the inside of the batter's box and open. When I say open, my right (front) leg faces a little bit more to the right-field side.

In other words, you are turning yourself a little bit.

A little bit. But I don't recommend that too much, because when you do, you may lose sight of the ball.

You would be off balance a little bit?

Sometimes yes. The only pitch you will hit good is the inside pitch. *It is better to go up to the plate and not try to pull the ball, but to go up there and hit the ball hard.*

Do you position yourself differently in the batter's box for a fast-ball pitcher as opposed to a "junk-ball" pitcher?

Well, I have two or three different styles. That's why I say every individual player must have his own style of hitting.

What about frequently changing your style of hitting?

Rod Carew gives you three or four different styles of hitting. There is only one Ron Carew. You know what I mean? He can do that because he is a smart hitter; he knows what he can do. One time he goes to the plate and wants to hit the ball to left field, another time to right field, another time through the middle, and the next time a bunt. He knows what he wants to do before he ever steps in the batter's box.

You mean he changes his stance depending on where he wants to hit the ball?

Yes, whatever he wants to do. Because he knows he can hit the ball that way.

Do most players do it that way?

No—just a few players do that. The guy who hits .300, or .290, or .280 is the guy who can adapt his style of hitting to different pitches. If he wants to go to left field, he hits to left field. If he sees a hole in right field, the hole is his target. Not too many guys can do that.

JOE TORRE ON HITTING

I would just like to talk about a couple of basic things that I use in hitting. First of all is discipline. When you go up to the plate, you have to have an idea in your mind what you are going to do. By that I mean the batter goes to the plate looking for the ball in a particular spot. If the ball is there, I know that I am going to hit it hard. Half the time I don't know what I hit—a fast ball, curve, or slider—because I am looking for the ball in that particular spot. If the ball is not there, I discipline myself not to swing. Now, with two strikes I think "up the middle." By doing this, you will hit the fast ball up the middle or to the opposite field and pull the off-speed pitches. In talking with Stan Musial on hitting, he said, as a left-hander, the outside pitch should be hit to left and the inside pitch to right.

Basically, thinking "through the middle" does several things. It makes you watch the ball. It keeps your shoulder in and aimed at the pitcher.

This will keep everything in there. If you pull your shoulder, your head follows. As a catcher, I am pleased to see a batter trying to pull everything. This gives the pitcher the outside half of the plate. The most exaggerated thing in baseball is the home run. To me it's rougher to hit a single with a man on second base than to hit a home run, because the pitcher is less apt to make a pitching mistake. I try to think line drive all the time. I think contact. Go up to the plate and hit the ball hard and don't worry about where it goes. This has worked out fine for me. So the keys are discipline, concentration, and self-confidence.

I would like to bring up the position of the hands. I find that the most comfortable position is close to my body. I keep my hands close, so I know where they are at all times. When the pitcher is out there looking at you, your hands are relaxed; you can get some kind of movement and not get tensed up. You'll do your best hitting when relaxed.

The top hand is my hitting hand. I try to keep my left hand firm and hold the bat in my fingers with my right hand. My hands are close to my body, and I concentrate on the pitcher and know what I'm looking for. I keep the bat in my fingers and swing to stay loose, keeping myself in some kind of motion so that if the ball breaks away from me or comes in, I'll still be able to hit it. It's similar to trying to catch a fly ball flat-footed—if the wind moves the ball a little you will have trouble, but if you are moving you go with it.

How far out in front of the plate do you hit the ball?

I try to wait as long as possible. Basically, I look for the breaking ball most of the time. I know this sounds terrible, but the reasons for this are that I know I can handle the fast ball and I know what the individual pitchers throw. Looking for the breaking pitch makes me watch the ball longer, and this gives me a better chance at hitting the ball hard. If you step incorrectly and the ball breaks, you will fail to get a good

swing because you are off balance. So I try to hit the ball in front of the plate as much as possible.

What is your feeling on waiting on a pitch?

If you are looking for a breaking ball, you've got to wait. You have to convince yourself that it is going to be a breaking pitch and wait for it to be in your hitting zone. If it's outside your hitting zone and it's a strike, then it's a pitcher's strike. If you take that pitch and wait for a ball in your zone, then you can hit it hard.

What about your hitch?

I did have a hitch, and that is why I was popping up. Now I try to keep myself as relaxed as possible and hold the bat up like Hank Aaron. If there is any movement with the hands and bat, it's up and over. I tell myself not to swing at anything above my hands. My hands are here by the "redbirds" on my shirt. Anything above is a ball and I take; anything below I know I can handle and hit hard. In the past they've been getting me out on pitches up and in, eight out of ten of which have been balls. So I lay off this pitch because no one can hit it with any consistency. It doesn't give you a chance to use your hands effectively. I hear people emphasizing quick hips, throwing the belly button, and taking a short stride. I believe it's the hands that trigger everything.

JAY JOHNSTONE ON HITTING

It is very hard to tell someone how to become a hitter. You just have to really work at it.

Are there any special exercises or routines?

Practice. Practice in hitting from a batting tee. You can pick one up almost anywhere. I just practice hitting the ball off the tee until I develop a stroke that becomes almost second nature. I don't have to think about it. (Using a batting tee is not just for Little Leaguers. It has real benefits at the highest level, too.) When I develop this stroke I then put it to use during a game, because I know if a ball is pitched in a certain situation I don't have to think about swinging the bat—it is just automatic, just a reaction. What I concentrate on is watching the ball, where it is pitched. If a ball is pitched away from me, I try to hit it to the opposite field. If it is inside, I know I have to be quick to pull it. A very important thing in hitting is watching the ball leaving the pitcher's hand. A lot of the guys don't pick up the ball until it is halfway up there, then they have to react very quickly. The ball gets there in hundredths of a second anyway, so the sooner you can pick it up and see where it is going, the quicker judgment you can make.

Then, you're saying that the whole science of hitting is that your practice has become automatic?

You don't have to think about it. You don't have to say, "I've got to swing this way at this pitch, I have to do that." It becomes second nature so that when you see the ball, you automatically react—you don't have to think about it.

BOB BOONE, CATCHER
PHILADELPHIA PHILLIES

Did growing up in a baseball atmosphere, the son of a major leaguer, help you achieve major league status?

No, it allowed me to be around the game at an early age with excellent instruction and to learn that I really loved the game, but as far as achieving anything, that came through a lot of hard work. I was blessed with some ability and the fact that I was around a major league camp really had no bearing.

At the earliest age, what would help a youngster develop skills such as you have for catching?

The best thing for a youngster to do is to go

out and play. Just play as much as he can to see if he likes it. The only way to develop skills is practice. There are many different theories about it. My theory is that you play. You refine your talents as you get older and can do some things. At first you just go out and have fun and see how it is playing.

What kind of special exercises would a person do, for instance, to build up his legs to stand the rigors of being a catcher?

Well, again you don't do anything, especially when you are young—just let your body develop. There are many things to develop, but nothing in particular for catching. Use a total conditioning program; if you are catching, the catching part will take care of itself. You don't have to develop anything special because you squat a lot. That's where you develop the skill. I'm just a strong believer in a total conditioning program. I really don't think you can isolate various parts of your body to do one particular thing. You have to make your body work as a whole. By doing so, as long as you are in condition, you will be able to handle any position.

Let's talk about catching itself. Is there a reason why left-handed catchers cannot make it, or is that a falsehood?

Well, the main reason left-handers do not make it is because of the numbers. There are just not the numbers in the major leagues. Maybe one in five million. It's just a matter of what you have. There are a hundred thousand right-handed catchers out there; if you only have ten left-handed catchers developing or working at it because they have always been discouraged from catching—it's the numbers.

It wouldn't have anything to do with the majority of batters being right-handed instead of left-handed, would it?

I guess that's the argument that is given in

Little League and what have you, but not really. You can throw through hitters regardless of at what side of the plate they are standing.

Is there any difference in catching with a right-handed batter opposed to a left-handed batter?

Well, you set up a little differently, but as far as throwing to second base, that hitter should really not become a factor in how you throw.

How about catching a right-handed pitcher opposed to a left-handed pitcher?

Well, the only difference is how you would react on different types of pitches. For example, a slider or curve ball set up anticipating a bad pitch is liable to bounce in the dirt. Depending on the side from which the pitcher throws the ball, the movement that pitcher's ball will take actually determines the adjustment you will make and the way the ball will bounce. Now, a left-handed curve ball that hits the dirt will bounce the opposite of a right-hander's curve ball in the dirt. Other than the fact that your pitch selection is going to be different to hitters, you don't do things much differently.

How do you determine how you will call the pitches? Is it by random selection or is it scientific?

Well, it is something that you develop through experience. It is a matter of a pitcher and a catcher working together. For a catcher it is getting to know a pitcher so that you know what he likes to throw in certain situations to a certain type of hitter. You adjust from there. It is not a random selection. There are some basic principles that you try to follow, and then you vary that as you get more and more refined.

There are different ways to change the signals through the course of a game, am I correct?

There are a number of ways of giving signs: pitchers counting the number of times you put your fingers down, to simple fingers, multiple signs, what we call "flaps" where you put your whole hand down and extend it. There are a number of ways you can give signs. I played for three years as a third baseman and they asked me to convert to a catcher. I was very leery of it at first because I was 23 years old, which is rather late to be changing positions. Now most performers in the major leagues have played their position for their entire lives. To make a change is pretty drastic, especially to catching. However, I was very fortunate. It was a good way for me to get into the major leagues. Now that I have an understanding of what I am doing and have had the experience, I love it and I'm glad I made the change.

If a person has the ability to make the major leagues, do you think he could convert to another position if asked to do so?

Again, that is a personal thing; it all depends on the individual. Some are blessed with the ability to play everywhere, and others are very specialized.

Let's talk a little about hitting. Is there a way to develop hitting?

Yes, but you need the basic ingredients of good reflexes and quick hands, then it's a matter of getting with somebody who really knows how to teach hitting. You must start with a pretty sound product, but it can be developed. Jay Johnstone made himself into an excellent hitter, just through a lot of hard work. It can be done.

How would a person change where he is going to hit the ball—pulling instead of hitting behind the runner?

There are ways of adjusting your stroke for that. My present philosophy is that you swing at the pitch where it is and don't really worry about where it goes. It is something that comes with time and experience. You know how to handle the bat and can move the ball inside out if you are going the other way. There are ways of moving the ball around on your own, but you should hit the ball where it is pitched and don't try to guide it or worry about its direction.

Do you actually see every pitch or do you sometimes speculate where it is going to be?

I see every pitch. You wait until you do see it.

On a breaking ball, do you guess where it is going or do you actually watch it?

You watch it. Through experience you know that a breaking ball you see at one point is soon going to be at another.

22 | Coaching Signs

**DICK HOWSER,
NEW YORK YANKEES**

Signs originate from the manager in the dugout and are relayed to the third base coach. With the sunken dugouts, most of the signs must be relayed from the waist up. Touching the throat might be the bunt, cap—take off, nose—hit-and-run, ears—squeeze, and chest—steal.

Then, your work as a third-base coach starts. Nothing will be on until you touch an indicator. Say the belt is the indicator. The first thing I touch after the belt will be the sign. We might use left leg—steal, right leg—hit-and-run, left chest—bunt, right chest—squeeze, cap—take. Skin on skin will take off any sign.

The easy way to change your signs is to change your take off or indicator. Another way is to go back to the indicator after you've given a sign which will lock it in.

A big key to coaching third base is *never* get someone thrown out at home plate with no one out.

You always try to get the tempo of a game while coaching. If your opponent has a tough pitcher going, you better think about bunting early and taking a few chances, because you may not get many runs.

EDDIE YOST ON SIGNALS

A good third-base coach uses both hands, if possible, simultaneously. The men taking the signs naturally have to know which hand counts. That is, if you say the left hand to concentrate on, that will be the one giving the signs. It could be either one. The guy receiving the signs must concentrate on the hand that counts.

Dick Howser, a master at giving signs at third base, at work. Is the right hand a decoy or is that the sign for the hit-and-run?

In other words, there is a check-off sign of some sort?

No. If I'm going to use my left hand and this is the sign that counts, you disregard the right hand entirely and concentrate only on the left hand. The reason you have to concentrate is because the coach is working with both hands at the same time, and if you don't concentrate, you can become easily confused.

Do hitters ever miss the signs?

They do occasionally, and a base runner might miss them too, but I would say that the reason for missing them is that they are not thinking about the game situation and strategy. Ordinarily, if they look at you and they know the signs, they'll get them.

Do the signs change during the game?

No, they might change during the season but not during the game, because they are a little complicated, and getting the whole club together during a game to give them new signs would be very difficult.

Can you give me an idea of different strategy in different situations?

That is a very broad question. It depends on the score and whether you are in the early or later part of the game. As far as hitting and running is concerned, managers generally like to hit-and-run on the first pitch or when the hitter is ahead in the count. Some managers, in order to advance a runner from first to second with one out in the latter part of a tie game, might hit-and-run with the count two strikes and a ball or two and two, just so that guy gets to second base. The guy who is hitting and running should get the ball on the ground, thereby avoiding the double play.

When should a runner steal second base?

If you have a guy who gets a good jump on the pitcher, runs well, and steals bases, he can be on his own many times. Naturally, if you have someone that can run, you give him more steal signs than one who can't. Once again that depends on the situation of the game. If the game is really close, you'll tell him to steal. If

you're way ahead or way behind, you don't do it. Send that guy to steal when the difference is two runs, one run, or a tie game.

In talking about signs, there is an indicator—something you touch on your body, face, or hat, meaning that the sign is the next one flashed. Say touching my chest is a bunt sign and my hat is the indicator, then hat to chest is a bunt sign. Go to my chest, pants, back to arm, to chest and face is nothing because I didn't touch the hat. On any given sign, you should touch as many things as possible so the opposition cannot pick it up. Then, if you touch all parts of your uniform, they are not sure what is what, as opposed to only touching one thing.

Can you ever pick up the catcher's signals? Is it hard to steal signals?

The way to do that is to have the runner on second base watch the catcher's signs to the pitcher. If he only gives one sign—which most clubs don't do—it is easy. He might put down one finger—the guy throws a fast ball. He puts down two, and it's a curve. Naturally, the man on second now has a good idea about the signs, and he can relay the information to the batter. If it is a fast ball, he can relay it by stepping toward third, stepping back toward second, moving an arm, or something like that.

Do the catchers also have sign indicators?

Yes, particularly when there's a man on second. The catcher will always use a more complicated set of signs. He might flash five signs, say one, two, three, three, and one, and his particular sign might be the sign that follows two. When he flashes the two, the following sign is the pitch.

Are there more variations? Do some catchers use other signs? Thurmon Munson moves all over the place with his hands. Johnny Bench just sits very quietly.

Munson uses outside signs, which means everything he does—touching his mask, shin guard, picking up dirt—is a sign. The finger or flap signs are a decoy. Bench uses inside signs. You can also move your glove to the right or left to indicate a sign.

Eddie Yost giving signs from third base. In photo 2, he's got the sign from the manager (the manager relays most of his signs from his waist up because some of the major league dugouts are sunken). Picture 7 looks like the key—left hand on the Boston letters. Now which one will be the sign after that; nose in photo 8; hands in 9, or clapping in 10? Perhaps he's taking the sign off in photo 12 by his right hand rubbing his left sleeve. And we thought Morse Code was tough!

23 | Your Baseball Charts, Situations, and Playbook

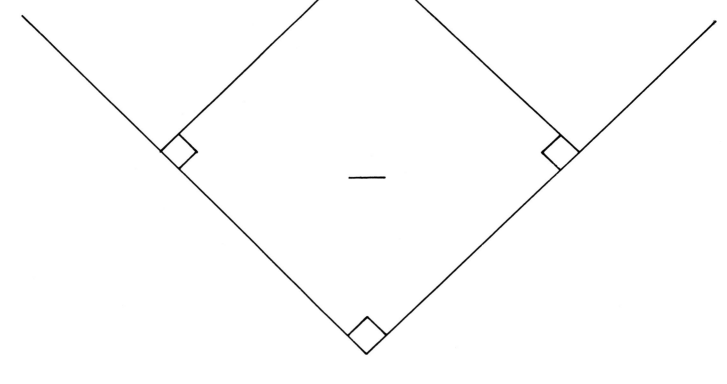

1. _____   26. _____
2. _____   27. _____
3. _____   28. _____
4. _____   29. _____
5. _____   30. _____
6. _____   31. _____
7. _____   32. _____
8. _____   33. _____
9. _____   34. _____
10. _____   35. _____
11. _____   36. _____
12. _____   37. _____
13. _____   38. _____
14. _____   39. _____
15. _____   40. _____
16. _____   41. _____
17. _____   42. _____
18. _____   43. _____
19. _____   44. _____
20. _____   45. _____
21. _____   46. _____
22. _____   47. _____
23. _____   48. _____
24. _____   49. _____
25. _____   50. _____

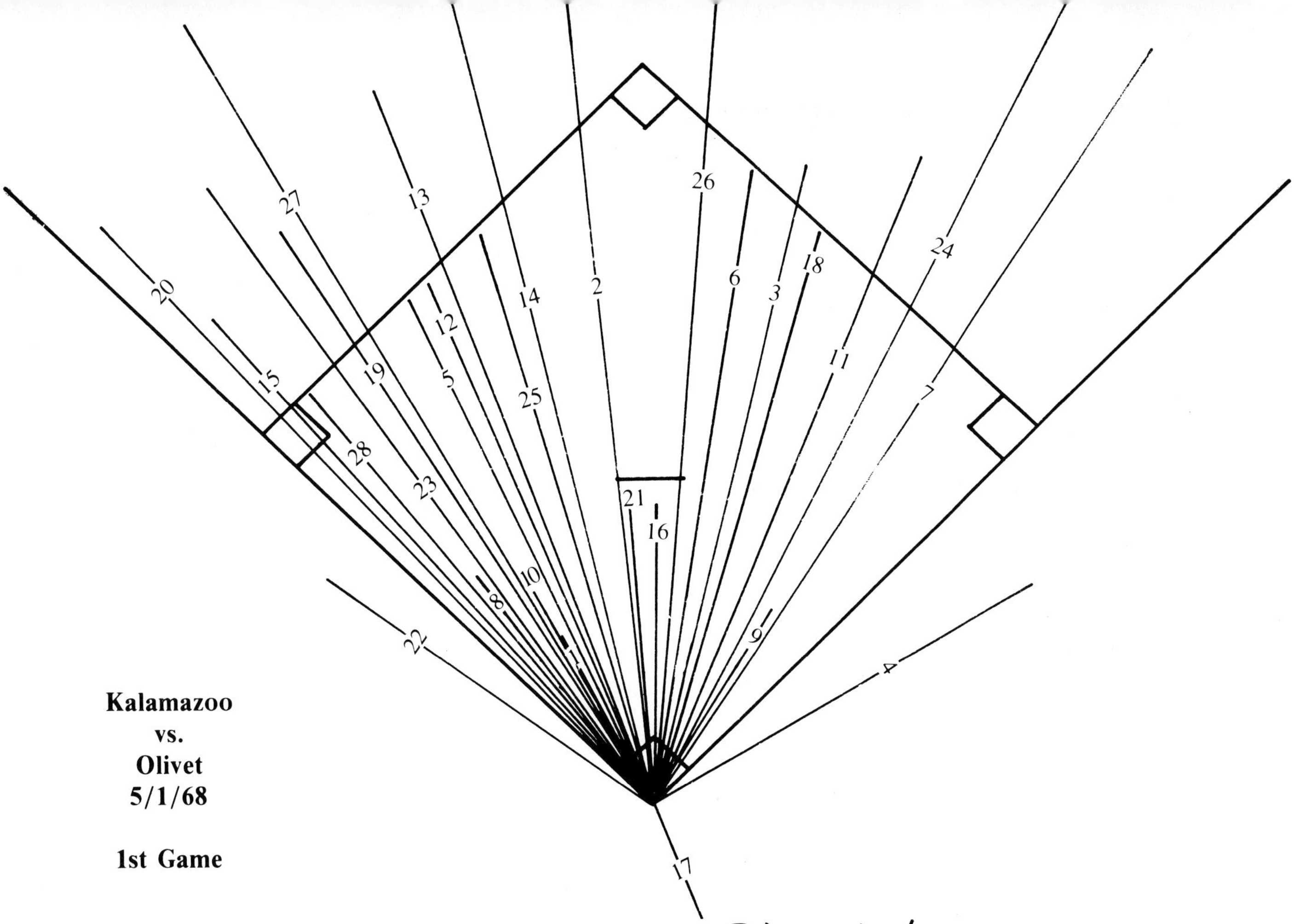

Kalamazoo
vs.
Olivet
5/1/68

1st Game

1. Gillie - sacrifice
2. Brian - single
3. Barny - ground out to second
4. Mike - foul out to first
5. Denny - ground out to short
6. Ken - line out to second
7. Clair - single
8. Joe - error
9. Gillie - sacrifice
10. Barry - bunt
11. Terry - single
12. Mike - single
13. Denny - fly out to left
14. Ken - fly out to center
15. Clair - single
16. Joe - error
17. Gillie - pop-up to catcher
18. Brian - ground out to second
19. Barny - single
20. Terry - single
21. Mike - double play ball
22. Denny - foul out to third
23. Clair - fly out to left
24. Joe - double
25. Gillie - ground out to short
26. Brian - single
27. Barry - fly out to left
28. Mike - fielders choice
29.
30.
31.
32.
33.
34.
35.
36.
37.
38.
39.
40.
41.
42.
43.
44.
45.
46.
47.
48.
49.
50.

233

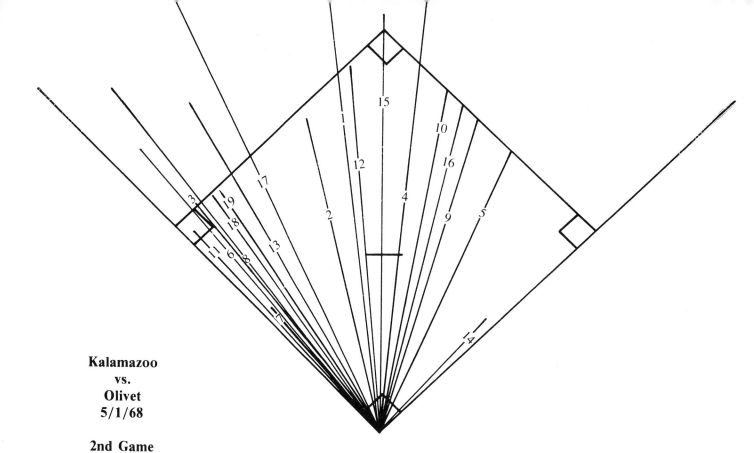

Kalamazoo
vs.
Olivet
5/1/68

2nd Game

1. Joe- single
2. Brian- ground out to short
3. Barry- double
4. Terry- line out to second
5. Jim- ground out to second
6. Ken- ground out to third
7. Denny- bounce out to third
8. Joe- fly to left
9. Brian- ground out to second
10. Terry- ground out to second
11. Denny- ground out to third
12. Steve- ground out to short
13. Mike- single
14. Denny- error
15. Brian- single
16. Barry- ground out to second
17. Terry- double
18. Dave- ground out to third
19. Paul- ground out to third
20.
21.
22.
23.
24.
25.

26.
27.
28.
29.
30.
31.
32.
33.
34.
35.
36.
37.
38.
39.
40.
41.
42.
43.
44.
45.
46.
47.
48.
49.
50.

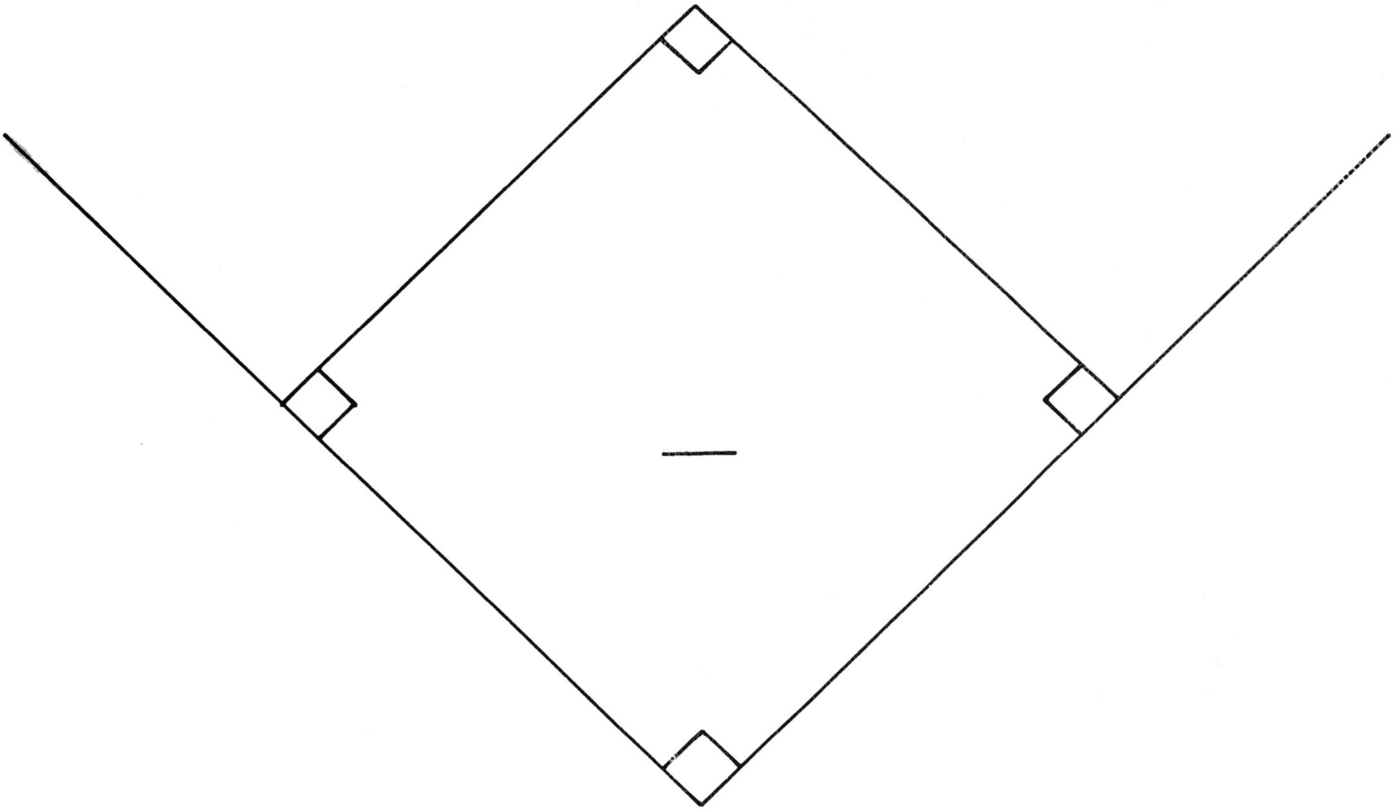

1. _____
2. _____
3. _____
4. _____
5. _____
6. _____
7. _____
8. _____
9. _____
10. _____
11. _____
12. _____
13. _____
14. _____
15. _____
16. _____
17. _____
18. _____
19. _____
20. _____
21. _____
22. _____
23. _____
24. _____
25. _____

26. _____
27. _____
28. _____
29. _____
30. _____
31. _____
32. _____
33. _____
34. _____
35. _____
36. _____
37. _____
38. _____
39. _____
40. _____
41. _____
42. _____
43. _____
44. _____
45. _____
46. _____
47. _____
48. _____
49. _____
50. _____

1. _____	26. _____
2. _____	27. _____
3. _____	28. _____
4. _____	29. _____
5. _____	30. _____
6. _____	31. _____
7. _____	32. _____
8. _____	33. _____
9. _____	34. _____
10. _____	35. _____
11. _____	36. _____
12. _____	37. _____
13. _____	38. _____
14. _____	39. _____
15. _____	40. _____
16. _____	41. _____
17. _____	42. _____
18. _____	43. _____
19. _____	44. _____
20. _____	45. _____
21. _____	46. _____
22. _____	47. _____
23. _____	48. _____
24. _____	49. _____
25. _____	50. _____

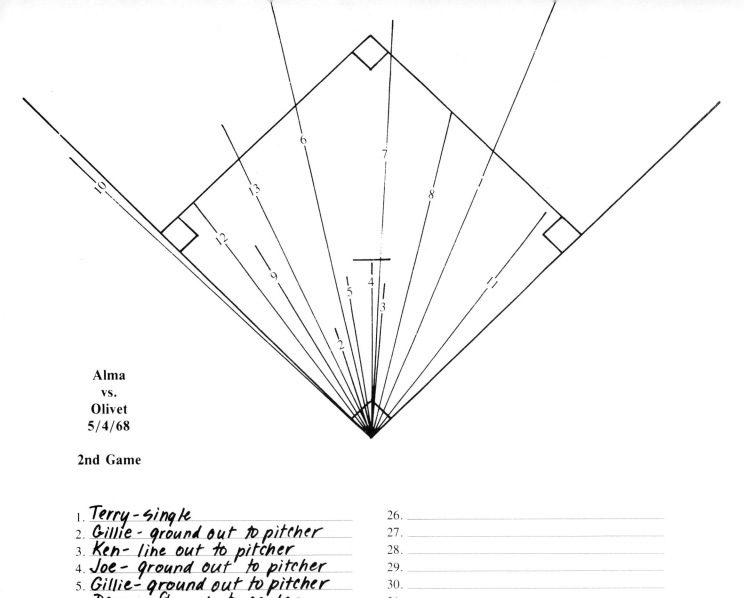

Alma
vs.
Olivet
5/4/68

2nd Game

1. Terry - single
2. Gillie - ground out to pitcher
3. Ken - line out to pitcher
4. Joe - ground out to pitcher
5. Gillie - ground out to pitcher
6. Denny - fly out to center
7. Ken - pop-up to second
8. Joe - ground out to second
9. Terry - error
10. Brian - foul fly out to left
11. Gillie - pop-up to first
12. Denny - ground out to third
13. Art - single
14.
15.
16.
17.
18.
19.
20.
21.
22.
23.
24.
25.
26.
27.
28.
29.
30.
31.
32.
33.
34.
35.
36.
37.
38.
39.
40.
41.
42.
43.
44.
45.
46.
47.
48.
49.
50.

237

↙ —Fast Ball
○ —Curve
𝕎 —Change
— —Slider
Ƨ —Screw Ball
✕ —Knuckle Ball

Team_____
Versus_____
At_____
Date_____
Prepared by_____

R   H   E

Weather_____

BATTER

PITCHER		FAST	CURVE	CHANGE	SLIDER	SCREW	KNUCKLE		TOTALS
	STRIKES								
	BALLS								
	STRIKES								
	BALLS								
	STRIKES								
	BALLS								
	STRIKES								
	BALLS								
	STRIKES								
	BALLS								
	STRIKES								
	BALLS								

Pop Flies to the Infield

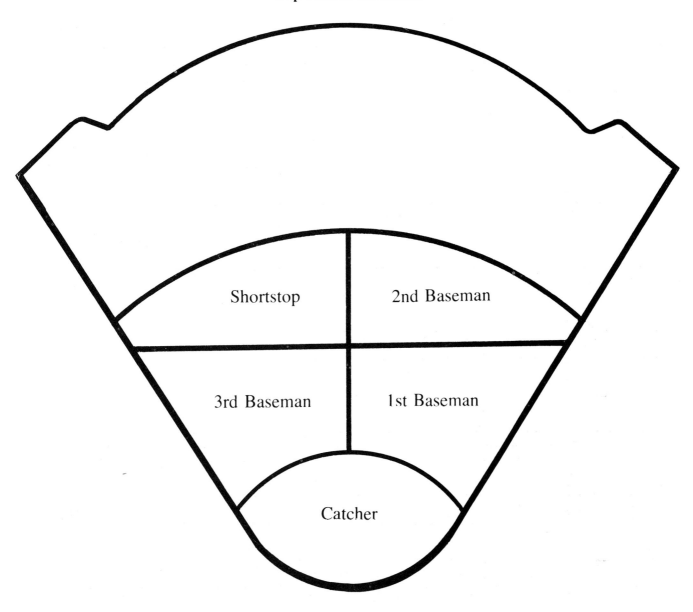

A. An infield pop fly will be all infielders' responsibility, and they must try for the ball until one fielder takes charge by calling for the play.
   a. When calling, yell loudly three or four times. Wave arms if possible.

B. Each infielder has his designated area, but he may take the play out of his area if he has taken charge of the play.
   NOTE: Especially on windy days, do not call for play too soon.

C. On questionable pop flies around the mound area and after one or more infielders has called for the play, the pitcher then calls the last name of the fielder he thinks is in the best position to make the play.

D. The catcher must not give up on pop flies too quickly.

E. All pop flies directly behind the first and third basemen will be the responsibility of the second baseman and the shortstop.

DEFENSE

DEFENSIVE CUTOFF AND RELAY PATTERNS

1. In all situations, keep each base covered where there is a possibility of making a play.
2. The cutoff man's importance cannot be stressed too much. He must think quickly, figure out plays instantly, and must decide which runner is most important to cut down or put out. This is especially true in the last inning or two of the games, when the tying or winning runs are involved. He cuts off throws to make possible the sure putout, especially when the runner caught is the tying or winning run. That is why all throws toward the cutoff man should be low enough for him to handle.
3. Outfielders must help each other on all plays when a ball is hit between them.
4. Infielders should station themselves inside a base while watching the runners tag the base in making the turn. Being inside the base has a tendency to make the runner take a wider turn at the base, thus increasing the distance he travels toward the next base.

Caution must be exercised not to interfere with the runner by being too close to the base.

5. On routine fly balls to the outfield with no one on base, the outfielders should get into the habit of making good, low, hard throws into second base. The shortstop should cover when possible on all balls to left and center field, and the second baseman should cover on balls hit to right field.

   This will get the outfielders into the habit of making this throw, so that when it counts, the good, low, hard throw will be automatic.
6. It is important that all players practice to overcome their weaknesses.
7. In cutoff plays, the standard rule is the position where each man should be on the routine cutoff plays.

WORD SIGNS USED BY CUTOFF MEN

1. Let it go: Let this throw go on through.
2. Cut: Cut this throw and be ready to throw.
3. Relay: Cut the throw, and relay the ball to the man calling "relay."

CUTOFF ASSIGNMENTS

FIRST BASEMAN. On all base hits and fly-ball scoring situations to right and center field, you are the cutoff man except for three situations:

a. Situation #17—Single to right field between first and second baseman with runner on second base.
b. Situation #19—Single to right field between first and second baseman with runners on first and second.
c. Situation #23—Double, possible triple, down right-field line with runner on first base.

When first base is occupied, you are the cutoff man on all extra base hits except the last one when you are a trailer.

When the third baseman dives for the ball and cannot recover to be the cutoff man, you become the cutoff man.

THIRD BASEMAN. You are the cutoff man in only four situations:

a. Situation #3—Single to left field with runner in scoring position.
b. Situation #5—Single to left field with runner in scoring position, a judgment play; the throw should go to second base.

c. Situation #17—When first baseman is pulled out of position on ground single between first and second with runner on second base.
d. Fly-ball situations to left field with a runner on third.

SECOND BASEMAN—You cover first base on five situations:

a. Situation #11—Single to center field with runner on second.
b. Situation #13—Fly-ball scoring situations to center and right field.
c. Situation #16—Single to right field with runner on second.
d. Situation #17—Single to right field between first and second.
e. Situation #19—Single to right field between first and second baseman with runners on first and second.

PITCHERS. You are the cutoff man on two situations:

a. Situation #19—Single to right field between first and second baseman with runners on first and second.
b. Pop Fly situation #2—Pop up in right field area.

Situation #1—Single to left field, no one on base.

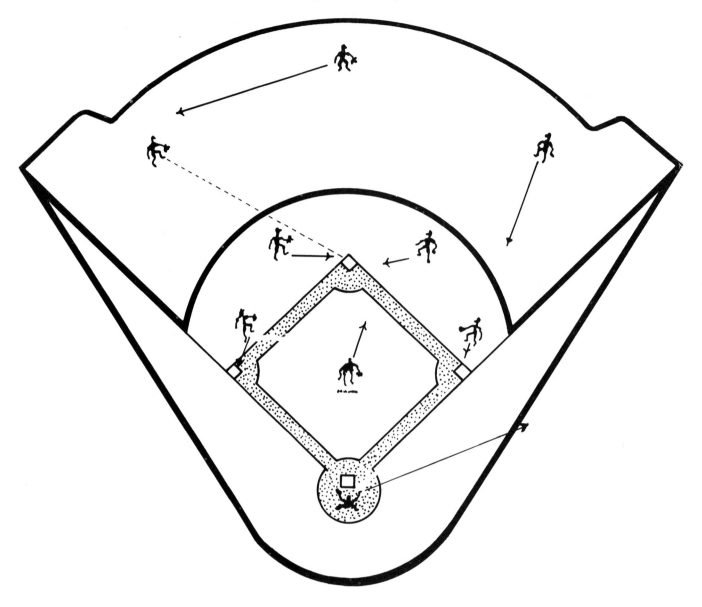

Pitcher:
Move to a position halfway between mound and second.

Catcher:
Follow runner down to first base.

First Baseman:
Make sure the runner tags the base in making the turn, then cover first base.

Shortstop:
Cover second to take throw from left fielder when possible.

Second Baseman:
Back up the left fielder's throw to the shortstop.

Third Baseman:
Protect third base area.

Outfielders:
Center fielder—back up left fielder. Right fielder—move in toward first base area.

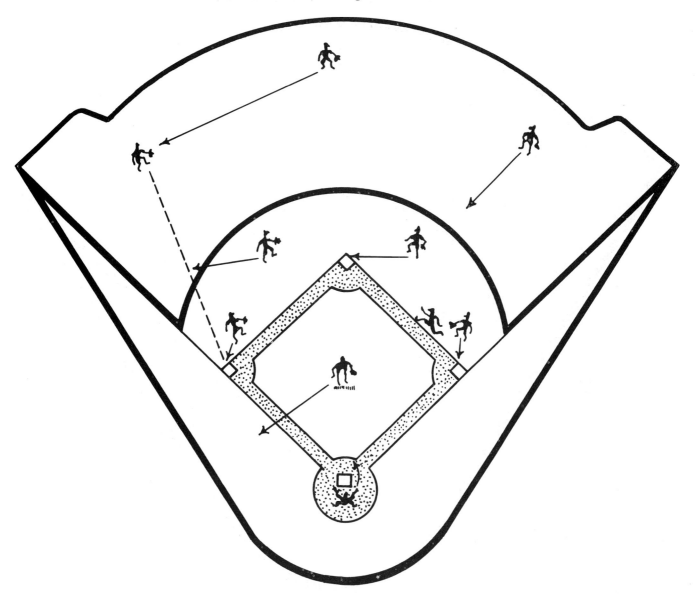

Man on first base.

Pitcher:
  Back up third base.

Catcher:
  Protect home plate area.

First Baseman:
  Cover first base.

Second Baseman:
  Cover second base.

Shortstop:
  Move into a position to be the cutoff man on the throw to third base.

Third Baseman:
  Cover third base.

Center Fielder:
  Back up left fielder.

Right Fielder:
  Move in toward infield area.

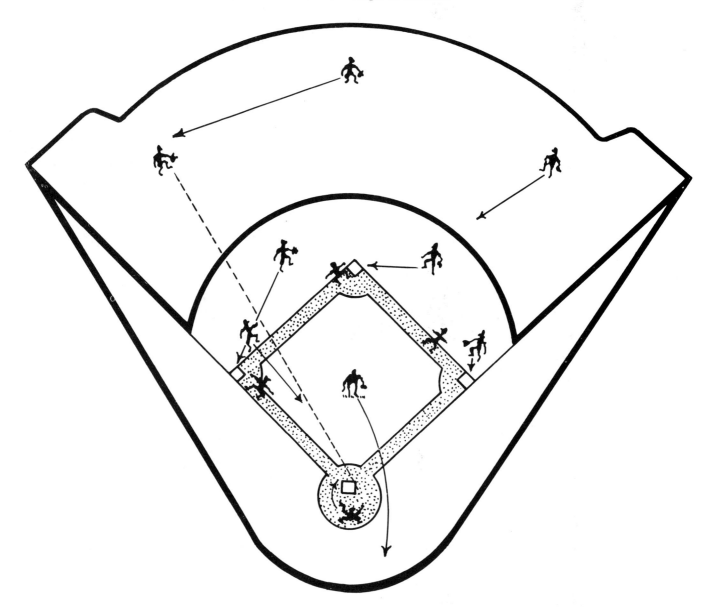

Man on second or men on first and second (or bases loaded)

Pitcher:
   Back up home plate.

Catcher:
   Cover home plate.

First Baseman:
   Cover first base.

Second Baseman:
   Cover second base.

Shortstop:
   Cover third base.

Third Baseman:
   Be the cutoff man.

Center Fielder:
   Back up left fielder.

Right Fielder:
   Move in toward second base area.

244

Situation #4—Single to left field between shortstop and third baseman.

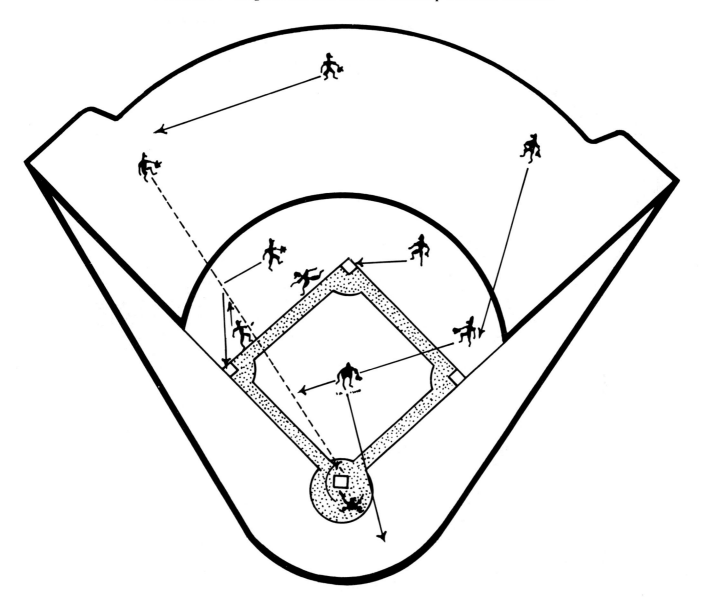

Man on second base or men on second and third bases.

Pitcher:
Back up home plate.

Catcher:
Cover home plate.

First Baseman:
Cutoff man. Take a position about 45 feet from home plate in line with left fielder and home plate.

Second Baseman:
Cover second base.

Shortstop:
May have to cover third if third baseman cannot recover.

Third Baseman:
Cover third if possible.

Left Fielder:
Make low throw to the plate.

Center Fielder:
Back up left fielder.

Right Fielder:
Come in quickly to try and cover first base.

Situation #5—Single to left field (Judgement Play)

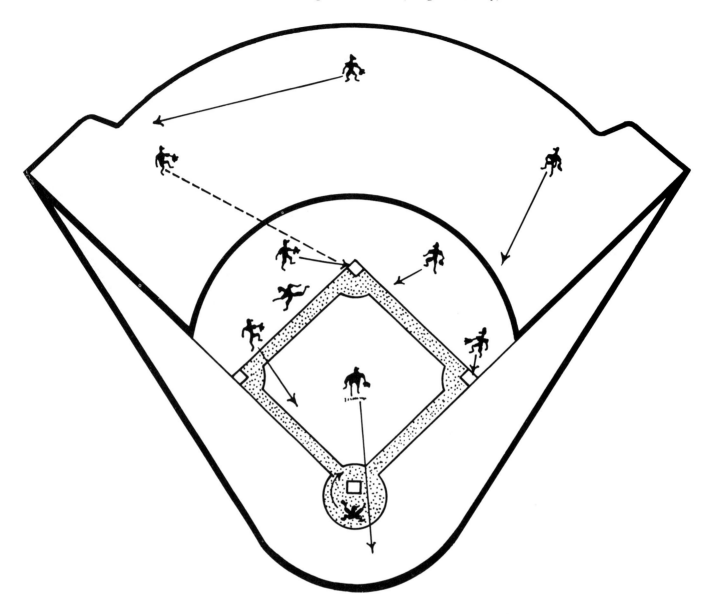

Man on second base—hitter is the tying run.

Pitcher:
Move off mound to back up home plate in case the left fielder makes the throw home.

Catcher:
Cover home plate.

First Baseman:
Cover first base.

Second Baseman:
Back up second base.

Shortstop:
Cover second base.

Third Baseman:
Move into position to be cutoff man in case the left fielder throws home.

Left Fielder:
Make low throw to second base to keep batter from advancing into scoring position.

Center Fielder:
Back up left fielder.

Right Fielder:
Move into position to help back up second base.

Never let the tying run get into scoring position at second base by making a foolish throw to the plate.

Situation #6—Double, possible triple, to left center.

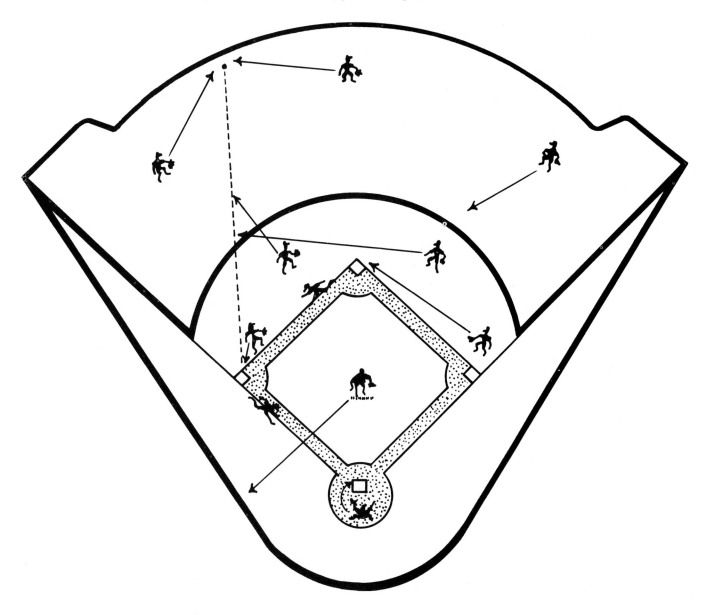

No one on base, or man on third base or second, or men on third and second bases.

Pitcher:
Back up third base in line with throw.

Catcher:
Protect home plate.

First Baseman:
Trail the runner to second base, cover the bag, ready for a play if runner rounds base too far.

Second Baseman:
Trail about 30 feet behind shortstop in line with third base.

Shortstop:
Go to a spot in left center to become relay man.

Third Baseman:
Cover third; stand on left side of base.

Center Fielder:
Back up the left fielder.

Right Fielder:
Move in toward second base.

Situation #7—Double, possible triple, to left center.

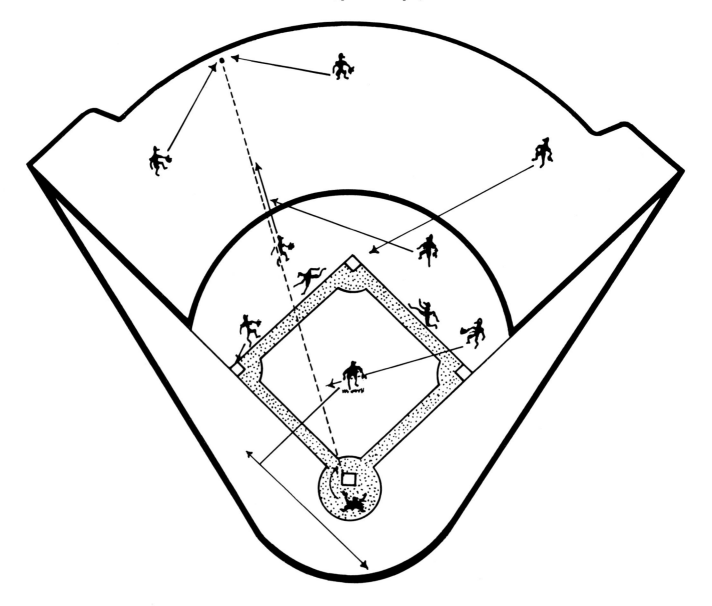

Man on first, man on first and second, or bases loaded

Pitcher:
Go halfway between home and third, then back up the base where throw is going.

Catcher:
Protect home plate.

First Baseman:
Be the cutoff man.

Second Baseman:
Trail and about 30 feet behind shortstop in line with third base.

Shortstop:
Go to a spot in left center to become relay man.

Third Baseman:
Cover third; stand on left side of base.

Center Fielder:
Back up the left fielder.

Right Fielder:
Move in to cover second base.

248

Situation #8—Double, possible triple, down left field line.

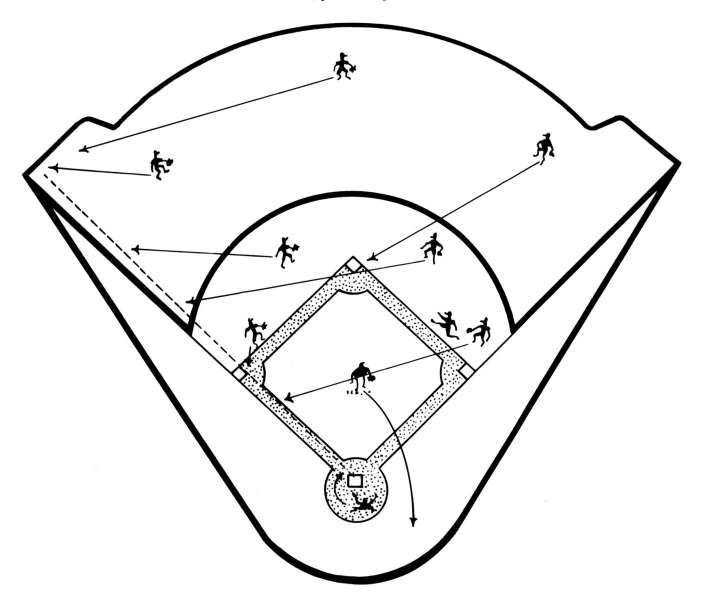

Man on first base.

Pitcher:
Back up home plate.

Catcher:
Cover home plate.

First Baseman:
Become the cutoff man.

Second Baseman:
Become trailer behind the shortstop.

Shortstop:
Relay man

Third Baseman:
Cover third.

Center Fielder:
Back up left fielder.

Right Fielder:
Cover second base.

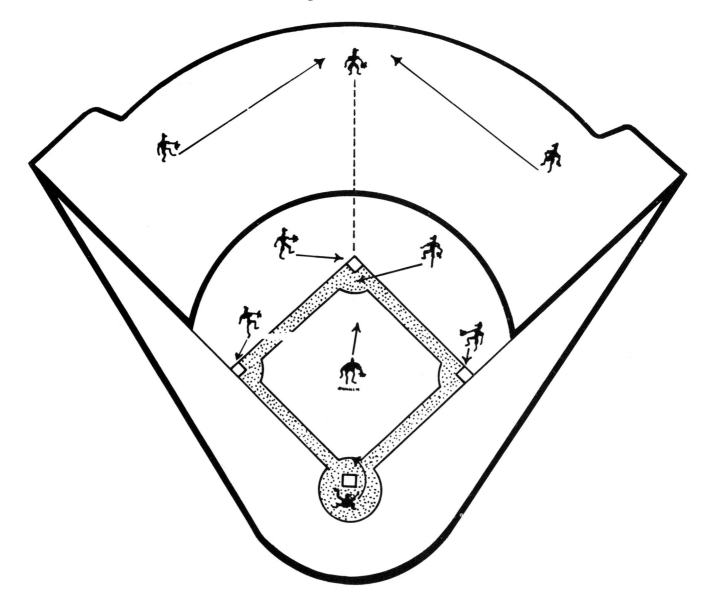

No one on base.

Pitcher:
Move to a position halfway beween mound and second.

Catcher:
Protect home plate area.

First Baseman:
Make sure the runner tags the base in making the turn, then cover first.

Shortstop:
Cover second to take throw from center fielder.

Second Baseman:
Back up the center fielder's throw to the shortstop.

Third Baseman:
Protect third base area.

Outfielders:
Left and right fielders—back up center fielder.

Situation #10—Single to center field

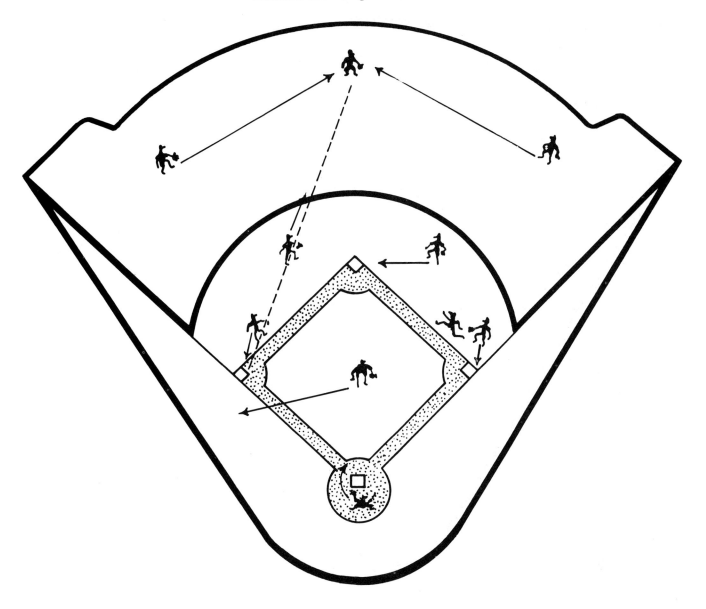

Man on first.

Pitcher:
  Back up third base.

Catcher:
  Protect home plate area.

First Baseman:
  Cover first base.

Second Baseman:
  Cover second base.

Shortstop:
  Be cutoff man on throw from center field to third base.

Third Baseman:
  Cover third base.

Left and Right Fielders:
  Back up center fielder.

Situation #11—Single to center field

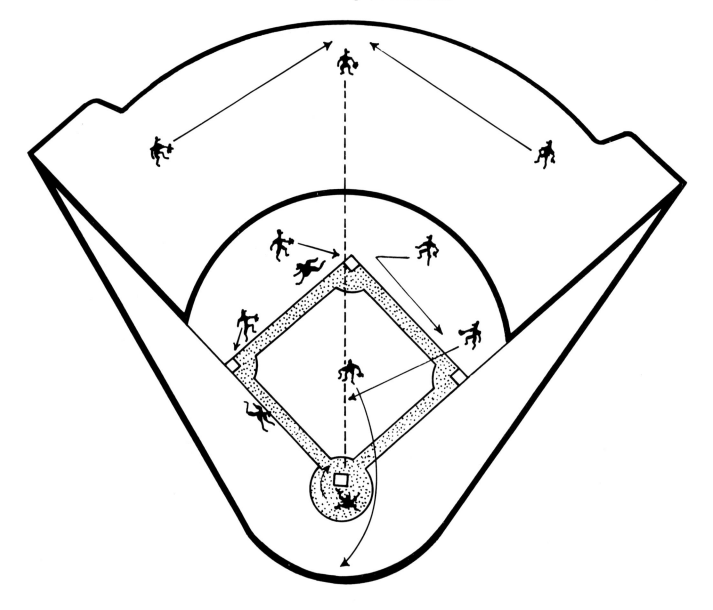

Man on second base, or men on second and third bases.

Pitcher:
Back up home plate.

Catcher:
Cover home plate.

First Baseman:
Be the cutoff man.

Second Baseman:
Go after ball. If possible, return to cover first base.

Shortstop:
Go after ball, then cover second base.

Third Baseman:
Cover third base.

Left Fielder:
Back up center fielder.

Right Fielder:
Back up center fielder.

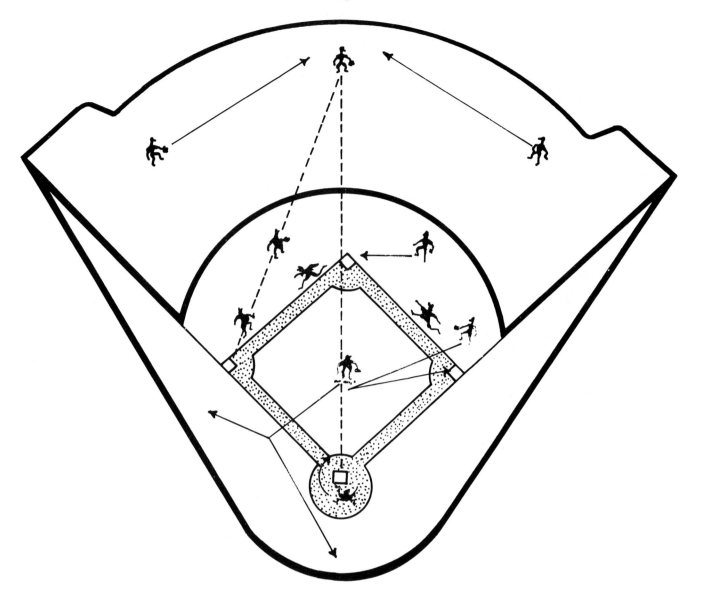

Men on first and second or men on first, second, and third.

Pitcher:
Go halfway between home and third base, then back up the base where the throw is going.

Catcher:
Cover home plate.

First Baseman:
Move into a spot 45 feet from home plate in line with the throw, to be cutoff man. If throw goes to third base, hustle back to first base to cover that bag.

Second Baseman:
Cover second base.

Shortstop:
Be the cutoff man for a possible throw to third base.

Third Baseman:
Cover third.

Left Fielder:
Back up center fielder.

Right Fielder:
Back up center fielder.

Situation #13—Fly ball to center or right field

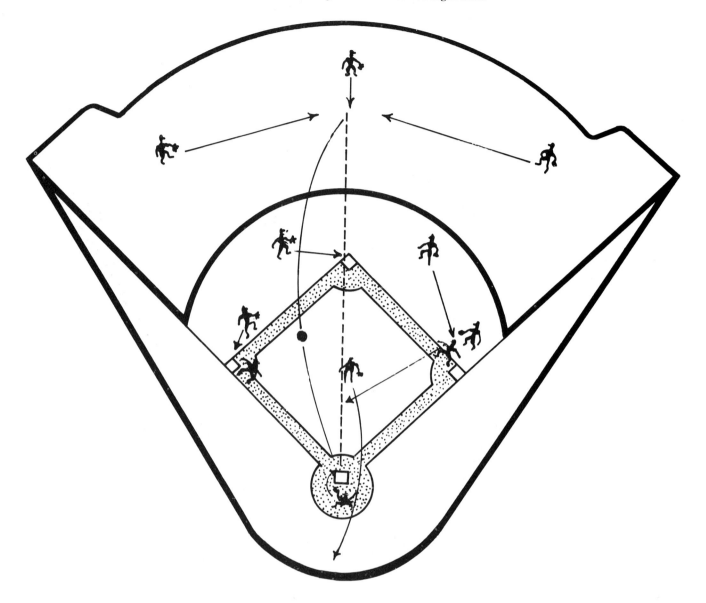

Runners on first and second or bases loaded.

Pitcher:
  Back up home plate.

Catcher:
  Cover home plate.

First Baseman:
  Be the cutoff man.

Second Baseman:
  Cover first base.

Shortstop:
  Cover second base.

Third Baseman:
  Cover third base.

Left Fielder:
  Move toward fly ball.

Right Fielder:
  Move toward fly ball.

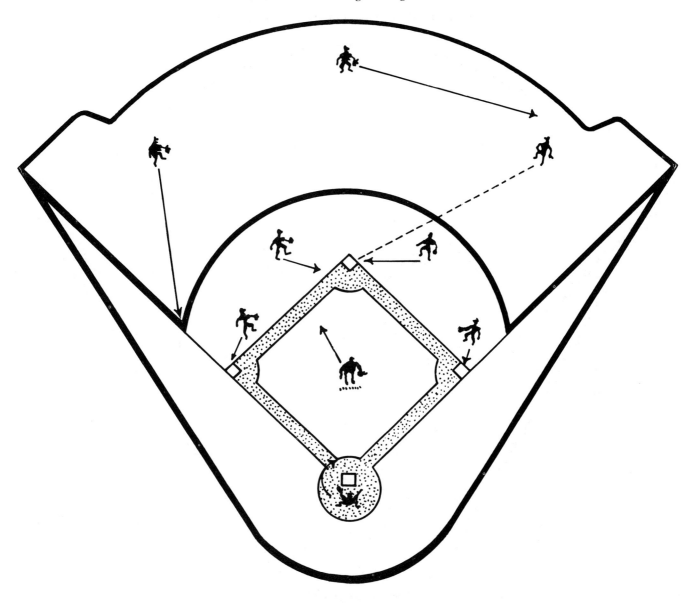

No one on base.

Pitcher:
Move to a position halfway between mound and second.

Catcher:
Protect home plate area.

First Baseman:
Make sure the runner tags the base in making the turn, then cover first.

Second Baseman:
Cover second, to take throw from right fielder.

Shortstop:
Back up right fielder's throw to second baseman.

Third Baseman:
Protect third base area.

Outfielders:
Center fielder—back up right fielder. Left fielder—move in toward third base.

Situation #15—Single to right field

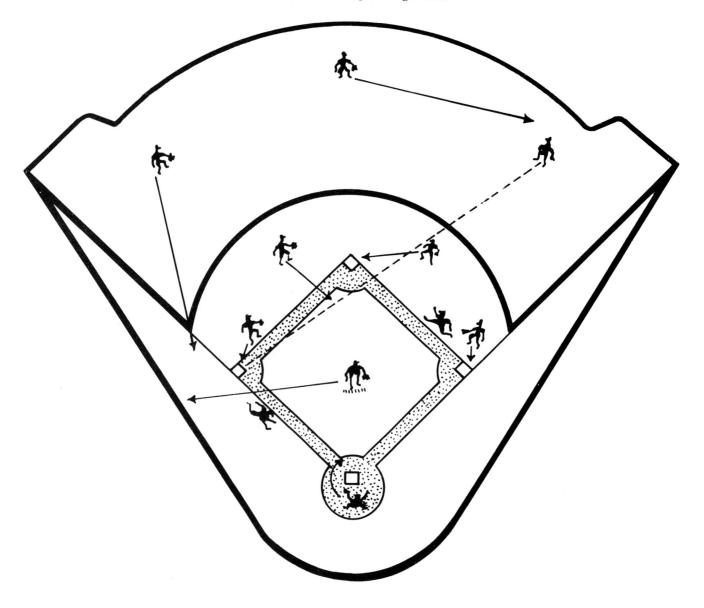

Man on first base, or men on third and first.

Pitcher:
Back up third base in line with throw.

Catcher:
Protect home plate.

First Baseman:
Cover first base. Make sure runner tags base.

Second Baseman:
Cover second. Make sure runner tags base.

Shortstop:
Station yourself about 45 feet from third base on a direct line from the base to the outfielder fielding the ball.

Third Baseman:
Cover third.

Left Fielder:
Move in toward third base.

Center Fielder:
Back up right fielder.

256

Situation #16—Single to right field

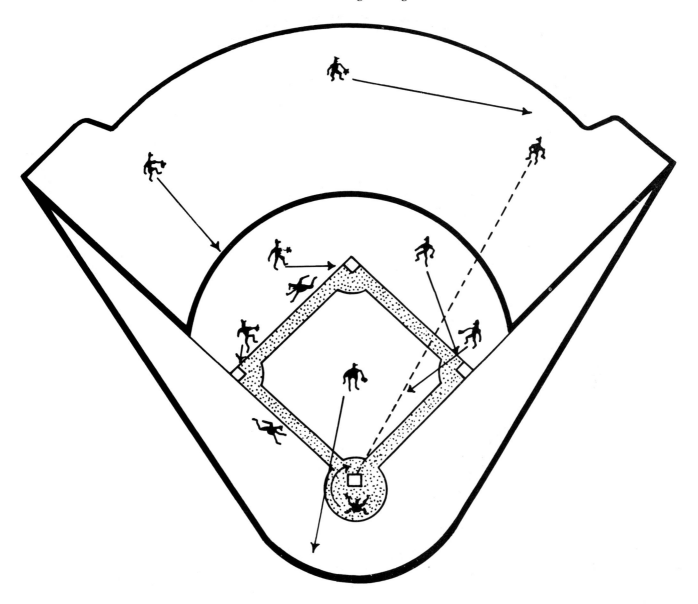

Man on second base, or men on second and third bases.

Pitcher:
  Back up home plate.

Catcher:
  Cover home plate.

First Baseman:
  Take position about 45 feet from home plate to become cutoff man.

Second Baseman:
  Cover first base.

Shortstop:
  Cover second base.

Third Baseman:
  Cover third.

Left Fielder:
  Move in toward second base.

Center Fielder:
  Back up right fielder.

257

Situation #17—Single to right field between first and second basemen.

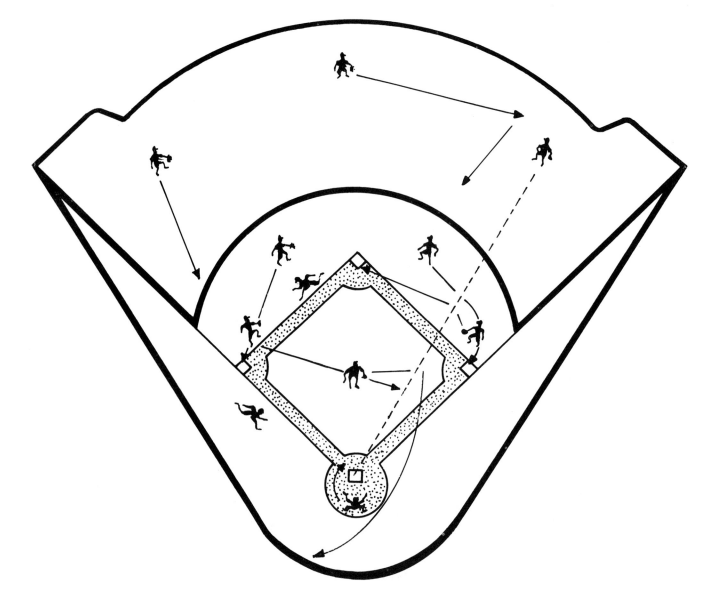

Man on second base or men on second and third bases.

Pitcher:
Start to cover first, then back up home plate.

Catcher:
Cover home plate.

First Baseman:
After attempting to field ball, continue to cover second base.

Second Baseman:
After attempting to field ball, continue to cover first base.

Shortstop:
Cover third base.

Third Baseman:
Be the cutoff man.

Left Fielder:
Move into area behind third base.

Center Fielder:
Back up right fielder, move in toward second base after ball is fielded.

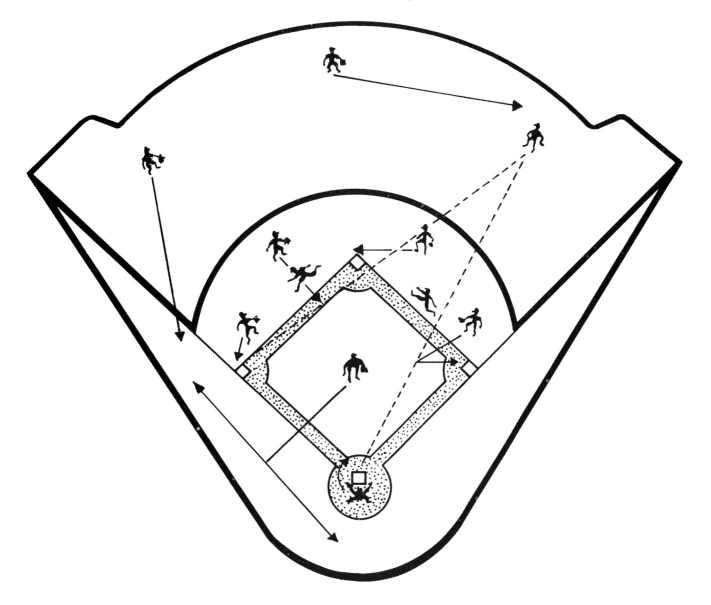

Men on first and second or men on first, second, and third.

Always **keep tying or winning run from going to third with less than two out. Give opposing team two runs to keep the tying run at second base in this situation.** *Never* **make a foolish throw to the plate.**

Pitcher:
Go halfway between third and home, then back up the base where the throw is going.

Catcher:
Cover home plate.

First Baseman:
Become a cutoff man in case the throw is made to the plate. If throw goes to third return and cover first base.

Second Baseman:
Cover second.

Shortstop:
Cutoff man for the throw to third base.

Third Baseman:
Cover third.

Left Fielder:
Move to a point near the line and back up third base.

Center Fielder:
Back up right fielder.

Right Fielder:
Make a low throw to the shortstop to keep the tying or winning run from going to third base.

259

Situation #19—Single to right field between first and second basemen.

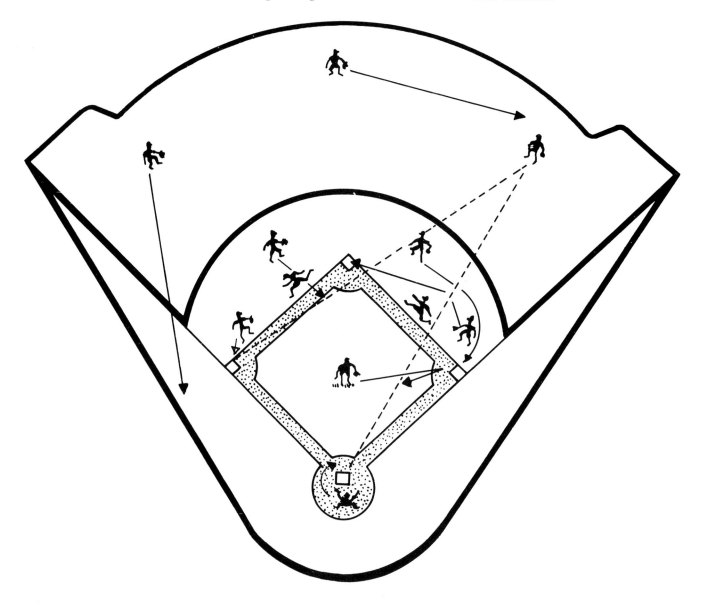

Men on first and second or bases loaded.

Pitcher:
Start to cover first base; when ball gets through, retreat to be cutoff man.

Catcher:
Cover home plate.

First Baseman:
When you can't field the ball, continue on and cover second base.

Second Baseman:
When you can't field the ball, continue on to cover first base.

Shortstop:
Cutoff man for a possible throw to third base.

Third Baseman:
Cover third.

Left Fielder:
Move into area behind third to back up.

Center Fielder:
Back up the right fielder.

Situation #20—Double, possible triple, to right center field

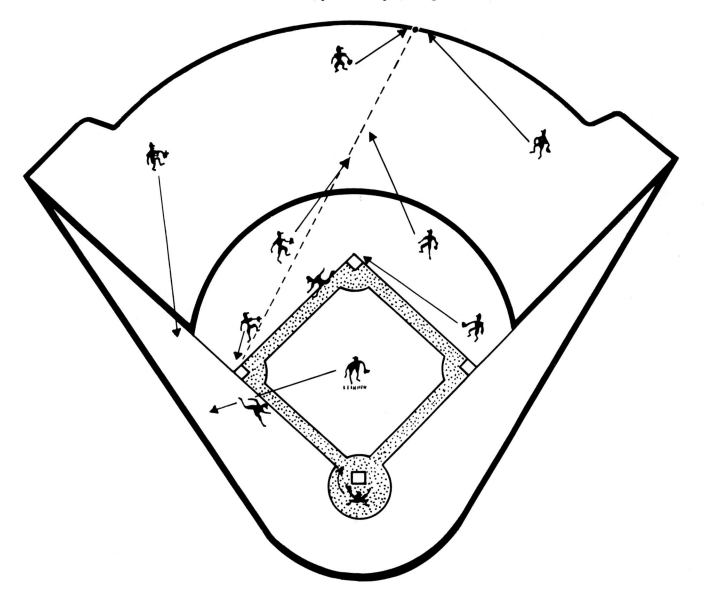

No one on base, or man on third or second base, or men on third and second bases.

Pitcher:
Back up third base. Get as deep as possible.

Catcher:
Protect home plate.

First Baseman:
Trail the runner to second base; cover the bag, ready for a play at that base.

Second Baseman:
Go to spot in center field in line with third to become relay man.

Shortstop:
Trail about 30 feet behind second baseman, in line with third base.

Third Baseman:
Cover third.

Left Fielder:
Move in toward third base.

Right Fielder:
Back up center fielder.

Situation #21—Double, possible triple, to right center field

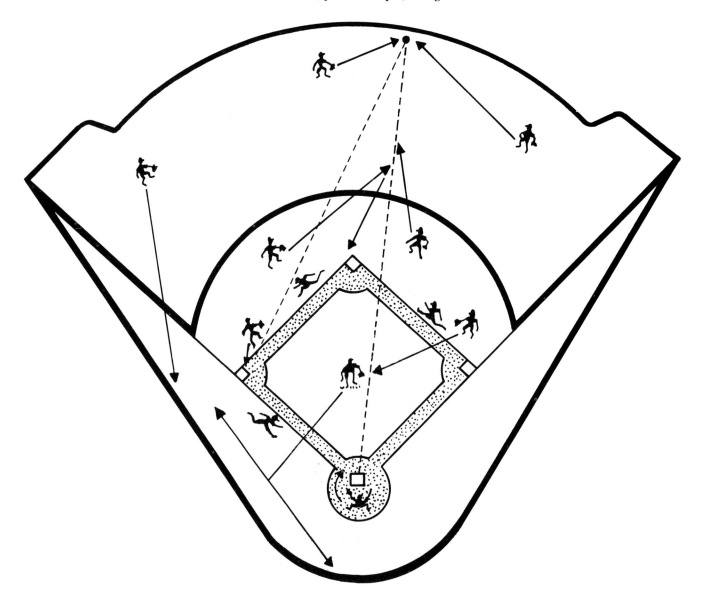

Man on first base, or men on first and second bases, or bases loaded.

Pitcher:
Go halfway between third and home to see where the throw is coming, then back up either base.

Catcher:
Cover home plate.

First Baseman:
Be the cutoff man.

Second Baseman:
Become relay man.

Third Baseman:
Cover third base.

Shortstop:
Be trailer relay man, then return and cover second base.

Left Fielder:
Move into area behind third base.

Right Fielder and Center Fielder:
Go after ball.

262

Situation #22—Double, possible triple, down right field line.

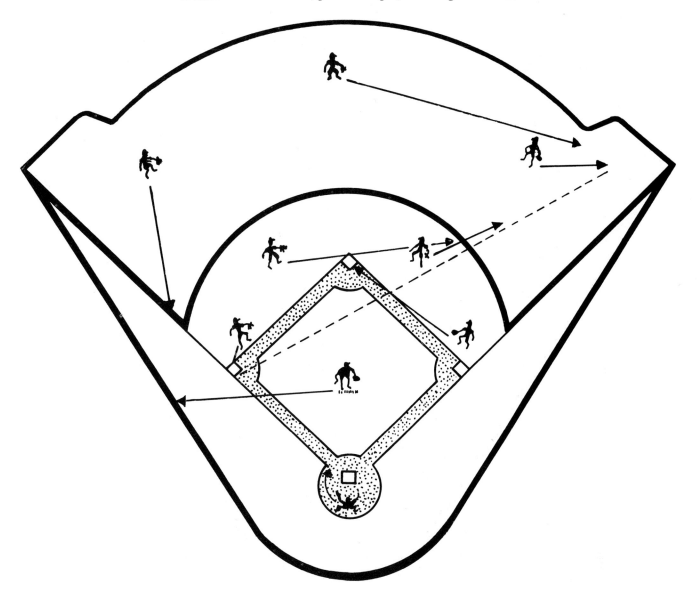

No one on base.

Pitcher:
  Back up third base.

Catcher:
  Protect home plate area.

First Baseman:
  Trail runner into second base.

Second Baseman:
  Become first relay man.

Shortstop:
  Become trailer relay man.

Third Baseman:
  Cover third base.

Left Fielder:
  Move into an area behind third base.

Center Fielder:
  Back up right fielder.

Situation #23—Double, possible triple, down right field line.

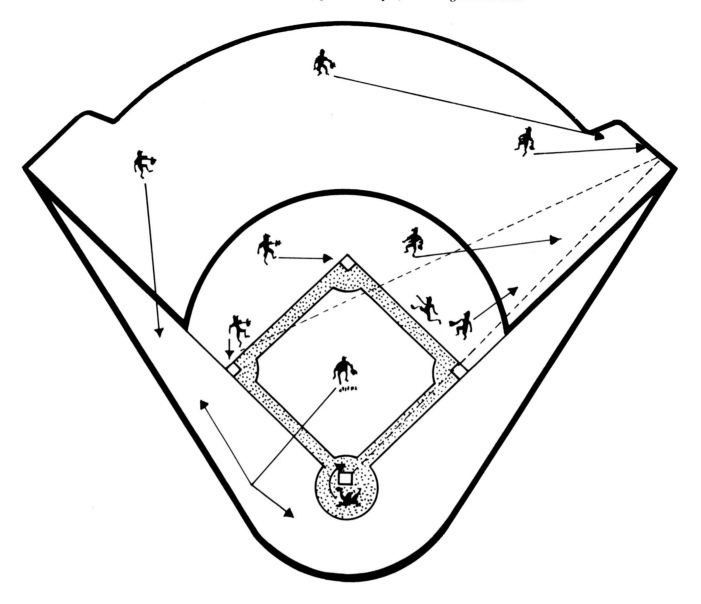

Man on first base.

Pitcher:
Go half way between third and home to see where throw is going.

Catcher:
Cover home plate.

First Baseman:
Trail second baseman—remain about 30 feet back.

Second Baseman:
Relay man. Go to a spot in right field along foul line in line with right fielder and home.

Shortstop:
Cover second base.

Third Baseman:
Cover third base.

Left Fielder:
Move in toward third base.

Center Fielder:
Back up right fielder.

DEFENSIVE ASSIGNMENTS FOR POP-FLY SITUATIONS

Situation #1—Foul fly behind the plate.

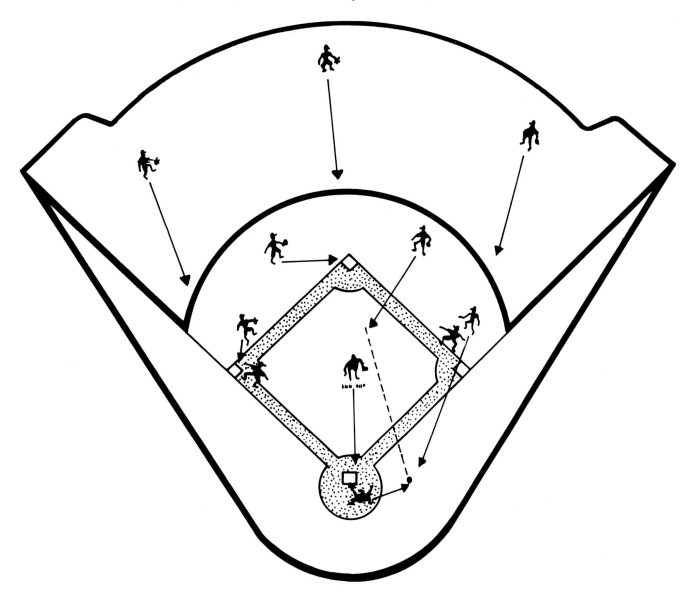

Runners on first and third, less than two out.

Both runners tag up and runner on first breaks for second. If there is no cutoff man, the runner on third will score easily when the catcher makes his throw to second base.

Pitcher:
Cover home plate.

Catcher:
Catch pop up and throw to cutoff man.

First Baseman:
Help on pop up.

Second Baseman:
Become cutoff man behind the pitcher's mound.

Third Baseman:
Cover third base.

Shortstop:
Cover second base.

Left Fielder:
Come in to help back up short and third base area.

Center Fielder:
Back up second base.

Right Fielder:
Cover first base.

Situation #2—Pop fly behind first base.

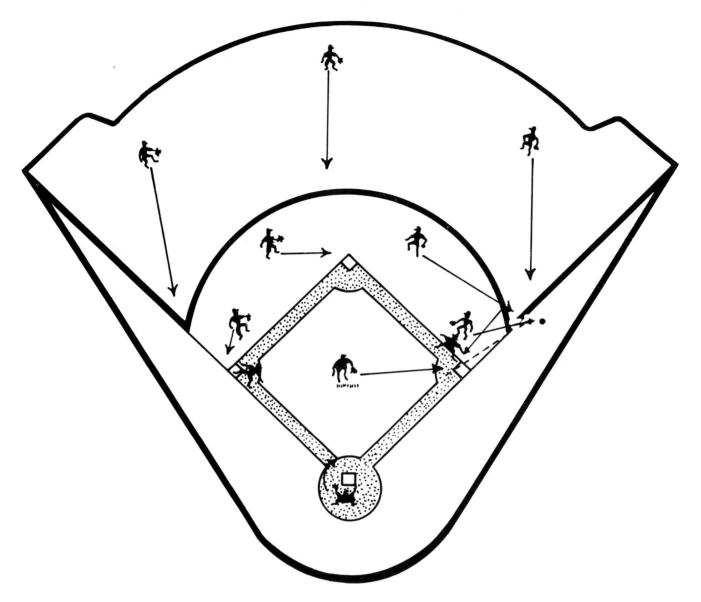

Runners on first and third, none out.
Both runners tag up and the runner on first breaks for second.

Pitcher:
Come to a point in the first base area to be the cutoff man.

Catcher:
Cover home plate.

First Baseman:
Catch the pop up and throw it to the pitcher.

Second Baseman:
Also go after the pop up; then hustle to cover first.

Shortstop:
Cover second base.

Third Baseman:
Cover third base.

Left Fielder:
Move into an area behind third for back-up man.

Center Fielder:
Back up second base.

Right Fielder:
Move in to help catch the pop up.

DEFENSIVE ASSIGNMENTS FOR WILD PITCHES AND PASSED BALLS

Situation #1

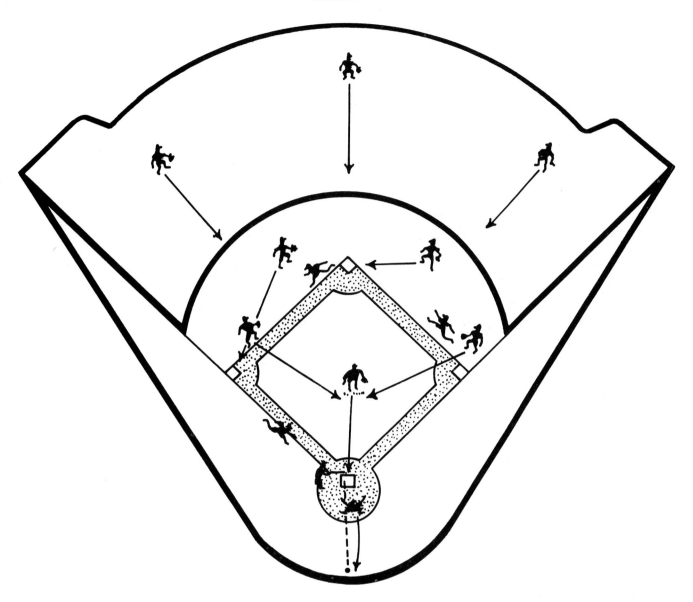

Runner on third, or first and third, or on first, second, and third.

Pitcher:
Cover home plate.

Catcher:
Retrieve the ball.

First Baseman:
Back up the plate.

Second Baseman:
Cover second base.

Shortstop:
Cover third base.

Third Baseman:
Back up plate at the mound.

All outfielders move toward the infield area to help where needed.

BUNT SITUATIONS

A. Man on first base:
   a. When you are anticipating the sacrifice bunt, charge when the pitcher throws the ball.
   b. If the ball is bunted hard to you, make the play to second base. (The catcher will call this play.)
   c. If play at second base is doubtful, make sure you get one out by throwing to first base.

B. Runners on first and second:
   a. The third baseman's judgment is the key to this play, and he is in full charge.
   b. Position is just inside of the line, four steps in front of the bag, and stationary.
   c. Tell the pitcher he must field the ball. Important: Know your pitcher's fielding ability.

NOTE: One out must be made in this situation.
   d. The bunted ball the pitcher can handle easily. The third baseman will cover the base without taking his eyes off the ball. Tag the base with your right foot for better balance, to be in position to make the throw to first base.
   e. On balls bunted down the line, the third baseman charges and runs the pitcher off.
   f. If your judgment is to go for the ball, run the pitcher off at all times. The play to first base is much easier for the third baseman in this situation.

C. Runners on first and second:
   a. Situation #3 is an option and must be controlled by a sign. The pitcher, first baseman, and third baseman charge toward the batter. The shortstop bluffs the runner back to second, then races to third.

Situation #1—Runner on first base and the bunt in order.

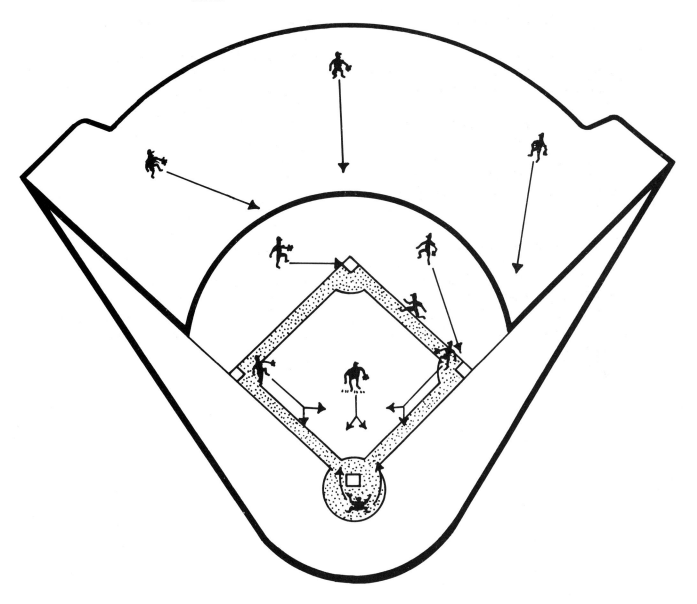

Pitcher:
Break toward plate after delivering the ball.

Catcher:
Field all bunts possible; call the play; cover third when third baseman fields the bunt in close to home plate.

First Baseman:
Cover the area between first and the mound.

Second Baseman:
Cover first base; cheat by shortening position.

Shortstop:
Cover second base.

Third Baseman:
Cover the area between third and the mound.

Left Fielder:
Move in toward second base.

Center Fielder:
Back up second base.

Right Fielder:
Back up first base.

269

Situation #2—Runners on first and second, bunt situation in order.

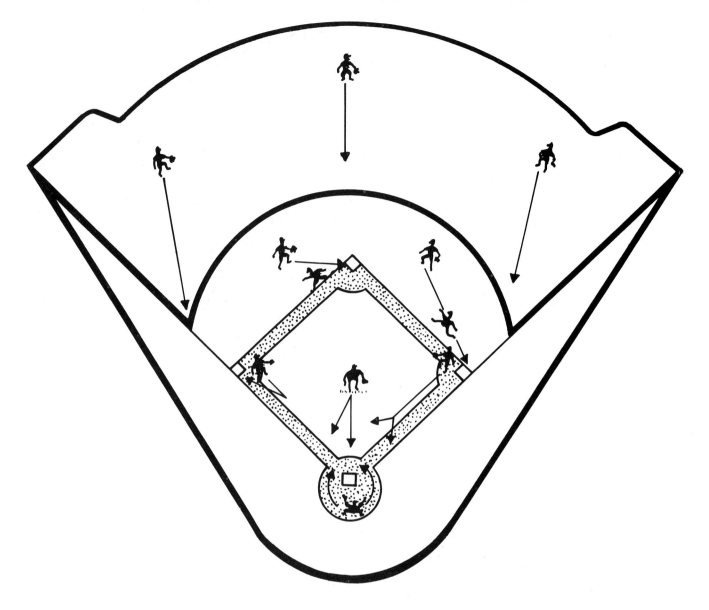

Pitcher:
Break toward third base line upon delivering the ball.

Catcher:
Field bunts in front of plate; call the play.

First Baseman:
Responsible for all balls in the area between first and a direct line from the mound to home.

Second Baseman:
Cover first base.

Shortstop:
Hold runner close to bag before pitch; cover second base.

Third Baseman:
Take position on the edge of the grass; catcher calls the play—whether the pitcher or the third baseman is to field the bunt.

Left Fielder:
Back up third base.

Center Fielder:
Back up second base.

Right Fielder:
Back up first base.

First objective is to retire the runner at third, but one runner *must* be retired.

Situation #3—Runners on first and second, bunt situation in order.

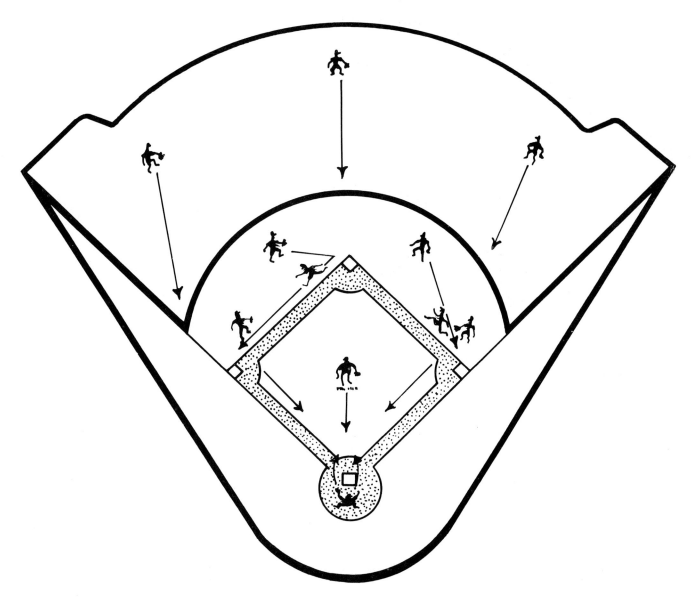

Pitcher:
Break toward the plate.

Catcher:
Field bunts in front of plate or call the play.

First Baseman:
Charge toward the plate.

Second Baseman:
Cover first base.

Shortstop:
Bluff runner back to second, then race to cover third.

Third Baseman:
Charge toward the plate.

Outfielders:
Move in toward infield area on all bunt situations.

THE RUNDOWN PLAY

There are several good rules to follow in making this play. The most important is run the man back to the bag from which he came.

1. Try to start this play when the runner is halfway between the bases.
2. Give the ball to the front man and let him run the man back to the bag from which he came.
3. The forward man should run hard at the runner, but not with a faking motion of the arm.
4. The tagger should stay in front of his gag, and inside the base line. This will give him the proper throwing angle.
5. When the runner is about ten feet from the tagger, the tagger should make a break toward the runner. This is the sign to the thrower to give the tagger the ball on his first step.
6. The thrower makes an easy, chest-high toss.
7. When play is worked right, one throw is all that is needed to get the runner at any base.
8. The man without the ball must avoid interfering with the runner.

RULES TO REMEMBER

1. Chase the runner back to the bag from which he came.
2. Run the runner hard.
3. The tagger and the thrower stay inside the base line.
4. The tagger must stay in front of his bag until making his break.
5. The thrower should make an easy, chest-high toss, not a quick, hard throw.

THE RUNDOWN PLAY

Situation #1

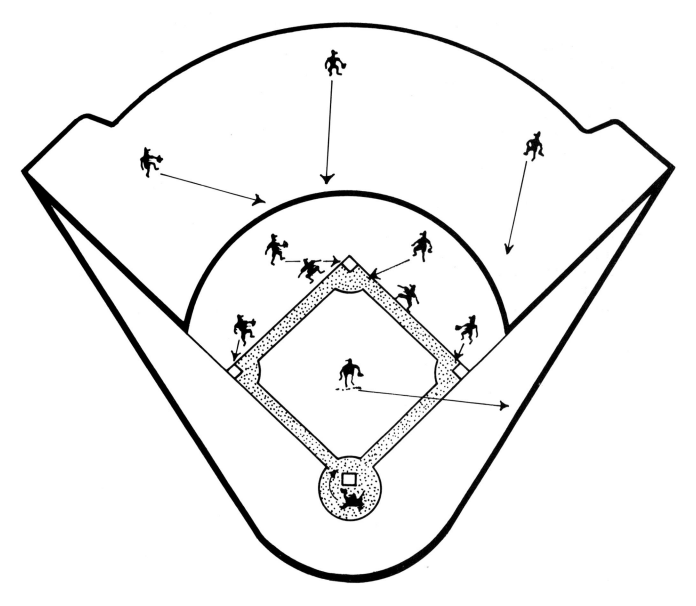

Men on first and second; man on first picked off.

Pitcher:
Back up first base.

Catcher:
Cover home plate.

First Baseman:
Cover first and be the tag man.

Second Baseman:
Cover second base and be the rundown man.

Shortstop:
Back up and cover second base, with possibility of being rundown man and tagger.

Third Baseman:
Cover third to keep runner on second from advancing.

Right Fielder:
Come in to help back up first base.

Center Fielder:
Come in to help back up second base.

Left Fielder:
Come in to help back up second base.

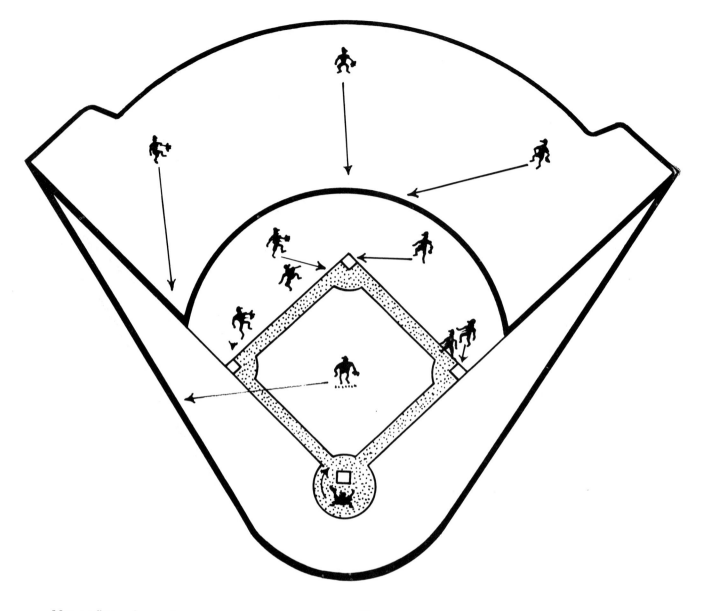

**Men on first and second,
man on second is picked off.**

Pitcher:
    Back up third base.

Catcher:
    Cover home plate.

First Baseman:
    Cover first base.

Second Baseman:
    Cover second base, with the possibility of being rundown man and tagger.

Shortstop:
    Cover second base and be the tag man.

Third Baseman:
    Cover third base and be the rundown man.

Right Fielder:
    Back up second base.

Center Fielder:
    Back up second base.

Left Fielder:
    Move into area behind third to back up.

274

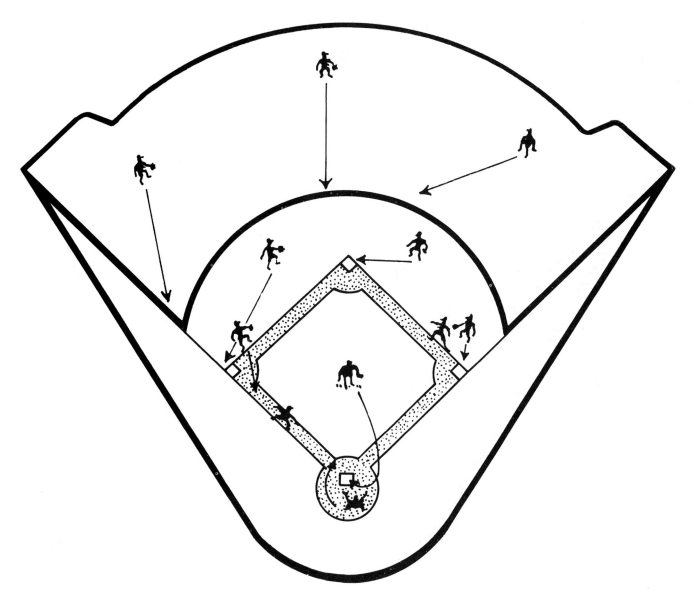

**Men on first and third,
man on third is picked off.**

Pitcher:
Cover home plate and back up catcher.

Catcher:
Cover home plate and be the rundown man.

First Baseman:
Cover first base to keep runner there from advancing.

Second Baseman:
Cover second base to keep runner on first from advancing.

Shortstop:
Back up third baseman.

Third Baseman:
Cover third base and be the tag man.

Right Fielder:
Move in to help back up second base.

Center Fielder:
Move in to back up second base.

Left Fielder:
Move in behind third to help back up.

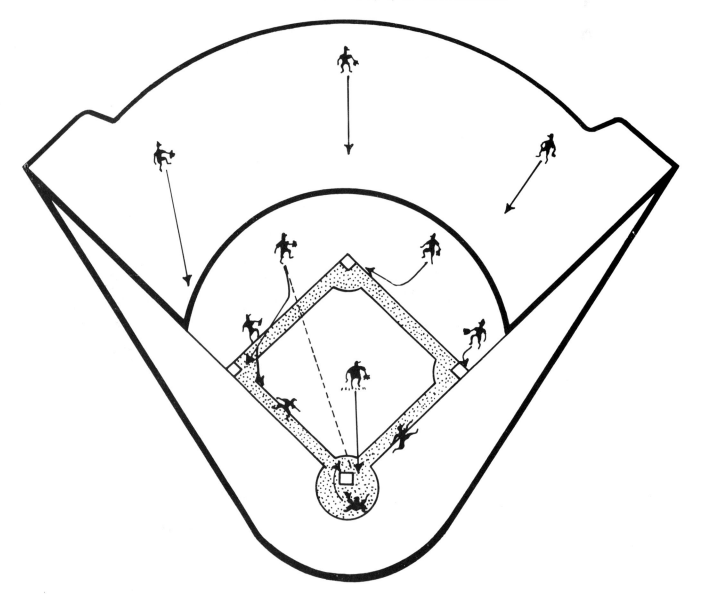

Man on third tries to score on ground ball to the infield when the infield is in.

Pitcher:
Cover home plate.

Catcher:
Cover home plate and be the rundown man.

First Baseman:
Cover first base.

Second Baseman:
Cover second base.

Third Baseman:
Follow in about 10 feet behind runner off third to make tag quickly, in order to keep batter from going to second base.

Shortstop:
Cover third base.

Left Fielder:
Back up third base.

Center Fielder:
Back up second base.

Right Fielder:
Back up area behind first base.

276

Ty Cobb

Lou Gehrig.
This is the only
known hitting sequence
pictures of the Yankee great.

Joe Medwick. Notice the unorthodox start in photo 1—front foot off the ground—but in picture 2, his hands are back in the launching position as the stride foot is about to come down.

Tom Tresh

A Picture of Happiness. Three of the greatest ballplayers of all time, truly having fun and enjoying what they're doing. Left to right: Lou Gehrig, Jimmie Foxx, Babe Ruth.

Index